Language, Learning and Teaching

Language, Learning and Teaching

IRISH RESEARCH PERSPECTIVES

EDITED BY

Fiona Farr and Máiréad Moriarty

PETER LANG

Oxford · Bern · Berlin · Bruxelles · Frankfurt am Main · New York · Wien

Bibliographic information published by Die Deutsche Nationalbibliothek.
Die Deutsche Nationalbibliothek lists this publication in the Deutsche Nationalbibliografie;
detailed bibliographic data is available on the Internet at http://dnb.d-nb.de.

A catalogue record for this book is available from The British Library.

Library of Congress Cataloging-in-Publication Data:

Language, learning and teaching : Irish research perspectives / Fiona Farr and Máiréad
Moriarty.
    pages cm
  "The work presented in this book stems from a postgraduate conference held by IRAAL
(The Irish Society for Applied Linguistics) at the University of Limerick in October 2010.
IRAAL was founded in 1975 to support research in applied and general linguistics in Ireland.
IRAAL is affiliated to the International Association for Applied Linguistics (AILA)."
  Includes bibliographical references and index.
  ISBN 978-3-0343-0871-7 (alk. paper)
  1. Language and education--Ireland--Congresses. 2. Education, Bilingual--Ireland--Con-
gresses. 3. Language and languages--Study and teaching--Congresses. 4. Intercultural
communication--Ireland--Congresses. 5. Language acquisition--Study and teaching--Con-
gresses. 6. Applied linguistics--Congresses. 7. Ireland--Languages. I. Farr, Fiona, 1971- editor of compilation. II. Moriarty, Máiréad, editor of compilation. III. Irish Association for
Applied Linguistics.
  P40.85.I75L3533 2012
  418.007--dc23

                              2012039216

Cover image courtesy of iStockphoto

ISBN 978-3-0343-0871-7

© Peter Lang AG, International Academic Publishers, Bern 2013
Hochfeldstrasse 32, CH-3012 Bern, Switzerland
info@peterlang.com, www.peterlang.com, www.peterlang.net

Printed in Germany

Contents

List of Tables and Figures

List of Tables

List of Figures

Acknowledgements

We would like to thank the many people who have helped in the preparation and production of this book. Its conception owes much to the stimulating Postgraduate conference hosted by IRAAL (Irish Association for Applied Linguistics) at the University of Limerick in October 2010. Versions of the chapters included were first aired as papers at that conference, and discussions and feedback that we received have helped shape the ensuing volume. We would like to sincerely thank the many reviewers, colleagues both old and new, who carefully reviewed each chapter and made the overall editorial process smooth and enjoyable (David Atkinson, Lorna Carson, Máiréad Conneely, Barbara Geraghty, Helen Kelly-Holmes, Freda Mishan, Oliver McGarr, Brona Murphy, Lelia Murtagh, Tadhg Ó hIfearnáin, Anne O'Keeffe, Muiris Ó Laoire, Stephanie O'Riordan, Ide O'Sullivan, Mary Ruane, Steve Walsh, and Paul Wickens). We would also like to acknowledge the anonymous reviewer of the book proposal for helpful and insightful comments which we hope that we have been able to address. Thanks also to Christabel Scaife at Peter Lang for help and guidance in the development of this book. We are grateful for the support of members of the executive of IRAAL in allowing us to realize the book. Above all we wish to thank each of the contributors for their patience, hard work and stimulating chapters and we wish them all ongoing success in their research endeavours.

FIONA FARR AND MÁIRÉAD MORIARTY

Introduction

Aim of the book

The work presented in this book stems from a postgraduate conference held by IRAAL (The Irish Association for Applied Linguistics) at the University of Limerick in October 2010. IRAAL was founded in 1975 to support research in applied and general linguistics in Ireland. IRAAL is affiliated to the International Association for Applied Linguistics (AILA) and pursues its aim of supporting research by organizing seminars, lectures, conferences and workshops. The IRAAL Postgraduate Conference presented an opportunity for new and emerging scholars to present and discuss their research. While the majority of the papers presented focused on Ireland as the context in which they address specific language problems, we also feel that the research has implications for the study of language and teaching in society more generally. As such, this book is a result of the desire to highlight the advances being made in research in the field within the context of Ireland. It is our belief that by focusing on macro issues of the relationship between language and its users within the micro context of Ireland, insights into interesting and innovative discussions which have implications for future avenues for Applied Linguistic research are provided.

The book is situated within the broad field of Applied Linguistics (AL). AL is an academic field of inquiry which connects knowledge about languages and its relationship to the social world. The tradition of applied linguistics established itself in part as a response to the narrowing of focus in linguistics with the advent in the late 1950s of generative linguistics, and has always maintained a socially accountable role, demonstrated by its central interest in language problems. The most widely cited definition of

AL comes from Christopher Brumfit who describes it as 'the theoretical and empirical investigation of real world problems in which language is a central issue' (Brumfit 1995: 27). Applied linguistics starts from the assumption that the relationship between language and society is an imperfect one and as a field of study AL seeks to solve many of the related problems. As Grabe (2002: 9) points out:

> (T)he focus of applied linguistics is on trying to resolve language based problems that people encounter in the real world, whether they are learners, teachers, supervisors, academics, lawyers, service providers, those who need services, test takers, policy developers, dictionary makers, translators or a whole range of business providers.

The aim of the present book is to provide examples of stimulating research which addresses two main themes within the field of AL. These include: language learning and teaching, and the study of language and some of its various discourses in context. In order to ensure the present volume has implications for as wide an audience as is possible, it is not theoretically focused, rather each chapter deals with a specific real world issue in context. The book endeavours to highlight real world language problems which are worth taking about. In this vein, the book aligns itself with Widdowson (2003: 14), who notes that applied linguistics 'does not impose a way of thinking, but points things out that might be worth thinking about'.

The purpose of this introduction, as well as outlining the contents of this volume, is to highlight a few of the major issues that have occurred to us as editors, in drawing the chapters together. The book is about the relationship between language and society in Ireland, with a strong focus on language learning contexts. Like the majority of contexts, language issues in Ireland have been influenced by global flows of people, ideas and technology. The relationship between language and society is complex and multi-faceted. Discussing it in this book is timely in the Irish context for a number of reasons. Firstly, to provide an account of language problems that have arisen given the increasing multilingual nature of Ireland; secondly, to examine the aspects of the current situation in relation to the Irish language; thirdly, to illustrate the potential for new technologies to enhance language learning and teaching.

With respect to the first aim, it is important to point out that during the period referred to as the 'Celtic Tiger' the number of immigrants to Ireland grew rapidly. According to the Central Statistics Office (<http://www.cso.ie>), immigration to Ireland peaked in 2006 and 2007 with numbers as high as 107,800 and 109,500 respectively. Thus, one can surmise that the number of speakers of languages other than English and Irish grew at a similar rate. As ever, it is difficult to accurately account for the number of languages spoken in Ireland on a daily basis, but recent research would point to something in the region of 180+ languages (cf. Carson and Extra 2010). While an increasingly diverse multilingual society creates many opportunities, it also creates new challenges in which language learning and teaching play a major role. Undoubtedly, Ireland's school-going population is likely to remain multilingual, multicultural and multinational, yet, there is little systematized provision and support for language learners, teachers and teacher educators. Some of the chapters in this book address these issues by focusing on the case of Polish migrants. By far the largest group of migrants to Ireland during the Celtic Tiger were Polish and while present economic conditions have forced some to return home, a significant number of Polish people have remained in Ireland. Machowska-Kosciak's chapter highlights the significance of the existing linguistic repertoires in forming part of the language socialization process of Polish learners of English. In this way, Machowska-Kosciak addresses a gap in the literature on multilingualism identified by Ó Laoire and Singleton (2009), who argue that there is little research available in the context of Ireland which uncovers the conditions through which prior knowledge of an additional language might influence subsequent acquisition processes. Baumgart, in her chapter, points to the need for a more systematic approach to teacher education in the context of EAL (English as an Additional Language) provision in Ireland. She offers a very timely critique of how EAL has been managed in Irish primary and post-primary schools to date. She provides a suggested strategy which has the potential to alter and improve the EAL provision in Irish schools.

The second aim which related to the Irish language is a theme that runs through many chapters of the book. The Irish language is the first official language of the Republic of Ireland, with English recognized as the second official language. The Irish language is an important marker of identity, yet after more than eighty years of status and acquisition planning, there are no monolingual Irish speakers, there are limited significant levels of inter-generational transmission both within and outside of officially designated Irish-speaking areas (the Gaeltacht), and the use of the language in contem-porary Irish society remains low. All of these factors combine to make Irish a minority language and much of the research presented in this book will have implications for many other minority language situations, as well as for other so-called 'bigger' languages that find themselves in a minoritized position. The chapters by Flynn, Kavanagh and Hickey, and Ó Murchadha address three of the major debates in current thinking on minority lan-guages. Flynn's chapter taps into the growth in literature on adult learners of heritage languages, and more specifically addresses the role that culture plays for these learners. Kavanagh and Hickey's chapter contributes to a growth in the research literature on immersion schooling. Their focus on parental involvement in children's experiences of Irish language medium schools, Gaelscoileanna, is particularly novel. Ó Murchadha's chapter also addresses a wider debate in current minority language scholarship on the notion of 'standard' and the ideological contestations that surround the vary notion of standard language.

The third aim of the book seeks to address the seemingly ubiquitous elements of new technologies that are currently impacting on language learning and teaching. Two of the book's chapters examine the potential for the use of such technologies in supporting language learning and con-tinued professional development amongst language teachers and learners. In her chapter, Riordan highlights the potential for the use of blogs as a space where novice teachers can engage in reflective practice. She argues that if student teachers engage in such reflective activity from the beginning of their career, it may give them a better understanding of themselves and their students, which can only serve to benefit them in their future careers. Healy and Onderdonk Horan's chapter offers an account of how corpora and concordancing software can be utilized to develop more authentic teaching materials for the teaching of Hotelspeak in Hotel Management ESP (English for Specific Purposes) pedagogy.

The three main aims of the book outlined here illustrate the robustness of the study of language, teaching and learning in Ireland. It is, of course, impossible to exhaustively address these aims herein and to this end we have organized the book under two main themes which we hope will allow it to serve the interests of linguists, educators and policy makers alike.

Structure of the book

The book opens with commentary from Prof. Michael McCarthy, who offers perspectives on the research presented herein and contextualizes it within the international applied linguistics arena. As the table of contents shows, we have organized the remaining chapters into sections that revolve around two major themes. Section One contains four papers that open the book by examining issues related to language learning and teaching. The first chapter in this section focuses on novel ways to activate learning in today's linguistically diverse classroom. Through an analysis of data gathered from an action research project in Irish post primary schools; Collins makes a case for mime as a significant tool in facilitating successful language acquisition. In the second paper, by Flynn, there is a focus on learner motivation and the role of cultural awareness in language learning. Specifically, the chapter focuses on adult learners of Irish. The results of a series of qualitative interviews conducted by the author supports the claim that taking learners' linguistic and cultural needs into consideration when designing language courses and classroom materials may lead to greater learner motivation and success in acquiring the target language.

The next chapter in Section One focuses on current trends in the scholarship of the Irish language. In their chapter, Kavanagh and Hickey examine how the rise in popularity of the Irish medium schools, Gaelscoileanna, has brought about changes in the typical profile of the students attending such schools and, as a result, the typical profile of an Irish-immersion parent. In their chapter they explore the barriers to parents' involvement in immersion schooling and how such barriers may impact on the linguistic outcomes of the children. The final paper in this section by Machowska-Kosciak takes a language socialization perspective on identity and knowledge construction in different educational settings in Irish post-primary education. The chapter is particularly concerned with the L1 (first language) and L2 (second language) language socialization processes among Polish immigrant students. The research examined how these students engage with issues of conflicting identities and competing language learning (English) and language maintenance (Polish) goals as they grow up and try to find their place in a new country and society. This chapter represents one of a relatively small number of studies to date which examine the experience of Polish learners of English in Ireland. This paper contributes to closing a gap that currently exists in the literature on the dual processes of language learning and heritage language maintenance experienced by immigrants and has benefits outside of the context of Ireland. In all, this section provides an account of a number of approaches to problems associated with language learning and teaching in contemporary societies categorized by globalized modernity and opens avenues for further research in the field relevant not only to Ireland.

The second section of the book also contains four chapters, which are organized around the theme of the study of language and discourse. The four chapters, many with a pedagogically-motivated research question, are focused around aspects of language study that have the potential to have significant impact in these globalizing times. The first chapter in this section by Baumgart looks at the discourse of multilingualism in the Irish education sector with a specific focus on teacher educators. Baumgart reports on research conducted amongst primary and secondary level teacher educators. The results of the research highlights how teacher education needs to address the issue of EAL more specifically and to provide structured workshops and sessions focussed around improving classroom practice through the use of policy tools and examples of best practice. She provides an up-to-date critique of the EAL provision in Irish schools and offers an avenue through which many of the issues outlined can be addressed. In their chapter, Healy and Onderdonk Horan focus on novel approaches to the creation of textbooks. In examining the discourse of the hospitality industry, the paper focuses on novel approaches to attempting an effective tool for the acquisition of English in educating future hotel managers. They describe how the Shannon College of Hotel Management in partnership with Cambridge University Press and Mary Immaculate College, Limerick, participated in a year-long research project aimed at capturing the language of native and non-native English speakers in hotel management training. The resultant corpus, they argue, will provide an up-to-the-minute invaluable resource for both lecturers and students in terms of their English language use. The data is analysed for Hotelspeak, demonstrating the shared repertoire of this community of practice (Wegner 1998), and can inform the development of more specialized and pragmatic teaching materials within this context.

In Chapter 7, Ó Murchadha focuses on issues surrounding notions of a language standard in the context of the Irish language. Ó Murchadha highlights the contested nature of 'standard'. He argues that it is mostly an ideology against which varieties of language are evaluated. Reporting on fieldwork data collected from teenagers in the Gaeltacht, he argues that the creation of a written standard for Irish has been detrimental to the vitality of the traditional Gaeltacht vernaculars. The results indicate that participants consider Gaeltacht youth speech and non-Gaeltacht speech more standard than traditional Gaeltacht speech. The final chapter in Section Two, by Riordan, sheds light on a significant avenue for continued profession development amongst language teachers. Riordan begins by highlighting the role of new technologies in allowing teachers to interact in ways that previously were not possible. Such technologies provide teachers and those involved in teacher education with an invaluable resource when it comes to aspects of continued professional development. Riordan's chapter focuses on reflective practice. In particular, she investigated the use of blogs as reflective diaries with student teachers on an MA in English Language Teaching programme. Using a corpus-based discourse analysis of the reflections of student teachers, Riordan highlights blogs as a significant tool in the promotion of reflective practice as a tool for professional development.

We hope that the book sheds light on a number of issues that are currently prominent in understanding applied linguistics in a multilingual and multimodal world. Inevitably, it also leaves many questions open, in need of further investigation and supporting data, which will allow us to continue the discussions around language problems not only within the context of Ireland.

References

Brumfit, C. (1995). 'Teacher professionalism and research'. In G. Cook and B. Seidl-hofer (eds), *Principles and Practice in Applied Linguistics*, pp. 27–42. Oxford: Oxford University Press.

Carson, L., and Extra, G. (2010). *Multilingualism in Dublin: Home language use among primary school children, report on a pilot survey*. Dublin: Centre for Language and Communication Studies.

Grabe, W. (2002). 'Applied Linguistics: An Emerging Discipline for the Twenty-first Century'. In B. Kaplan (ed.), *Oxford Handbook of Applied Linguistics*, pp. 3–12. Oxford: Oxford University Press.

Ó Laoire, M. and Singleton, D. (2009). 'The role of prior knowledge in L3 learning and use: Further evidence of psychotypological dimensions.' In L. Aronin and B. Hufeisen (eds). *The Exploration of Multilingualism*, pp. 79–102. Amsterdam: John Benjamins.

Wenger, E. (1998). *Communities of Practice. Learning, Meaning, and Identity*. Cambridge: Cambridge University Press.

Widdowson, H.G. (2003). *Defining issues in English Language Teaching*. Oxford: Oxford University Press.

MICHAEL MCCARTHY

Applied linguistics research: Connecting with the bigger picture

There is (fortunately) no one single agreed definition of Applied Linguistics (AL), though most scholars would agree that AL should always be concerned with practicalities in the real world in relation to which knowledge about language plays a pivotal role. Schmitt and Celce-Murcia (2010: 1) refer to AL's aim to 'achieve some purpose or solve some problem in the real world' by using what we know about language, how it is learned and how it is used. I might in addition, if the reader will permit such vanity, refer to a definition from one of my own works, which includes 'the belief that linguists can offer insights and ways forward in the resolution of problems related to language in a wide variety of contexts' (McCarthy 2001: 1). Meanwhile, the editors of the present volume have added further definitions to the mix (see p. 2). What emerges is a discipline that is very catholic in its scope, covering a spectrum that ranges from the application of theories and descriptions of language in general and particular languages on one side, to chalk-face and e-learning preoccupations on the other, which, while dominated by problems of language learning, by no means exclusively function within that domain. Aside from the issues of language and language learning in classrooms and more recently online, the discipline has, in the last few decades, expanded to include forensic applications and the broad domain of information technology. Being rooted in the real world, AL has also of necessity allied itself with sociolinguistic preoccupations and analyses and critiques of social and linguistic phenomena as reflected in educational linguistics, cultural studies, bilingualism, multilingualism, code-switching, literacy and (critical) discourse analysis, to name but a few.

How, then, does the present volume fit into this picture? Firstly, and most importantly, its roots are in Ireland, though its insights most certainly will be of interest to practitioners in a vastly wider, global context. In the past, it often seemed to me, as a British outsider, that AL in Ireland struggled to assert itself in the shadow of its historically dominant neighbour. Small departments in a small constellation of universities funded by a small economy, located on the farthest-flung western fringe of Europe, were somewhat suffocated by the giant across the water with its many universities and the critical mass of scholarship in AL thus generated. However, in all probability the outsider will, like me, have been woefully ignorant of the long and fertile tradition of linguistic and applied linguistic work concerning the Irish language, as well as the excellent lexicographic and grammatical studies of the English language in Ireland represented by scholars such as Dolan (1998) and Filppula (1999). It is probably fair to say that relatively few AL scholars researching in the Irish context were known beyond Erin's green shores. However, all that was to change rapidly in the last years of the twentieth century and the opening decade of the twenty-first, such that anyone following even half-heartedly the AL literature in English in the last decade or so cannot fail to have noticed the emergence into international scholarship of a new generation of Irish AL researchers.

The new generation surfed the tide of several developments, not least the so-called Celtic Tiger economy with its increased funding opportunities for research and international collaboration and the expansion of university departments, along with the boom in MA and teacher education programmes in the field of AL and TESOL/ELT and the growing numbers of international students choosing to study in Ireland.

Two allied developments contributed to the growth of critical mass in international terms for Irish AL. The first was the transformation of Irish society from being a two-language culture to its current profile as a multilingual and multicultural nation. Such a development, as in other nations, brought with it both benefits and downsides, and both provided a new impetus for AL researchers. The present volume is replete with examples of such problems and prospects and good-sense responses to them, and Ireland-based AL has shown its ability to offer valuable insight into issues around intercultural communication (e.g. Chambers and O'Baoill 1999). The second development was the explosion of technology, which in turn had two aspects from which AL in Ireland has benefitted. On the one hand, technology released the potential of corpus linguistics, with major corpora being built in Irish and Irish English, e.g. the Royal Irish Academy (2004) Irish language Corpus, the Irish and English Nua-Chorpas na hÉireann / New Corpus for Ireland (Foras na Gaeilge 2012), ICE Ireland, a member of the world-wide International Corpus of English project (Kallen and Kirk 2008), the L-CIE spoken Irish English corpus (Farr, Murphy and O'Keeffe (2004) and some smaller Irish English corpora serving specific projects (e.g. O'Keeffe 2006; Clancy 2011). On the other hand, the advent of e-learning in terms of CALL, ICT, Data-Driven Language Learning (DDL) and blended and online learning provided Irish AL scholars with home-based research opportunities that possess far-reaching and global consequences (Chambers 2010; Chambers et al. 2011). Meanwhile, the technology envelope has been pushed forward within innovative AL frameworks in collaborative enterprises between linguists and non-linguists in the Dublin Institute of Technology's projects in spoken language analysis in the context of language learning (Campbell et al. 2009).

As a result of this growth in Irish-based AL, outsiders like me now see a confident and self-assured body of researchers uninhibited by the long shadow cast by the scholarship of its neighbour across the Irish Sea, 'doing' AL against a national, European and global backdrop. It is a community of scholars receiving due recognition as a robust and energetic group of professionals, outward-looking in their research perspectives and methods, but firmly grounded in the home territory and serving the community that supports and invests in it. In particular, Irish English, as a variety of English, has earned itself the status of equal partner in studies of World Englishes and has shed its historical baggage as a minority dialect within the 'British' Isles. Alongside this, the Irish language has assumed a more confident place in the broader debate on multilingualism and language and heritage within the Irish nation.

The present volume is one of the fruits of the healthy flourishing of AL in Ireland. However, although home-grown in its practical preoccupations, a most powerful index of the health and calibre of Irish AL is the contextualizing of its research within established global methods and processes as well as cutting-edge approaches. The international profile of AL has changed in the last couple of decades in tandem with the way AL has grown and changed in Ireland. In the context of language teaching and learning, several strands have come to the fore in the last two decades which are accurately and faithfully reflected in the chapters of the present volume. These embrace the fields of language acquisition, teacher education, technology and minority and heritage languages. Much has changed in the three decades that I have dared call myself an applied linguist. From positivist and generative theories of language acquisition to the emergence of sociocultural theory championed by scholars such as Lantolf, Appel and Thorne (Lantolf and Appel 1994; Lantolf 2006; Lantolf and Thorne 2006) and theories of language socialization (Duff and Hornberger 2008), the emphasis has been less on the language learner as rat-in-the-laboratory and more as a whole person building upon existing knowledge, thriving under guidance and scaffolding while acquiring a language as a social and cultural resource. Nowhere more marked is this urge to develop as a social being than in the challenging environment encountered by incoming populations, including school-age children. Papers in the present volume by Machowska-Kosciak and Collins testify to an awareness of these significant developments in AL.

Multilingualism and multiculturalism involve questions of identity, and language and identity has been another significant thread in the fabric of AL in recent years. The notion of a monolithic identity has been questioned by sociolinguists and sociocultural theorists, with identity now typically conceptualized as multiple, flexible, dynamic and reconstructed continuously in interaction. Identity has been seen both in terms of the social positioning that is often triggered by language use and in terms of broader ethnic and national identities (Spolsky 1999: 181). Furthermore, there is the question of whether individuals associate with particular community identities or distance themselves from them, an issue which applies in classrooms as well as in broader social contexts (Norton 2000; Toohey 2000; Maybin 2006; Block 2007). As Flynn puts it in the present volume: 'A person's sense of self is often connected to issues of culture and language' (p. 41), arguing that motivation is also affected by sense of self, a preoccupation addressed in the papers in Dörnyei and Ushioda (2009).

Irish, like the language of its near-neighbour and my own nation of birth, Welsh, depends for its health, survival and growth partly on the existence of immersion education (in Wales in the form of the Ysgolion

Cymraeg / Welsh Schools), as well as investment and commitment to reinforcement via the media and the 'linguistic landscape' (Howell 1982; Shohamy et al. 2010). An important trend in Educational AL has been the recognition of schools as a collaborative environment where success is enhanced not only by appropriate pedagogy but by parental and broader local and social involvement. Immersion education, in particular, is often viewed by immigrant parents as an investment in social capital, which can be achieved alongside the preservation of heritage languages, as Canadian evidence suggests (Dagenais 2003). Kavanagh and Hickey in the present volume ground their research in this perspective. However, no-one can gainsay the importance of teacher education in any paradigm shifts in pedagogical AL. Wright (2010), in an important survey article on Second Language Teacher Education, points to a shift away from what he calls the old 'demonstrate and delivery' pattern of teacher education with its roots in traditional AL towards an emphasis on reflective practice and school-based training, where the school is seen as a social context for teachers learning to teach. Additionally, action research and the role of the teacher as researcher-practitioner have come greatly to the fore, along with a recognition of the importance of teacher cognition and beliefs (Borg 2006). The classroom itself is seen as the arena for the development of a particular type of competence: classroom interactional competence (Walsh 2011: ch. 8), another kind of social capital often raising difficulties for immigrant pupils and a new challenge for teacher education in multicultural contexts. Baumgart in this volume tackles some of these questions head-on, aligning teacher-educators' perceptions with institutional and policy critiques. An awareness of the delicate strands that link, push and pull between teachers, classrooms, the home environment, the canons of teacher education and political and institutional policy inform all the papers in the present volume which confront the practical issues of language pedagogy.

It could be argued that it is in the area of technology that AL has seen the greatest upheavals in the last couple of decades, with the challenges of computer literacy for both teachers and pupils in language teaching and learning set alongside developments in Applied Corpus Linguistics and blended and online learning. Corpus linguistics has offered AL more than just the ability to search massive textual databases. Especially in the

development of spoken corpora, traditional perspectives on language use
and teaching materials have been challenged (McCarthy 1998; McCarten
2010). Healy and Onderdonk Horan's paper in the present volume presents a classic case of the modelling and compilation of a vocationally-ori-
ented spoken corpus, created collaboratively with British-based colleagues,
research into which is not only grounded in the widely cited notion of
Community of Practice (Wenger 1998), but is also aimed at extremely practical and useful ends in preparing hotel managers and allied professionals in
the hospitality industry. One further comment about the impact of spoken
corpora that must be made is the emergence, hopefully, of a greater respect
for the spoken language, not only in pedagogy but in relation to major issues
such as the promotion of standard varieties of languages. Recent years have
seen a growth of understanding of the importance of varieties of English
and of the role of English as lingua franca, along with the development
of spoken learner corpora (Granger 2004). If smaller languages such as
Welsh and Irish are to flourish, their spoken forms must be acknowledged
and given proper priority, as Ó Murchadha adumbrates in this book. As
mentioned towards the beginning of this exordium to the present volume,
computational technology has penetrated a number of areas of language
pedagogy, and of the many insights to come out of the advent of blended
and online learning, perhaps the most striking is the new spaces in which
teachers and learners can interact and thus develop more social kinds of
learning, including online journals, fora and blogs. Building on the work
of scholars such as Yang (2009), where blogs are seen as enhancing the
development of communities of practice among novice teachers and the
exchange of ideas and beliefs that blogs facilitate, Riordan brings corpus
linguistic techniques to bear on her data in this volume, thus marrying two
aspects of the technological revolution in AL.

When I was invited to write this introductory piece, in which I have
attempted to place the papers in the present volume in a wider AL context,
I read the contributions with a view to getting some sense of the state of
health of AL in Ireland. My conclusion is that it is in excellent shape, that its
practitioners as represented in these papers have forged a unique combination of research into important questions for Ireland while grounding their
scholarship in current and cutting-edge approaches within international

AL. My own collaboration with Ireland-based scholars has been enriched by the community of researchers in the IVACS (Inter-Varietal Applied Corpus Studies) group. IVACS was founded in Ireland and has reached out to researchers in corpus studies around the world, bringing together a wealth of insights into language use and functioning as an exemplary AL community. Its members are well-represented in the editors, contributors and scholarly references in the papers of this book. I hope that all its readers will take the same pleasure and edification from it as I have done.

Cambridge, July 2012

References

Block, D. (2007). *Second Language Identities*. London: Continuum.

Borg, S. (2006). *Teacher Cognition and Language Education*. London: Continuum.

Campbell, D., McDonnell, C., Meinardi, M., Pritchard, C., Richardson, B. and Wang, Y. (2009). 'DIT's Dynamic Speech Corpus'. *Proceedings of the 43rd IATEFL 2009 Conference*, 108–110.

Chambers, A. (2010). 'Computer-Assisted Language Learning: Mapping the territory.' *Language Teaching*, 43 (1): 113–122.

Chambers, A. and O' Baoill, D. (eds) (1999). *Intercultural Communication and Language Learning*. Dublin: Irish Association for Applied Linguistics in association with the Royal Irish Academy.

Chambers, A., Farr, F. and O'Riordan, S. (2011). 'Language teachers with corpora in mind: From starting steps to walking tall.' *Language Learning Journal* 39 (1): 85–103.

Clancy, B. (2011). 'Complementary perspectives on hedging behaviour in family discourse: The analytical synergy of variational pragmatics and corpus linguistics.' *International Journal of Corpus Linguistics* 17 (4): 371–390.

Dagenais, D. (2003). 'Accessing imagined communities through multilingualism and immersion education.' *Journal of Language, Identity and Education* 2 (4): 269–283.

Dolan, T.P. (1998). *A Dictionary of Hiberno-English: The Irish Use of English*. Dublin: Gill & Macmillan.

Dőrnyei, Z. and Ushioda, E. (eds) (2009). *Motivation, Language Identity and the L2 Self*. Bristol: Multilingual Matters.

Duff, P.A., and Hornberger, N.H. (eds) (2008). *Language Socialization*. Encyclopedia of language and education, 2nd edition, Vol.8. Boston: Springer.

Farr, F., Murphy, B. and O'Keeffe, A. (2004). *The Limerick corpus of Irish English: Design, description and application*. Teanga, 21: 5–29.

Filppula, M. (1999). *The Grammar of Irish English*. London: Routledge.

Foras na Gaeilge (2012). *The New Corpus for Ireland*. Online at <http://www.focloir.ie/corpus-based-lexicography>.

Granger, S. (2004). 'Computer Learner Corpus Research: Current Status and Future Prospects'. In Ulla Connor and Thomas A. Upton (eds), *Language and Computers, Applied Corpus Linguistics. A Multidimensional Perspective*, pp. 123–145. Amsterdam: Rodopi.

Howell, W.J. (1982). 'Bilingual broadcasting and the survival of authentic culture in Wales and Ireland.' *Journal of Communication* 32 (4): 39–55.

Kallen, Jeffrey L and John M. Kirk (2008) ICE-Ireland A User's Guide. Belfast: Ció Ollscoil na Banríona.

Lantolf, J.P. (2006). 'Sociocultural theory and second language learning: State of the art.' *Studies in Second Language Acquisition* 28: 67–109.

Lantolf, J.P., and Appel, G. (eds) (1994). *Vygotskian Approaches to Second Language Research*. Norwood NJ: Ablex.

Lantolf, J.P., and Thorne, S.L. (2006). *Sociocultural Theory and the Genesis of L2 Development*. Oxford: Oxford University Press.

Maybin, J. (2006). *Children's Voices: Talk, Knowledge and Identity*. London: Palgrave Macmillan.

McCarten, J. (2010). 'Corpus-informed course book design'. In A. O'Keeffe and M.J. McCarthy (eds), *The Routledge Handbook of Corpus Linguistics*, pp. 413–427. Abingdon: Routledge.

McCarthy, M.J. (1998). *Spoken Language and Applied Linguistics*. Cambridge: Cambridge University Press.

McCarthy, M.J. (2001). *Issues in Applied Linguistics*. Cambridge: Cambridge University Press.

Norton, B. (2000). *Identity and Language Learning: Gender, Ethnicity and Educational Change*. Harlow: Longman.

O'Keeffe, A. (2006). *Investigating Media Discourse*. Abingdon: Routledge.

Royal Irish Academy (2004). *Corpas Na Gaeilge 1600–1882. Focloir na Nua-Ghaeilge, The Irish Language Corpus*. Dublin: Royal Irish Academy.

Schmitt, N. and Celce-Murcia, M. (eds) (2010). 'An Overview of Applied Linguistics.' In N. Schmitt (ed.), *An Introduction to Applied Linguistics*, pp. 1–15. London: Hodder & Stoughton Ltd.

Shohamy, E., Ben-Rafael, E. and Barni, M. (2010). *Linguistic Landscape in the City.* Bristol: Multilingual Matters.

Spolsky, B. (1999). 'Second-language learning.' In J. Fishman (ed.), *Handbook of Language and Ethnic Identity*, pp. 181–192. Oxford: Oxford University Press.

Toohey, K. (2000). *Learning English at School: Identity, Social Relations and Classroom Practice.* Clevedon: Multilingual Matters.

Walsh, S. (2011). *Exploring Classroom Discourse.* Abingdon: Routledge.

Wenger, E. (1998). *Communities of Practice. Learning, Meaning, and Identity.* Cambridge: Cambridge University Press.

Wright, T. (2010). 'Second language teacher education: Review of recent research on practice.' *Language Teaching* 43 (3): 259–296.

Yang, S.-H. (2009). 'Using blogs to enhance critical reflection and community of practice.' *Educational Technology and Society* 12 (2): 11–21.

Exploring Language Learning and Teaching

MANDY COLLINS[1]

1 Teacher Acts, Class Speaks: Mime activating learning in today's linguistically diverse classroom

> 'what you get is someone telling you that our classrooms have changed, as if you needed to be told that, but not showing you techniques for teaching these students.'
>
> — LYONS and LITTLE, 2009: 45.

Introduction

Teacher Acts, Class Speaks (TACS) is one of three pedagogical interventions being developed within an Action Research project, aiming towards meeting the need identified in the quotation above, which is from a language support teacher responding to questions about in-service training related to teaching international students in Irish post-primary schools. The project addresses the challenge linguistic diversity in the classroom represents for teachers. The three pedagogical strategies are developed over one school year, to support the academic language development of all pupils, both native and non-native English speakers, within Irish post-primary classrooms. Teachers' attitudes towards these interventions are recorded during one-to-one conversations with the researcher and group discussions. Pupils' attitudes towards these interventions are recorded in writing through the use of student research notebooks and through discussion in focus groups. Criteria from Systemic Functional Linguistics (Halliday

---

1   The author would like to thank Gareth Brugha, Peter Edwards and the anonymous reviewers for their valuable comments.

& Matthiessen 2004) and school genre theory (Schleppegrell 2004) are employed to analyse pupils' written work, for features of academic English.

This paper offers a description and analysis of TACS, weaving together theoretical perspectives from Gesture Studies and Sociocultural Theory, with findings from research into communication and language pedagogy, as well as established language teaching approaches. It begins by explaining the recent shift in the linguistic profile of Irish post-primary classes and the implications of the resulting linguistic diversity for teachers. Drawing on research into bilingual education (Cummins 2000) it highlights the challenges facing the small minority of English language learning pupils typically found in Irish post-primary classrooms. The process and purpose of TACS is then described, and further illuminated with reference to Gesture Studies for a theoretical description of TACS mime, research involving mime, deaf children's communication, and language teaching involving gesture. The conclusion of this literature survey is to place TACS in the gestural category of 'pantomime'. Following this analysis, the paper argues that TACS addresses the linguistic diversity found in contemporary Irish classrooms, from the perspective of sociocultural theory, a viewpoint further supported in the form of two examples of the use of silence in second language pedagogy. The paper concludes with concerns about how appropriate teachers and pupils may find this use of mime in the classroom.

Today's linguistically diverse classroom

The linguistic profile of post-primary classes in Ireland has undergone a significant transformation over the last fifteen years, reflecting the pattern of immigration into Ireland, which is in turn located within the context of increasing migration worldwide (Mac Éinrí & White 2008: 164). In the mid-1990s the trend of outward migration was reversed by the return of many Irish migrants due to the economic boom. With European Union enlargement in 2004, this trend of immigration became dominated by migrants from other EU countries, particularly the new accession States

(Smyth et al. 2009: 17). In April 2006 non-Irish nationals representing 188 different countries were living in Ireland (CSO 2008: 8) and by 2007 immigrants comprised about 11 per cent of the population, an increase of 60 per cent in ten years (Taguma et al. 2009: 16). Ireland experienced net immigration each year from 1996 until 2009, when the trend reverted to net outward migration. Estimated figures for the year ending April 2010, supported by preliminary findings from the 2011 census (CSO 2011), indicate that levels of immigration almost halved during 2010, while the overall level of emigration from Ireland remained constant. However, a much higher percentage of emigrants were Irish nationals in the year up to April 2010 (42 per cent compared to 28 per cent during the previous year), while the number of non-Irish nationals leaving the country declined by approximately 20 per cent (CSO 2010).

Consequently, over the last decade, there has been a shift in the linguistic profile of post-primary school classes from typically monolingual or English/Irish bilingual to heterogeneously multilingual. Estimates based on limited data suggest that approximately 5 per cent of the children currently attending Irish post-primary schools speak a language other than English or Irish as their mother tongue (Smyth et al. 2009: 1–11, Taguma et al. 2009: 27). Approximately 90 per cent of post-primary schools record newcomer students; '[i]n general, newcomer students are well dispersed in schools throughout the second-level sector' (Smyth et al. 2009: 46). In each post-primary school between 2–9 per cent of students are international newcomers (Smyth et al. 2009: xiv). These children spend most or all of their school day in mainstream subject classes. It is therefore clear that linguistic diversity is a mainstream issue of Irish post-primary education and that Ireland represents one example of the current worldwide reality of increasing cultural, racial and linguistic diversity in schools (Miller et al. 2009: 3, Hammond 2009: 56, Cummins et al. 2007: 40).

The Irish post-primary class now typically contains a small minority of English language learners: one, two or three pupils in a class of approximately thirty. While there is widespread consensus on the importance of a whole school approach to English as an Additional Language provision in Irish schools (DES 2009; Smyth et al. 2009; Wallen 2007; NCCA 2006), there is also general agreement that in view of the diversity and heterogeneity of student populations, a one-size-fits-all approach is not appropriate: '[a] one-size-fits-all approach to teaching ELLs [English language learners] is bound to fail because students bring varying linguistic and academic backgrounds to learning' (Lucas et al. 2008: 364). Keogh and Whyte (2003) conducted a study to explore the experiences and aspirations of immigrant students in four Dublin post-primary schools. They argue: '[s]ome of the teachers in this study identified themselves as subject teachers, yet found themselves having to be language teachers also and felt unequipped to deal with the situation' (Keogh & Whyte 2003: 48). The theme of teachers feeling ill equipped for this situation due to inadequate training and resources recurs in other studies within the Irish context (Lyons & Little 2009: 52–70; Smyth et al. 2009: 185; Taguma et al. 2009: 10; Nowlan 2008: 261; Wallen 2007; Healy 2007: 93; Devine 2005: 59; Ward 2004: 31). The linguistic diversity of today's post-primary classroom clearly presents a significant challenge for teachers.

English language learning pupils face multiple challenges; in addition to the usual tasks of studying school subjects, they need to acquire English for social purposes as well as academic English, which is the language of instruction at school. Cummins (1979) coined the terms basic interpersonal communicative skills (BICS) and cognitive academic language proficiency (CALP). BICS refers to the type of social language that most native-speaking children master before they start primary school. Basic interpersonal communicative skills consist of 'accent, oral fluency and sociolinguistic competence' (Larsen-Freeman & Long 1991: 39). CALP is the type of language needed to fully access the post-primary curriculum and perform well in examinations. Native English speaking children develop their cognitive academic language proficiency throughout their time at school and the career paths pupils follow 'depend very much on how successfully they acquire this specialized language required to gain academic qualifications and carry out literacy-related tasks and activities' (Cummins 2000: 53). English language learning pupils usually acquire BICS within their first two years at school in Ireland and may appear fluent in social situations. However, acquiring CALP to the same level as their peers involves trying to catch up with a moving target and research suggests that this takes longer than students spend at post-primary school.

Research in the Irish context has identified that subject-specific terminology takes English language-learning pupils longer to acquire than day-to-day conversational fluency (Smyth et al. 2009: 181). As well as acquiring lexical items, however, pupils must learn to 'use language in ways that meet the school's expectations' (Schleppegrell 2004: 6), which involves mastering genres and grammatical structures not usually found in BICS. Schleppergrell quotes Mehan: 'to be successful in the classroom, students not only must know the content of academic subjects, they must learn the appropriate form in which to cast their academic knowledge' (Mehan 1979: 133). The current study, which includes the piloting of TACS, addresses the issue of supporting pupils' development of academic language on the levels of genre, the sentence and lexical item; TACS is the classroom intervention addressing the level of the sentence.

A recent small-scale study, which surveyed seventeen English language support teachers in Irish post-primary schools, found 100 per cent of the participants willing to mime for the sake of their English language learning pupils (Collins 2009: 32). This study developed materials for teachers to use in the context of newly arrived pupils' initial orientation and assessment at their new school, a situation where multiple factors may obscure the pupils' level of English proficiency. Given that teachers have expressed their feelings of being inadequately trained and equipped for the current challenge of linguistic diversity, teaching strategies employing mime may be welcomed as one way of addressing the challenge of supporting all pupils' development of academic English, of both the native speakers and the non-native speakers. Teacher Acts, Class Speaks (TACS) is one short activity during which the teacher mimes for the class.

Teacher Acts, Class Speaks (TACS)

TACS in progress in the classroom closely resembles a teacher playing the game Charades with her class. The most significant feature is that the teacher does not speak, but uses mime and visual aids, silently encouraging the class to provide words to match her actions. The pupils may be quiet while they first watch the mime, they may speak amongst themselves and they will eventually shout out suggestions of words, both lexical and grammatical, to see if the teacher accepts them as part of the target language. Looking to the teacher for silent guidance, the class co-re-construct the target language, which is predetermined by the teacher and contains subject-specific terminology conveying the key concepts of the lesson, formulated in an academic structure appropriate to the classroom.

The purpose of TACS is to equip teachers with a technique for introducing new concepts and the associated academic language at the level of the sentence. It enables each individual pupil in a class, irrespective of their mother tongue or proficiency in academic language, to access their prior knowledge about the subject matter of the lesson and build on that knowledge to acquire the key concepts, as well as academic English lexis and syntax to express those concepts. This learning is activated through peer collaboration as the pupils work together to re-construct the teacher's prescribed target language.

As an illustrative example, consider the TACS target language for a Geography lesson on glacial erosion: 'U-shaped valleys are formed by glaciers.' This sentence contains the subject-specific lexical terms 'U-shaped valley' and 'glacier' as well as being in the passive voice, a grammatical form common in academic language, but unusual in everyday conversation. The teacher might take as much as 5 minutes to elicit the exact sentence 'U-shaped valleys are formed by glaciers.' through mime and the use of visual aids. Consider the silent representation of the term 'U-shaped valley'. While the teacher is miming 'valley', the pupils are likely to gain the familiar context of mountains, high ground and low ground and possibly the presence of water. 'U-shaped' is a highly visual lexical item; to elicit the word 'shape', the teacher might draw shapes such as a square, circle, triangle and plus sign on the board. Once the pupils have suggested 'shape', the teacher indicates that this is the correct word, but that a morphological change (to 'shaped') is needed; these indications are also made silently, so the teacher uses mime both to represent meanings and to comment on the form and structure of the target language. From 'shaped' the teacher and class together produce 'U-shaped' and thence 'U-shaped valley'. While remaining silent the teacher is free to listen to what the pupils are saying, enabling her to gauge knowledge levels of the topic and associated terminology.

TACS elicits language from the pupils visually. It is an unusual classroom scenario, as the teacher has a clear message to convey, but refrains from verbal expression and explanation, instead employing gesture. Gesture does not normally occur in the context of artificially imposed silence; the discipline of Gesture Studies provides descriptions of how gestures are used.

TACS mime as gesture

Kendon (1972) and McNeill (1979) supplied the theoretical framework for modern Gesture Studies in the 1970s when they independently concluded that gesture and speech are two aspects of the same process (Stam and McCafferty 2008: 5). McNeill (2005) sees language as inseparable from imagery; the imagery being embodied in gestures which occur with speech and places the discipline of Gesture Studies 'at the intersection of the humanities, linguistics, psychology, social science, neuropsychology, and computer engineering/computer science' (McNeill 2005: 15).

Emblems and spontaneous gestures (gesticulations)

Stam and McCafferty (2008) propose two basic types of gesture: emblems, and spontaneous gestures or gesticulations. Emblems can occur without speech and are conventionalized in that they carry a definite meaning within their cultural setting. The 'thumbs up' gesture, for example, is an emblem expressing approval in contemporary Irish culture. Emblems mirror lexical items and can fill a grammatical slot. Emblematic gestures make up part of the TACS mime repertoire, particularly on the meta-level when the teacher comments on the words suggested by the pupils; for example, the teacher can use the 'thumbs up' emblem to signal that a suggested TACS target item is correct. However, TACS mime is not composed solely of emblematic gestures. Clearly TACS mime cannot be classified as gesticulation either, as gesticulations only occur during speech. The 'two basic types of gesture' model fails to provide an adequate framework to describe TACS mime.

Gestures without speech for communicative purposes

Goldin-Meadow et al. (1996) describe speech and accompanying gesture (gesticulation) as parts of an integrated system in which each perform a distinct role: speech conveys information in a linear and segmented fashion and gesture conveys information in a global and non-compositional manner (Goldin-Meadow et al. 1996: 34). Their study asked 'what happens when speech is removed?' and found that 'gesture does not remain global and mimetic but rather immediately switches its form' (Goldin-Meadow et al. 1996: 52). Mimetic gestures mimic or imitate their referent. Goldin-Meadow et al. conducted experiments during which hearing adult participants with no knowledge of any kind of sign language, first explained in words and later expressed with their hands, various short film scenes involving small objects moving across space. The participants all used gestures in both parts of the experiment: the gesture + speech condition and the gesture condition. While speaking, the participants' gestures displayed the global and mimetic qualities of gesticulations. When the participants were asked to use only their hands to communicate, the language-like properties of segmentation and hierarchical combination immediately appeared in their gestures.

> By breaking the bond between gesture and speech, silence frees gesture from the constraints imposed by being part of an integrated system with speech-only to force gesture into the constraints imposed by carrying the full burden of communication, that is, the constraints of a language-like system. (Goldin-Meadow et al. 1996: 50)

TACS mime is also made up of gestures, which are more language-like than gesticulations as the meanings they are trying to convey are not supported by linear and segmented speech and so have to take on these speech-like properties to be interpretable by the class. Furthermore, as well as functioning on the level of meaning, TACS mime is used to explicitly comment on a meta-level about language. For example, gestures are used to indicate the need for a morphological change to a word, in order to reach the exact target item; if the target item is 'formed' in 'U-shaped valleys are formed by glaciers', the teacher indicates through mime to the class, the need to adjust suggestions such as 'formation' or 'forms'. Thus, in the absence of accompanying speech, TACS gestures are more language-like than the gestures characteristic of gesticulation.

Goldin-Meadow et al. compare the gestures of their hearing adult experiment participants with the gestures of ten deaf children (observed by Goldin-Meadow and her colleagues: Feldman, Goldin-Meadow & Gleitman 1978; Goldin-Meadow 1979; Goldin-Meadow & Feldman 1977; Goldin-Meadow & Mylander 1984; 1990). These deaf children had not been exposed to a conventional sign language, but had developed 'home signs', their own systems of gestures for communicative purposes. Goldin-Meadow et al. categorize the deaf children's gestures into three major types: i) deictic, ii) characterizing, and iii) marker gestures. Deictic gestures point out a referent. The marker gestures were used to modulate the children's messages, expressing such qualities as affirmation, negation and doubt. 'Characterizing gestures were stylized pantomimes, the iconic forms of which varied with the intended meaning of each sign (e.g. A fist pounded in the air as if someone was hammering)' (Goldin-Meadow et al. 1996: 38). The deaf children combined their gestures into structured strings comparable to spoken sentences of young hearing children. The gestures were also composed of meaningful parts (morphemes). In other words, the deaf children's home signs employed combination and segmentation. However, like the experiment participants' gestures and TACS mime, the deaf children's home signs are less sophisticated and so less language-like than conventional sign languages such as American Sign Language.

Gestures with speech for pedagogical purposes

Allen (2000) conducted an observational analysis inquiry of one foreign language teacher, referred to as Mrs. Keifer, who was selected for her extensive use of the target language, Spanish, as the language of instruction and her natural use of nonverbal behaviour as part of her teaching style. Allen cites Moskowitz (1976), who found that outstanding foreign language teachers exhibit more nonverbal behaviour than typical foreign language teachers (Allen 2000: 156). Allen video-recorded a succession of classes and then grouped examples of Mrs. Keifer's nonverbal behaviour according to Burgoon, Buller and Woodall's categories (1989), finding that she used kinesics, vocalics and artifacts in her teaching (three of their seven categories of nonverbal behaviour). Within the kinesics (gesture) grouping Allen observed Mrs. Keifer using emblems, illustrators, affect displays and self-adaptors purposely to convey meaning. After the lessons, the students expressed in writing 'overwhelmingly' that their teacher's gestures and other body movements helped them understand Spanish. One representative response quoted by Allen (2000: 169) included:

> When the teacher uses her hands and gestures, it helps me to understand better what she's trying to say. Especially when she is speaking only in Spanish, because the motions help me to visually comprehend what I may not understand at all if she was just standing there talking. It also keeps my attention when she is constantly moving as opposed to boring the students to death. The movements set a more relaxed and casual atmosphere.

Mrs. Keifer's kinesic behaviour accompanied speech (in the target language) but did not resemble gesticulation. She used emblems to make comments on the meta-level of discourse, such as cupping her hand behind her ear to indicate that she had not heard a student and acknowledging a correct response with a 'thumbs up'. She also used emblems to convey the meaning of vocabulary, for example, rubbing the fingers and thumb of one hand together to demonstrate 'mucho dinero' (a lot of money). Such uses of emblems are typical of TACS mime, where they are performed silently, to elicit suggestions for target items from the pupils. The silence allows each pupil to think in their own terms before looking to the teacher to guide the class towards the target academic English terms. From the kinesics subcategory 'illustrators', Mrs. Keifer conveyed meanings using diectics (pointing out), kinetographs (acting out) and pictographs (drawing in the air) while speaking the target language, aiming to build on her students' knowledge of Spanish that had already been covered in class. A teacher using TACS is attempting to build on each pupil's prior knowledge, without imposing a language while the initial associations are being made. Mrs Keifer used intentionally exaggerated affect displays and self-adaptors, for example holding her stomach while speaking about becoming ill from bad food. Mrs. Keifer's nonverbal accommodations represent pedagogically motivated artificial behaviour, characteristic of pantomime and fundamentally different from gesticulation.

A framework for describing TACS gestures

McNeill provides a framework for analysing gestures, using four categories proposed by Kendon (1988): gesticulation, emblems, pantomime, and sign language, arranged in differing orders along four separate continua based on: (1) their relationship to speech, (2) their relationship to linguistic properties, (3) their relationship to conventions, and (4) their semiotic characteristics (global or segmented, and synthetic or analytic) (McNeill 2005). Gesticulation and sign language are consistently positioned at the two extremes of the continua, with emblems and pantomime between them in different orders. McNeill defines pantomime as 'dumb show, a gesture or sequence of gestures conveying a narrative line, with a story to tell, produced without speech' (McNeill 2005: 5). TACS mime can be positioned with pantomime on each continuum. Firstly, like pantomime, TACS mime occurs in the context of the obligatory absence of speech. Secondly, linguistic properties are absent from TACS gestures and pantomime, for example, a teacher using TACS is free to represent 'mountains' as a series of pyramid images, with the tips of the fingers of each hand touching in front of the teacher or sweeping arm gestures, drawing the landscape in the air; there are no linguistic constraints governing the gestures. Thirdly, as in pantomime, any conventions employed in TACS mime are flexible, serving the teacher's purpose. Fourthly, like pantomime, TACS mime is most likely to be composed of global and analytic gestures, understood as a whole but relating to one lexical item. 'Global' carries the sense that 'the meanings of the "parts" of the gesture are determined by the meaning of the whole' (McNeill 2005: 10).

So, in terms of McNeill's model, TACS mime can be described as 'pantomime'. TACS gestures share some characteristics with gesticulation: linguistic properties are absent and the gestures are not ruled by conventions. However the lack of accompanying speech demands the presence of language-like characteristics in TACS gestures for the sake of intelligibility/ interpretability. McNeill (2005) extends Vygotsky's (1986) model concerning the relationship between thinking and speaking by adding gesture; for McNeill thinking, speaking and gesture are the three components of an interactive model, each influencing the others in dialectical tension. McNeill's hypothesis concerns gesticulation, where gesticulation (image) is inseparable from language (speech) in spontaneous spoken communication. TACS mime artificially imposes a separation of image and language in order to elicit language from the observers (the pupils).

Sociocultural theory addresses diversity

Sociocultural principles originally proposed by Vygotsky (1986) concerning the nature of knowledge, how it is acquired and expressed, provide a useful framework for addressing the linguistic diversity of today's classroom because it allows for all pupils in a class to progress in their knowledge, each from their own particular starting point, despite each pupil beginning the lesson with a different level of knowledge about the subject and a different level of language proficiency. From a sociocultural perspective, learning involves building on prior knowledge. Vygotsky (1986) characterizes knowledge in two ways: as everyday concepts and scientific concepts;

everyday concepts are acquired through life's experiences and relation-ships within social contexts while scientific concepts are acquired through instruction. Everyday concepts are expressed in conversational language (BICS) whereas scientific concepts are more likely to be conveyed through specialized academic language (CALP). Progressing through school, chil-dren encounter more and more scientific concepts. School pupils' think-ing is transformed as they internalize, that is, master and become able to manipulate scientific concepts, using the mediating tool of language. Language is a vital tool for development, 'The child's intellectual growth is contingent on his mastering the social means of thought, that is, language' (Vygotsky 1986: 94). Academic lexis carries subject specific concepts; once acquired and internalized these concepts and the names for them are used to deepen knowledge of the subject.

Learning occurs in an individual's zone of proximal development, Vygotsky's (1986) metaphor for the potential for learning in collabora-tion with others beyond what an individual can learn alone and unaided. English language learners may struggle to access their prior knowledge of the content of a lesson delivered using English subject-specific lexis and academic language, and thus get locked out of the learning process on both levels: English language and subject content. TACS aims to bring each pupil in a class to the upper threshold of their knowledge of the subject at the beginning of a lesson, that is, to the boundary of their zone of proximal development. While the teacher acts, pupils gain the opportunity to access their knowledge of the lesson's subject area. Because the teacher is silent, each pupil can do this in their own language initially, and so each individual arrives at the threshold of their own zone of proximal development. The teacher is not imposing any level of linguistic knowledge or even any one language. Pupils can participate in the lesson in a way in which they would not be able to do on their own, as they activate their prior knowledge and collaborate with their peers to identify the prescribed target language. Through this collaboration each pupil's knowledge and comprehension increase; each collaborating pupil pushes back the boundary of their zone of proximal development. 'These boundaries are not immutable but rather constantly changing as the learner becomes increasingly independent at successively more advanced levels' (Brown & Campione 1998: 160).

Referring again to the example of the 'U-shaped valley': each pupil may have very different prior associated knowledge about valleys, for example, while watching the teacher's mime, one pupil may be visualizing mountainous countryside where they go walking with their family, one may be recalling scenes from a film set in the mountains, another may have relatively extensive knowledge about glacial erosion and be trying to remember the terms for different types of moraine, while another may be wondering about the speed of ice-flow. Through such associations made with the teacher's actions, the subject of the lesson gains meaning for every participating child; each pupil has a concept to build on, whether it is an everyday concept arising out of normal life experience or a scientific concept, learned through educational means. TACS builds on the prior knowledge of each of the pupils, encourages collaboration with others to co-re-construct the target language, and draws on the collective lexical and grammatical knowledge of the class, enabling the pupils to achieve something together that they might not be able to achieve alone. In sociocultural terms, this constitutes learning. The silence of the teacher facilitates this learning by creating a space, a verbal vacuum, for pupils to fill with suggestions of target words.

Silence activating learning in second language pedagogy

Language lessons differ from other school subject lessons in that all the pupils share the same aim of learning an additional language. The target language is the subject content. A post-primary language class, such as Irish, French or German, where no pupil speaks the target language as their mother tongue, represents a level playing field for a multilingual class when the target language is the language of instruction. Second language pedagogy has employed silence in various ways. Presented below are two contrasting examples: on a macro level, Gattegno's 'Silent Way', which employs teacher silence as a main characteristic of a language teaching approach, and on a micro level, an example of a classroom activity for use within a second language lesson, during which pupils mime to each other.

The Silent Way

The Silent Way aims to free students from unhelpful constraints and create a state of heightened awareness for optimal learning. During 'Silent Way' language classes the teacher remains silent, ideally all of the time and elicits language from the students. The teacher uses a pointer to tap out rhythms and direct students' attention to special colour-coded wall charts, using symbols to show pronunciation and colour to link groups of words. There is a strong emphasis on pronunciation (Richards & Rogers 1986: 105), although the language being worked on may not always be intelligible to the students. 'If they [students] observe the rules, what they utter may make total sense to natives and none at all to them' (Gattegno 1976: 22). This approach differs significantly from TACS, which is only an introduction, taking up about 5 minutes at the beginning of a lesson, and aims to facilitate all pupils' comprehension of key terminology. However, in both teaching methods learners are encouraged to collaborate with their peers to solve problems about how to manipulate and produce language. The teacher chooses the target language, which the learners produce. Both the Silent Way and TACS are based on the principle that teacher silence can facilitate student engagement, collaboration and learning.

Communicative techniques

There are many publications available to English language teachers, which give examples of communicative techniques including role play and mime. A very good model can be found in the work of Klippel (1984) in the role play activity, 'Hotel receptionist', where a guest in a hotel (one learner) has lost their voice and so mimes messages of immediate personal relevance to the receptionist (a small group of learners). The group collectively acting as the receptionist must reproduce the exact message. This exercise engages the learners in recalling appropriate lexis and collaborating to use it to construct a grammatically correct message together. Learners listen to each other's suggestions and may discuss points of grammar. The amount of time spent on re-constructing the messages depends on the learners' familiarity with the target language, including grammatical structures, with most attention being paid to linguistic items not yet mastered. TACS represents a similar process, but with only one target message, which defines the aim of the lesson it introduces. During TACS the whole class focuses on the teacher's silent actions, discussing possible target language items amongst themselves and calling out suggestions to the teacher; it is potentially very noisy. Both Klippel's exercise and TACS require the target language to be exactly reproduced and so linguistically are highly controlled. A necessary part of the procedure is pupils suggesting 'non-target' items, which get rejected; however, this is a valuable aspect of TACS as it generates a pool of subject-specific lexical items from the pupils, which are likely to recur in the lesson, as a by-product of the introductory activity. The Silent Way, Klippel's miming game and TACS all involve the use of silence to encourage learners to discover target language prescribed by the teacher and to collaborate with their peers; from a sociocultural perspective such collaboration facilitates learning.

Conclusion

TACS is being piloted within a research context exploring the appropriateness for the contemporary Irish classroom of three classroom interventions designed to support academic language development, on the levels of genre, sentence (TACS) and lexical item. Distinctive characteristics of TACS include the dramatic element of pantomime, the teacher's silence and the noise, which is encouraged from the pupils as they collaborate with each other and shout out suggestions for the target language. This paper argues that TACS provides optimal conditions for learning: pupils build on their prior knowledge through collaboration with each other and their teacher, and cites research and practice in support of this sociocultural perspective. Students' attitudes and teachers' attitudes are triangulated with findings from the linguistic analysis of pupils' written work, focusing on features of academic English, to look for converging evidence concerning the appropriateness of TACS for the contemporary post-primary classroom in Ireland.

Goldin-Meadow et al.'s (1996) experiment demonstrates the ease with which hearing adults can adapt their gestures to become more language-like when they are asked to mime. Pantomime-like gestures can be found being effectively exploited in conjunction with speech in instructional contexts, as researched by Moskowitz (1976) and illustrated by Allen's (2000) study of Mrs Keifer. The two examples from Gattegno (1976) and Klippel (1984), illustrate how silence can be used to motivate pupils and encourage peer collaboration. However, is TACS appropriate for contemporary post-primary education in Ireland? Are teachers willing to mime in front of their classes as an introductory exercise to a lesson? Are pupils (as well as teachers) comfortable with the necessary noise levels of TACS or might this aspect exacerbate potential discipline problems in the classroom? Is Irish society ready for the shift in classroom power relations that such pedagogical strategies represent? The noise involved is an indicator that collaboration amongst the pupils and between the class and the teacher is in progress. As collaboration facilitates learning, Teacher Acts, Class Speaks is proposed as one of a range of techniques to activate learning in today's linguistically diverse classroom.

References

Allen, L.Q. (2000). 'Nonverbal accommodations in foreign language teacher talk', *Applied Language Learning*, 11 (1), 155–176.

Brown, A.L., and Campione, J.C. (1998). 'Designing a community of young learners: Theoretical and practical lessons'. In N.M. Lambert and B.L. McCombs (eds), *How Students Learn: Reforming Schools Through Learner-Centred Education*, pp. 153–186. Washington DC: American Psychological Association.

Burgoon, J., Buller, D.B., and Woodall, W.G. (1989). *Nonverbal communication: The unspoken dialogue*. New York: Harper and Row.

Central Statistics Office (CSO). (2008). *Census 2006: Non-Irish Nationals Living in Ireland*. Dublin: The Stationery Office.

Central Statistics Office (CSO). (2010). *Population and Migration Estimates April 2010*, <http://www.cso.ie/releasespublications/documents/population/current/popmig.pdf> accessed December 2010.

Central Statistics Office (CSO). (2011). *Census 2011 Preliminary Report*, <http://www. cso.ie/census/documents/Prelim per cent20complete.pdf> accessed August 2011.

Collins, M. (2009). *Orientation and assessment of newly arrived non-native English speaking post-primary students: A framework for teachers*. Unpublished MA dissertation, University College Cork.

Cummins, J. (1979). 'Cognitive/academic language proficiency, linguistic interdependence, the optimum age question and some other matters'. *Working Papers on Bilingualism*, 19, 121–129.

Cummins, J. (2000). *Language, Power and Pedagogy: Bilingual Children in the Crossfire*. Clevedon: Multilingual Matters.

Cummins, J., Brown, K., and Sayers, D. (2007). *Literacy, Technology and Diversity: Teaching for Success in Changing Times*. Boston: Pearson.

Department of Education and Science (DES). (2009). Circular 0015/2009. *Meeting the needs of pupils learning English as an Additional Language (EAL)*. Dublin: DES.

Devine, D. (2005). 'Welcome to the Celtic tiger? Teacher responses to immigration and increasing ethnic diversity in Irish schools'. *International Studies in Sociology of Education*, 15, 49–70.

Feldman, H., Goldin-Meadow, S., and Gleitman, L. (1978). 'Beyond Herodotus: The creation of language by linguistically deprived deaf children'. In A. Lock (ed.), *Action, Symbol, and Gesture: The Emergence of Language*, pp. 351–414. New York: Academic Press.

Gattegno, C. (1976). *The Common Sense of Teaching Foreign Languages*. New York: Educational Solutions Inc.

Goldin-Meadow, S. (1979). 'Structure in a manual communication system developed without a conventional language model: Language without a helping hand'. In H. Whitaker and H.A. Whitaker (eds), *Studies in Neurolinguistics vol. 4*, pp. 125–209. New York: Academic Press.

Goldin-Meadow, S., and Feldman, H. (1977). 'The development of language-like communication without a language model', *Science*, 197, 401–403.

Goldin-Meadow, S., and Mylander, C. (1984). 'Gestural communication in deaf children: The effects and non-effects of parental input on early language development', *Monographs of the Society for Research in Child Development*, 49, (3–4, Serial No. 207).

Goldin-Meadow, S., McNeill, D., and Singleton, J. (1996). 'Silence is liberating: Removing the handcuffs on grammatical expression in the manual modality', *Psychological Review*, 103 (1), 34–55.

Halliday, M.A.K., and Matthiessen, C.M.I.M. (2004). *An Introduction to Functional Grammar*. London: Hodder Education.

Hammond, J. (2009). 'High challenge, high support programmes with English as a Second Language learners: A teacher-researcher collaboration', in J. Miller, A. Kostogriz and M. Gearon (eds), *Culturally and Linguistically Diverse Classrooms: New Dilemmas for Teachers*, pp. 56–74. Bristol: Multilingual Matters.

Healy, C. (2007). *On Speaking Terms: Introductory and Language Programmes for Migrants in Ireland*. Dublin: Immigrant Council of Ireland.

Kendon, A. (1972). 'Some relationships between body motion and speech'. In A. Siegman and B. Pope (eds), *Studies in Dyadic Communication*, pp. 177–210. Elmsford, NY: Pergamon Press.

Kendon, A. (1988). 'How gestures can become like words'. In F. Poyatos (ed.), *Cross-Cultural Perspectives in Nonverbal Communication*, pp. 131–141. The Hague: Mouton.

Keogh, A.F., and Whyte, J. (2003). *Getting On: The experiences and aspirations of immigrant students in second level schools linked to the Trinity Access Programmes*. Dublin: Children's Research Centre, Trinity College Dublin.

Klippel, F. (1984). *Keep Talking*. Cambridge: Cambridge University Press.

Larsen-Freeman, D., and Long, M.H. (1991). *An Introduction to Second Language Acquisition Research*. Essex: Longman.

Lucas, T., Villegas, A., and Freedson-Gonzalez, M. (2008). 'Linguistically responsive teacher education: Preparing classroom teachers to teach English language learners'. *Journal of Teacher Education*, 59, 361–373.

Lyons, Z., and Little, D. (2009). *English Language Support in Irish Post-Primary Schools: Policy, challenges and deficits*. Dublin: Trinity Immigration Initiative, English Language Support Programme.

Mac Éinrí, P., and White, A. (2008). 'Immigration into the Republic of Ireland: A bibliography of recent research'. *Irish Geography*, 41 (2), 151–179.

McNeill, D. (1979). *The Conceptual Basis of Language*. Hillsdale, NJ: Lawrence Erlbaum Associates.

McNeill, D. (2005). *Gesture and Thought*. Chicago: The University of Chicago Press.

Mehan, H. (1979). *Learning Lessons: Social Organization in the Classroom*. Cambridge, MA: Harvard University Press.

Miller, J., Kostogriz, A., and Gearon M. (eds) (2009). *Culturally and Linguistically Diverse Classrooms: New Dilemmas for Teachers*. Bristol: Multilingual Matters.

Moskowitz, G. (1976). 'The classroom interaction of outstanding foreign language teachers', *Foreign Language Annals*, 9, 135–157.

National Council for Curriculum and Assessment (NCCA). (2006). *Intercultural education in the post-primary school*. Dublin: NCCA.

Nowlan, E. (2008). 'Underneath the Band-Aid: Supporting bilingual students in Irish schools'. *Irish Educational Studies*, 27 (3), 253–266.

Richards, J.C., and Rogers, T.S. (1986). *Approaches and Methods in Language Teaching*. Cambridge: Cambridge University Press.

Schleppegrell, M.J. (2004). *The Language of Schooling: A Functional Linguistics Perspective*. Mahwah: Lawrence Erlbaum Associates.

Smyth, E., Darmody, M., McGinnity, F., and Byrne, D. (2009). *Adapting to Diversity: Irish Schools and Newcomer Students*. Dublin: The Economic and Social Research Institute (ESRI).

Stam, G. and McCafferty, S.G. (2008). 'Gesture studies and second language acquisition: A review'. In S.G. McCafferty and G. Stam (eds), *Gesture: Second Language Acquisition and Classroom Research*, pp. 3–24. New York: Routledge.

Taguma, M., Moonhee, K., Wurzburg, G., and Kelly, F. (2009). *OECD Reviews of Migrant Education: Ireland*. Organisation for Economic Co-operation and Development (OECD) <www.oecd.org/edu/migration> accessed November 2010.

Vygotsky, L. (1986). *Thought and Language*. Cambridge, Massachusetts: The MIT Press.

Wallen, M. (2007). 'The need for a long-term, comprehensive approach to EAL instruction in Irish schools', *NALDIC Quarterly*, <http://www.naldic.org.uk/docs/members/documents/NQ4.3.6.pdf> accessed January 2011.

Ward, T. (2004). *Education and Language Needs of Separated Children*. Dublin: City of Dublin VEC.

COLIN JOHN FLYNN

2   The role of culture in minority language learning: The case of adult learners of Irish[1]

Introduction

The importance of culture and cultural awareness in language teaching and learning has been highlighted by many authors (e.g. Badger & MacDonald 2007; Byram & Grundy 2003). Language and culture are generally considered to be interconnected in complex ways and, therefore, one must be accounted for in teaching/learning the other. A person's sense of self is often connected to issues of culture and language. Learning a second or foreign language in adulthood may, in some contexts, be the realization of a person's attempt to develop features of his or her individual identity. This may be particularly true of minority language learners in cases where learners were unable to successfully learn the target language during childhood.

Though learners are often introduced to a new culture when learning a foreign language, this may or may not be true when learning languages spoken in other regions of the learners' home country. For historical, political or cultural reasons learners may have been removed from the target language or its community and may, in some cases, need to reacquaint themselves not only with grammatical and pragmatic elements of the target language system, but also with the culture associated with the language and its speakers if the learning experience is to be successful. It is argued in the sections to follow that developing language and cultural awareness in both learner and instructor will greatly enhance the language learning experience.

1   The author would like to thank the editors and the anonymous reviewers for their very useful suggestions which helped to improve this chapter greatly.

In the second half of this paper this argument is supported by findings from a small-scale study involving a group of adult learners of Irish in
Dublin, Ireland. The results of this study show that high levels of language
and cultural awareness in these learners could potentially serve as a source
of motivation to complete culture-related tasks in the classroom.

Culture in language learning

Cultural awareness

Cultural awareness may be defined as perceptions of one's own culture,
perceptions of a foreign/secondary culture, or a combination of the two.
In the context of language teaching and learning, the relationship between
language and culture is complex. Language is generally regarded as being
a key element of cultural identity and the principal means by which cultural values and customs are transmitted. Simply put, 'language expresses,
embodies and symbolizes cultural reality' (Kramsch 1998: 3). From this,
we may infer that culture and cultural awareness play vital roles in language
teaching and learning, and that cultural awareness may facilitate greater
language proficiency.

   Williams and Burden (1997: 116) argue 'that language learning will be
[...] affected by the whole social situation, context and culture in which
the learning takes place'. In other words, language learning does not take
place in a vacuum, but rather the process is influenced by the attitudes
and actions of other stakeholders both inside and outside the classroom
context. In light of this, it becomes clear that issues of cultural awareness
have major implications not only for language learners, but for language
teachers and course designers (Badger & MacDonald 2007; Byram, Nichols
& Stevens 2001; Hall 2002).

   The above-mentioned interconnections between language and culture
demonstrate that language learners need to be aware of the culture of the

target language if they are to successfully communicate with its speakers. This raises the issue of *intercultural communicative competence*, a conceptual expansion of *communicative competence* (Byram 1997). Littlewood (1981: 6) posits four domains of skill which make up a person's *communicative competence*: (1) the learner must develop a linguistic competence allowing him to manipulate the linguistic system of rules; (2) the learner must be able to distinguish between the linguistic competences he has acquired and the communicative functions they perform; (3) the learner must develop skills and strategies for effectively communicating meaning; (4) the learner must become aware of the social meaning of language forms.

In developing the learner's intercultural communicative competence, the above four domains of skills must be considered within the social, political and cultural settings of the target language. The extent to which a language learner wishes to join, as it were, the target language speech community raises a number of questions. For example, to what extent should the learner model his linguistic and cultural behaviours on that of native speakers of the language (Byram 1997; Lee 2005)? Moreover, in the context of learning a second language spoken in one's native country or region, a person may, or may not, wish to adopt or imitate the native speaker's culture for personal, political or social reasons (Ó Baoill 1999). Nevertheless, in either situation, the learner will need to be aware of the social and cultural practices in the community where the language is spoken in order to engage in meaningful communication with its members.

Fostering cultural awareness

The previous section has highlighted the importance of cultural awareness in the language learning process; however, we cannot presuppose the existence of cultural awareness in the learner. Teachers and course designers must consider how their language courses might aim to develop such awareness.

Tomlinson and Masuhara (2004) make a useful distinction between *cultural knowledge* and *cultural awareness* and have outlined how the latter may be developed in the language learner. These authors define cultural knowledge as 'information about the characteristics of our own and other people's cultures' (p. 5), and cultural awareness as 'perceptions of our own and other people's cultures' (p. 6). This subtle distinction is made more apparent when we consider the characteristics of each. Cultural knowledge is generated externally, is static in nature and can only be articulated by what words can express. We acquire this information by learning facts and statistics, making generalizations and basing this knowledge on given examples, all of which are at times misrepresentative. For example, Tomlinson and Masuhara (2004: 2) argue that in the context of a business trip to Japan, being told that Japanese people are hardworking and serious might be useful, but a generalization of this kind may lead one to conclude that the Japanese don't enjoy going out after work. Cultural awareness on the other hand is internal, dynamic, variable, multi-dimensional and interactive. We acquire this awareness through a series of internal processes whereby we witness culture in action, make connections and comparisons between cultures and experiences, resolve conflicts and accommodate differences, reflect on and interpret cultural encounters and behaviours, suspend judgment and tolerate ambiguity. Though developing cultural awareness is clearly a more complex process, it is achievable through regular contact with the target culture, whether directly, that is, visiting the individuals or societies where the culture is practiced, or indirectly through film, music or literature (Tomlinson & Masuhara 2004).

How can we foster the development of this awareness in the classroom? The learner's challenge of acquiring the intricacies of the grammar, lexicon and phonetics of the target language is made even more complex when coupled with the need to learn the pragmatic importance of linguistic cues, turn taking, socio-cultural meanings of phrases and vocabulary, etc. Of course, acquiring a pragmatic competence is only one element of developing a wider cultural awareness about the target language and its speakers, but it is undoubtedly an important one. The learner may, for example, succeed in acquiring a variety of the target language without being fully aware of the social or cultural implications of using that variety in a given context. Experience will certainly aid the learner in determining when and where certain types of language are acceptable, but s/he will benefit more, at least in the short term, from the input of the course instructor on such matters. Unfortunately, many newly qualified language teachers have limited communicative experience with the target language community and have rarely spent any length of time living among them. This creates a situation where 'those [...] entering a career in language teaching with an adequate knowledge of the culture and society of their language are a small minority' (Byram & Morgan 1994: 62).

In the context of minority language education this problem is often compounded by the general lack of suitable teaching materials in the target language. This places the burden on teachers to draw on their personal experience, yet, teachers who are second language L2 learners themselves may not have had much experience of the target language culture, despite it being part of their national culture (Ó Baoill 1999). In light of this, teacher training, both pedagogical and cultural, is paramount if it is to aid in the development of cultural awareness in the learner.

Once a language teacher has developed his or her own knowledge of the culture and community of the language they are to teach, s/he must find ways of imparting that knowledge to the learner. Tomlinson and Masuhara (2004), for example, argue that a cultural awareness approach to language teaching should incorporate the following elements:

- Start and finish an activity in the minds of the learners (e.g. by getting them to think about an experience in their own culture before providing them with a similar one in another culture; by getting them to 'translate' a new experience in another culture into an equivalent experience in their own culture);
- Provide cultural encounters (e.g. through visits, video, songs, literature, simulations);
- Facilitate connections between the old and the new (e.g. by encouraging the learners to constantly think of comparable personal experiences);
- Stimulate multi-dimensional representation of cultural experiences (e.g. through visualization and inner voice activities);
- Focus initially on intake responses rather than input responses (e.g. get learners to articulate their own personal response to a story before getting them to study its text);
- Provide focused discovery activities which guide the learners to find out things for themselves;

- Contribute your [the teacher] personal interpretations but don't provide them as definitive answers;
- Contribute your [the teacher] personal experiences of other cultures. (Tomlinson & Masuhara 2004: 7–8)

Of course (and as recognized by Tomlinson and Masuhara), unless the explicit aim of the course is to highlight cultural differences between languages and language communities, it is not necessary to make use of culture-related materials and activities in every class. Nevertheless, introducing such materials at various instances throughout the course may aid the learner in developing his or her own awareness of the cultural significance of language use in the target community which may in turn increase levels of motivation.

The links between cultural awareness and language learning goals is an area which has received relatively little attention to date. The literature on minority language learning and attitudinal/motivational factors in second language learning has featured discussions of culture, but until now it has not been a common theme. This may be the result of the difficulties associated with defining the concept of culture (Kramsch 2006) and measuring cultural awareness in the context of second language learning. Nevertheless, cultural identity, awareness of one's own culture and/or interest in the target language culture should not be overlooked as possible sources of motivation to learn an additional language.

Cultural motivation in the language learner

A great deal of research has been conducted on L2 motivation over the last fifty years and the field has embraced a number of different explanatory models. The present section does not permit an extensive discussion of the merits and shortcomings of each model (see Chapter 4 in Dörnyei 2005 for an excellent overview). Instead, we will focus on Gardner's (1985; 2001) Socio-Educational Model of Second Language Acquisition, and Dörnyei's (2005; 2009) more recent model, The L2 Motivational Self System.

The work of Gardner and Lambert (e.g. Gardner 1985; Gardner & Lambert 1972) has done much to illuminate the complexities of second language learner motivation. Their research, and that of their associates, has resulted in a distinction between *integrative* and *instrumental* orientations in second language learners. Learners with an integrative orientation wish to interact with, or become similar to, members of the target language community, while learners with an instrumental orientation take a utilitarian view of the language learning situation, seeing the potential pragmatic gains of learning the target language (e.g. getting a promotion at work or to pass a required exam). These orientations are not motivations in themselves; they simply give rise to motivation in the learner and direct it towards a set of goals with either a strong integrative or instrumental quality (Gardner 1985; Gardner 2001; Gardner & Tremblay 1994).

At the heart of Gardner's socio-educational model is an *integrative motive*, which he defines as a 'motivation to learn a second language because of positive feelings towards the community that speaks that language' (Gardner 1985: 82–83). The integrative motive comprises of three factors: integrativeness (i.e. interest in foreign languages and attitudes towards the L2 community), attitude towards the learning situation and motivation. The early work of Gardner and his colleagues suggested that, in the Canadian context at least, L2 achievement was most strongly correlated with an integrative motivation (e.g. Gardner & Lambert 1972), however, research in a wider variety of learning contexts has in some cases provided contradictory results (cf. Ellis 2004). Instrumental orientation, though seen initially as an external factor, since it does not feature in Gardner's Integrative motive model (Gardner 1985), has been shown to play an important role where learners take a more pragmatic view of the language learning experience, e.g. where direct contact with the target language community is not an immediate goal (cf. Csizér & Dörnyei 2005; Dörnyei & Csizér 2006).

A more recent model coincides with current trends in L2 motivation research which seek a more eclectic approach to the description of the phenomenon. Dörnyei's (2005; 2009) conceptualization of L2 motivation, 'The L2 Motivational Self System', was born out of the growing concern about the theoretical content of Gardner's integrativeness/integrative motive concept of motivation and its limiting qualities in some learning contexts.

According to Dörnyei (2009: 9), '[t]he L2 Motivational Self System represents a major reformation of previous motivational thinking by its explicit
utilization of psychological theories of the self, yet its roots are firmly set in
previous research in the L2 field'. Dörnyei's latest model is promising in its
attempts to incorporate traditional integrative/instrumental accounts of
motivation with theories of self in recent psychology research (e.g. Markus
and Nurius 1986; Oyserman, Bybee, Terry & Hart-Johnson 2004; see
Dörnyei 2005 for an overview). This model also includes aspects of the
intrinsic/extrinsic motivational dichotomy and situated factors.

The model comprises of three components: (1) *Ideal L2 Self* – the
L2-specific component of one's 'ideal self'; (2) *Ought-to L2 Self* – attributes
that a person believes he/she ought to possess in order to meet expectations
and evade potential negative outcomes; (3) *L2 learning Experience* – the
situated or executive motives connected to the immediate learning environment (e.g. the teacher, the curriculum) and experience (e.g. peer groups,
successes). And, although this line of inquiry is relatively new and has not
been the focus of a great deal of empirical research, it contains elements
that would seem to have great explanatory power for L2 motivation in
learning contexts other than traditional preparatory courses, whether they
are examination-orientated or aimed at preparing learners to integrate into
a society. For example, the extended opportunities for further education
currently available in most European societies provide language learners
with the possibility of learning a second or additional language for more
personal, self-orientated reasons. Minority language learners, for instance,
may benefit from these types of cultural or identity-based motivations.

Minority language learners and cultural motivation

The learning of minority languages presents a unique set of issues for consideration. In general, learners of more commonly spoken languages (MCSLs)
have more opportunities for exposure to the target language. Although
face to face encounters with native speakers may not be the norm in some
contexts, learners of MCSLs will generally have better access to various
other types of input (e.g. media, music, literature) than learners of less

commonly spoken languages (LCSLs). For learners of LCSLs, teachers, authentic learning materials and authentic language use contexts may be difficult to access. In fact, in some cases the classroom setting may be the learner's only exposure to the target language (for the case of Irish see Ó Laoire 2000; Singleton 1987).

Despite numerous limitations, LCSL learners often have some emotional or practical motivation that will drive them to learn the target language. This motivation may be linked to the linguistic heritage of the region where the learner resides or a desire to recapture some lost aspect of his or her own culture. Alternatively, the learner may have relocated (or wish to relocate) to a region where the target language is spoken, in which case learning the lesser spoken language may be advantageous for social purposes. Finally, the learner may have some ancestral link to the language, culture, region, or speech community, and this may be the motivation for learning the LCSL.

Language and culture in the teaching of Irish

The sociolinguistic position of Irish is unique. Firstly, despite being an indigenous minority language, it is has been given status as the country's first national language as well as an official working language of the European Union. This official status becomes all the more important when one considers that it is the first language (at least in sequential terms) of not more than 80–100,000 people in Ireland (Carnie 1996; Singleton 1987). Secondly, Irish would appear to be in direct competition with the world's most powerful international language, English, which is the second official language of the State and the first language of the majority of the island's inhabitants.

The most recent census data for the Republic of Ireland (Central Statistics Office 2012) has recorded that a little more than 1.77 million people claim some ability to speak Irish. However, only 158,686 people

(9 per cent of the total number of Irish speakers) use the language on a regular basis, that is, daily or weekly, outside the educational system, while just over 1.04 million (59 per cent of all speakers) use it less often or never. Of the 519,181 people who use Irish within the educational system, only 38,480 use the language daily outside the educational system. These figures imply a complex relationship with the language for the majority of Irish people. Despite having been exposed to the language in the educational system (in most cases for thirteen years), only a small number actually use the language on any sort of regular basis outside that context. This suggests that most people who claim the ability to speak Irish do not have much contact with the language's regular speech community and, therefore, are likely not to be completely familiar with their specific cultural practices. This might be viewed as an extension of what Ó Baoill (1999: 190) refers to as 'cultural distance', which, as he argues, provides a complex set of issues for the teaching and learning of Irish.

Minority language teaching differs from other language teaching contexts in that course designers and/or instructors are generally not seeking to prepare learners for situations of so-called linguistic survival. In the case of more dominant languages, learners may hope to find themselves in a situation where they need the target language for communication purposes. Littlewood (1984: 54) points out that the nature of the social community in which the learner finds himself often determines whether or not there is a communicative need to learn a language. For example, it has been observed (Ó Baoill 1999; Singleton 1987) that, since nearly all L1 speakers of Irish are balanced bilinguals, having at least a near-native command of English, there is no need to use Irish in order to communicate and/or socialize. Furthermore, when learners do engage with the native speaker in conversation, the native speaker will often switch to English when difficulty is encountered (Singleton 1987). This situation challenges the fundamental aims of communicative language teaching and removes the element of linguistic survival.

In light of the above, it is fair to say that, apart from customer service roles which require state agencies to provide service through Irish if requested,[2] there is no immediate communicative need for Irish, which might act as a motivating factor in learners. There is, on the other hand, the possibility of a cultural need for Irish which will motivate learners. Alongside a desire to use Irish to celebrate Ireland's unique cultural and linguistic traditions, an interest in Gaelic culture (e.g. history, literature, music, art) may serve as a means for engaging with one's linguistic heritage. Though there is a viable argument for labelling this type of motivation 'integrative', it is possible that this motivation is fuelled by more than just a desire to join the Irish language speech community, communicate with other Irish speakers or even read texts or listen to songs in Irish (what Csizér and Dörnyei (2005) labelled 'Cultural Interest'). Learners of Irish, in particular adult learners, may, at least in some instances, be driven by a desire to simply be an Irish speaker, which may or may not be connected to a desire to use the language as a regular means of communication. This type of motivation would be in line with Dörnyei's conceptualization of the L2 Motivational Self, since 'the central theme of the emerging new theory [is] the equation of the motivational dimension that has traditionally been interpreted as "integrativeness/integrative motivation" with the Ideal L2 Self' (Dörnyei 2009: 27). The language learning process may aid an individual in becoming his or her ideal self, one that speaks the Irish language. Taking the emphasis away from integration creates a situation where the learner is freer to explore his or her own interests as well as to serve personal needs.

The challenge, then, is for course instructors to meet these needs and tailor the course to the learner's interests. Mac Mathúna (1996) has suggested incorporating lessons into Irish courses which deal with personal names, surnames and local place-names, for example, as well as language awareness issues such as the uniqueness of Irish morphosyntactic structures, in order to respond to learners' cultural interests. Indeed, the range

---

2　The Official Languages Act 2003 provides a statutory framework for the delivery of services through the medium of Irish, e.g. correspondence to be replied to in the language in which it was written, providing information to the public in the Irish language, or in the Irish and English languages, bilingual publications of certain key documents, use of Irish in the courts, etc.

of possibilities for cultural awareness components in Irish language courses is very broad and may include anything from 'early literary and artistic output to folklore and contemporary expressions of Irishness through language, art, music, dance, sport, etc.' (Ó Laoire 2004: 10). Nevertheless, lessons aimed at engaging with cultural aspects (both cultural artefacts and sociolinguistic features) of the language and the linguistic community might provide learners with the cultural experience they seek.

In the next section of this paper some findings from a small-scale exploratory study conducted by the author (Flynn 2009) with a diverse group of adult learners of Irish are discussed. The study aimed to explore the extent to which learners were integratively motivated to learn Irish and their attitudes towards cultural activities in the classroom.

Culture in the adult Irish classroom: some preliminary findings

In the above-mentioned exploratory study of integrative and cultural motivation in adult learners of Irish, two separate qualitative methods were employed, semi-structured interviews, and a focus group, both of which were conducted by the author using the same participant sample.[3] There were three reasons for using both data collection methods with the same participants. Firstly, it was felt that a combination of the two interview types would provide the study with a diverse data set since the two methods are inherently different and might elicit different types of information from

---

3   The interview schedule for both interview types consisted of two lines of questioning, (a) introductory questions which gathered background information about the participants, their past Irish language experiences and courses attended; (b) questions focused on affective issues such as reasons for learning Irish, goal-setting, cultural/ linguistic background in relation to the course and/or language, importance of completing culture-related tasks in an Irish language course, and reactions of family, friends and colleagues to their learning Irish.

participants (Morgan 2008). Secondly, it was felt that participants might reveal more (or different) information in a private session as opposed to in a group setting, or *vice versa* (Morgan 2008). Finally, since these data were collected as part of a master's level postgraduate course, the time constraints of the study did not allow for multiple interviews, the second meeting in the form of a focus group would serve as a follow-up interview with at least some of the participants.

The study's twelve participants comprised of seven male and five female learners aged twenty-six to sixty-five. Although the learners were all living in Ireland at the time of the study, Irish (n=6), English (n=1), French (n=1), German (n=1), Norwegian (n=1) and Scottish-born (n=2) learners were represented. All of the Irish, English and Scottish-born learners had English as their L1 and Irish as an L2. The French, German and Norwegian learners all had a language other than English as their L1, English as an L2 and Irish as their L3.[4]

The learners were all attending Irish language courses run by the same Dublin-based provider at the beginners' or elementary level at the time of the study. According to the course provider, these two course levels correspond to the A1 and A2 levels of the Common European Framework of Reference for Languages (Council of Europe 2001). Eight of the participants were attending general conversation courses and the remaining four were taking a specialized training course at the A2 level organized by a public sector organization and taught by the same course provider. Though the types of data produced in individual interviews and the focus group were different in some instances, discussion surrounding cultural issues relevant to this analysis did not differ greatly, therefore, the participants' responses included in the remainder of this chapter have all, with one exception (see below), been taken from the individual interviews since these were the most informative.

---

4   Data on participants' other languages was not explicitly gathered in this study, therefore, the labels L2/L3 are being used here to indicate additional languages in sequential terms. This means that although it is unknown whether participants for whom English is their L1/L2 speak other languages, it is known that English was learned by these participants before Irish.

The recordings of individual sessions were transcribed verbatim and a content analysis was performed. The data was coded according to five salient motivational categories as they emerged from the data set: integrative, instrumental, culture-heritage-related, goal-oriented, and significant-other-related (for a full account see Flynn 2009). A more comprehensive analysis of the full range of motivational types represented in this group of learners is currently underway (Flynn and Harris in preparation). The data subset which is being presented here concerns those findings which relate to cultural motivation in learners and the use of culture-related tasks in the classroom.

Cultural background

Six of the participants were born in Ireland and had received their primary and secondary education here. All of these learners recognized a cultural connection to the language but in many cases struggled to identify it. In response to the questions '*How does your own linguistic and/or cultural background relate to the course? Do you have any connection to Irish?*', statements like the one below were common with three of these six participants finding it difficult to articulate what cultural connection they might have to the language:

> 'Only in the fact that I'm Irish, and that there is an expectation probably that the people that have been taught in school have something … they'd have remembered some small part of it. I'd listen to the news in Irish, but I've no interest in it, but I'd hear different things and I wonder what it is.' (participant 3)

Two of the Irish born learners initially provided a negative response to the above questions, stating that they had no connection to the language, but at a later stage in the interview made statements, such as the following one, which indicated that they felt that Irish people should feel a connection to the language:

> 'We should use it a lot more. People should be proud of it. Unfortunately, people don't … it's sad.' (participant 11)

Of the six remaining participants who were born outside Ireland, three indicated a familial connection to Ireland. Two of these learners identified this as being a major motivating factor for learning Irish. The importance of this connection was expressed in statements like the following:

> 'Well, you know, as I am half Irish. I don't know, for me it's really important you know ... I am very, very interested in the Irish culture, because I did somehow grow up a little bit in the Irish culture, I did do some Irish dancing in Munich and other things. My father is actually ... well, he claims that he speaks fluent ... he cannot prove it yet but I am trying ... and yeah, I would like, I really would like to catch up and be able to speak a bit of Irish with my father.' (participant 2)

The other non-Irish born learner with an Irish family background stated that his background was not a motivating factor to learn Irish. However, he did say that the fact that he is married to an Irish woman was one of the reasons he wanted to learn Irish. The couple had also just bought a house in a Gaeltacht (Irish speaking) region and he was eager to learn Irish as 'it would be handy to see whether they were talking about me and join in the conversation' (participant 6). The remaining three non-Irish born learners who did not have a family background connection to Ireland provided varied reasons for learning the language, which included a general interest in languages, interest in the cultural fortunes of their current country of residence, and schooling issues related to their children.

In terms of background, the participants in this study can be divided into three groups: (i) learners born in Ireland; (ii) learners born outside of Ireland but who have an ancestral link to Ireland; and (iii) learners who were born outside of Ireland and who have no ancestral link to Ireland. Different learner backgrounds will normally bring with them different reasons for learning a language. For this group of learners it is not clear how strong or otherwise a cultural motivation stemming from their family or cultural background might be when compared to other types of motivation. However, for the first two groups a family connection to Ireland, background or otherwise, appears to be one motivating factor. In the case of the third group, it may be the learners' own non-Irish cultural background or their new Irish cultural links that has brought them to the learning situation.

Linguistic awareness/language awareness

In the first half of this chapter it was argued that language and culture are clearly linked. It follows then that language awareness and cultural awareness must be linked on some level as well. Masny (1997) provides a useful distinction between language and linguistic awareness in second language learning. In her view, *language awareness* is 'an effective tool in language instruction [...] [which] allows teachers to draw attention to similarities and differences between the two language codes (the L1 and the TL)', whereas *linguistic awareness* is rooted in psycholinguistic and cognitive theories, and 'refers to individuals' ability to reflect on, and match intuitively, spoken and written utterances with their knowledge of the language' (p. 106). Though these types of awareness are distinct from one another, there are undoubtedly areas of overlap between them. For example, if a language teacher draws attention to particular forms in the target language through a comparison to learners' L1 (language awareness), it is likely to inspire reflection about these, and perhaps other, target language forms (linguistic awareness). Furthermore, the statements below suggest that, for some learners, such types of awareness may be linked to their motivation to learn:

> 'One of the things I did find interesting in the course was why Irish people use English the way they do. [...] I wasn't really aware that they came from Irish, I was aware that it was Irish English, like "the food in that restaurant does be nice" was something that I'd never heard anybody but Irish people say, but I didn't realize it came from Irish.' (participant 8)

> 'Literature as well, going back some of the old writing, the old script as well. It'd be fascinating to be able to read that. Another reason to learn the written language, I've got a book by Seán Óg de Paor and it's all in Irish. That's the mission to read that start to finish.' (participant 1)

> 'I'd love to be able to go to Donegal and speak their Irish, go to Galway and speak their [Irish], and go to Kerry. I love that for a week. But I would have to do classes.' (participant 11)

Since no question directly addressed the issue of how these types of awareness developed, it cannot be established whether they have come as a result of formal consciousness-raising by course instructors or through personal reflection on the part of the learners. It is also possible that they have come about as a result of a broader cultural awareness (see next section). In any case, from the above statements we can see that some participants in this study demonstrated a great deal of both linguistic and language awareness in relation to Irish. They appear to be aware of differences between old and new orthographic scripts, the influence of Irish on some forms of English spoken in Ireland and the dialectical variations between regional varieties of the language. A desire to engage with these elements of the language would also appear to be present in these learners, though admittedly it would take further probing on this issue to determine to what extent these learners are actually motivated by these factors.

Cultural awareness and culture-related tasks

Measuring the participants' cultural awareness, that is, their perceptions of their own culture(s), the culture of the Irish language and the Irish language classroom, was not the aim of the study which produced the data presented in this section. Nevertheless, we can gain some insight into the level of cultural awareness in these learners by looking at their responses to questions dealing with the use of culture-related tasks in the classroom. When learners were asked whether or not it was important for them to complete culture-related tasks as part of their course (e.g. discussing traditional Irish music, listening to and understanding an interview with an Irish author, reading and understanding an article about life in Ireland), they provided mixed reactions. Just over half of the participants (seven out of twelve) indicated that they would be interested in some types of culture-related classroom activities. However, only two of the learners indicated a strong feeling in favour of such activities with statements like:

> 'For me personally, I think that's very important, because you know, it's also part of the whole thing ... if you learn a language, of course, you also learn something about the culture of that country.' (participant 2)

The other five learners who responded positively qualified their statements in some way, to demonstrate that they would like to engage in activities of this type at a later stage. For example, some learners' hesitation about engaging in culture-related activities in the classroom was related to the course level. Four learners felt that culture-related tasks would only be important in courses at a higher level:

> 'For me at the moment, it's not very important, but maybe when my level goes up it will become more important. So at the moment it's not very important but it will be as I progress.' (participant 7)

Among the Irish born participants, the responses were again mixed. Three of these learners said that they would like to engage in culture-related activities in the classroom while three said they would not be interested. One Irish-born learner who said that he would not be interested in cultural activities did feel that such activities would benefit non-Irish born learners:

> 'In my case, not at all. I don't see any benefit in that at all. However, considering that I am the only Irish person in the class, all of the others are from different European countries, I can see that they may benefit from an exposure to different Irish cultures.' (participant 5)

Though it is not entirely clear from the data available why the Irish-born learners who responded negatively were not interested in such culture-related activities, one possible explanation was provided in the focus group data. In this session some of these learners expressed the opinion that culture-related activities were something they could do on their own, outside of class. Furthermore, one of the Irish-born participants felt that because learners born in Ireland have been exposed to the Irish culture for so long and because they are constantly surrounded by Irish culture there was no need for them to engage with it in the Irish language classroom.

Finally, an important element of these learners' socio-cultural awareness is that they were, in general, aware of the limited opportunities they would have for using Irish outside the classroom. This was expressed by participants in two ways. Some learners commented on their own low proficiency level, while others recognized the limited domains of use for Irish in the broader context:

'Who would I talk to? I'd talk to the four walls in Irish, you know! I don't have anybody that I know who would talk to me in Irish.' (participant 3)

'[...] there's nobody at home who speaks Irish more than the force-fed bits of *Peig* from school. No, I don't really have anybody to talk to, but we do that in class a lot, a lot of the focus in class was about conversations.' (participant 8)

Discussion

Though the data included here shed only a small amount of light on the complexity of addressing issues of culture in the Irish language classroom, they do draw attention to elements of language and cultural awareness in adult learners of Irish. In making their decision to (re)invest in the learning experience, these learners appear to have taken their own cultural and linguistic background into consideration. Furthermore, although it is difficult to generalize the findings of a subset of data such as the one presented here, it is clear that the learners in this study demonstrate great consciousness of the importance of links between their personal, cultural and linguistic background and their language learning endeavours. This may well contribute to a manifestation of their ideal L2 selves and help form, in part, 'a "package" consisting of an imagery component and a repertoire of appropriate plans, scripts and self-regulatory strategies' (Dörnyei 2009: 37) for achieving this.

Certain learners in this study clearly value the completion of culture-related tasks in the classroom, though some of them feel that this type of material should be introduced later in the learning process, that is, when they progress to a higher level. In light of this, tasks focused around literary works, traditional songs and music, cultural stories and pastimes, for example, would be a desirable addition to the communicative tasks adult learners normally encounter in the Irish language classroom. From the data presented here it is also evident that these learners are very much aware of the sociolinguistic realities surrounding the Irish language. They are aware that they have just begun the learning process and that there is a long road ahead of them, but they do not appear to be discouraged by the limited prospects for using Irish now and in the future. This finding would appear to support Singleton's (1987) observation that at least some Irish language learners may seek to realize a cultural need for the language, in lieu of a communicative need. Ó Baoill (1999) takes this idea further in stating that, in his opinion, it is unlikely that learners have a desire to integrate with the Gaeltacht community. The evidence provided here does not support this claim, but it does highlight these learners' awareness of the difficulty of interacting with Irish-speakers inside or outside the Gaeltacht.

In general, it would appear that the participants in this study were not divided on culture-related issues according to their own personal background. These learners were, for example, as likely to be aware of sociolinguistic status of Irish and the limited domains of use for the language whether they were born in the country or not. This was also true of participants' positive/negative reactions to questions about culture-related tasks. One interesting difference in this regard is that three of the four learners who felt that culture-related activities would only be important in courses at a higher level were not native to Ireland. Although it is difficult to interpret this finding, it is possible that some non-Irish learners feel that they have enough to contend with in the classroom without trying to interpret foreign cultural meaning and practices. Conversely, Irish born learners who are in favour of cultural activities, regardless of level, might have already had enough exposure to the native culture to feel comfortable with it being included in the course syllabus.

Conclusion

This paper has outlined some key issues surrounding language, culture and self-image in the context of language learning and teaching. Cultural awareness has been discussed in the broad context of language learning as well as the specific context of minority language learning, to show the importance of cultural awareness for learners in these contexts. We have seen that existing models of L2 motivation do account for some cultural motivation in learners and that Dörnyei's latest conceptualization, The L2 Motivational Self System does hold promise for exploring and explaining some of the complexities that drive individual learners to continue to invest in the learning experience, even in contexts where contact with the target language community may be limited. Finally, Irish language learning has been examined in brief to show that cultural components are an important aspect of any course that aims to meet the needs of its learners. These issues were shown to be particularly relevant to learners included in the small-scale study reported here.

It should be emphasized that although the ideas and findings presented in this paper may be welcomed by both researchers and teachers concerned with Irish language teaching, they surely warrant further research. We simply do not know enough about the role cultural awareness plays in learning Irish. A certain focus on culture exists in course syllabuses available for adults learners (e.g. Little, Ó Murchú & Singleton 1985), but the extent that these elements are incorporated into the day to day teaching of the language and how learners engage with them has not yet been systematically investigated.

In closing, courses aimed at meeting the needs of a diverse group of adult learners of Irish should be tailored to account for the cultural interests and motivations of the learner group. The emphasis on cultural awareness in this paper should not be seen as taking anything away from the teaching of communicative language skills, but attempts to incorporate culture-related activities alongside traditional communicative language teaching promises to aid learners in reaching their desired level of language proficiency and cultural knowledge. However, this is by no means an easy task. The practicalities of meeting the individual needs of learners pose great challenges for course designers and instructors, but meeting these challenges may produce excellent results.

References

Badger, R. and MacDonald, M.N. (2007). 'Culture, language, pedagogy: the place of culture in language teacher education', *Pedagogy, Culture & Society*, 15(2), 215–227.
Byram, M. (1997). *Teaching and Assessing Intercultural Communicative Competence.* Clevedon: Multilingual Matters.
Byram, M. and Grundy, P. (2003). *Context and Culture in Language Teaching and Learning.* Clevedon: Multilingual Matters.
Byram, M. and Morgan, C. (1994). *Teaching-and-Learning Language-and-Culture.* Clevedon: Multilingual Matters.
Byram, M., Nichols, A. and Stevens, D. (2001). *Developing Intercultural Competence in Practice.* Clevedon: Multilingual Matters.
Carnie, A. (1996). 'Modern Irish: a Case Study in Language Revival Failure', *Papers on Endangered Languages, MIT Working Papers in Linguistics*, 28, 99–114.
Central Statistics Office. (2012). *This is Ireland: Highlights from Census, 2011, Part 1.* Dublin: Stationery Office.
Csizér, K. and Dörnyei, Z. (2005). 'The internal structure of language learning motivation and its relationship with language choice and learning effort', *Modern Language Journal*, 89(1), 19–36.
Dörnyei, Z. (2005). *The Psychology of the Language Learner: Individual Differences in Second Language Acquisition.* London: Lawrence Erlbaum.
Dörnyei, Z. (2009). 'The L2 Motivational Self System'. In Dörnyei, Z. and Ushioda, E. (eds), *Motivation, Language Identity and the L2 Self*, pp. 9–42. Bristol: Multilingual Matters.
Dörnyei, Z., Csizér, K., and Németh, N. (2006). *Motivation, Language Attitudes and Globalisation: A Hungarian Perspective.* Clevedon: Multilingual Matters.
Ellis, R. (2004). 'Individual Differences in Second Language Learning.' In A. Davies and C. Elder (eds), *The Handbook of Applied Linguistics*, pp. 525–551. Oxford: Blackwell.
Flynn, C.J. (2009). 'Integrative and Cultural Motivation in Adult Learners of Irish: An Exploratory Study'. Unpublished M.Phil. dissertation, Trinity College Dublin.
Flynn, C.J., and Harris, J. (in preparation). 'Integrative and cultural motivation in adult learners of Irish.'
Gardner, R.C. (1985). *Social Psychology and Second Language Learning: The Role of Attitudes and Motivation.* London: Edward Arnold Publishers.
Gardner, R.C. (2001). 'Integrative motivation and second language motivation'. In Dörnyei, Z. and Schmidt, R. (eds), *Motivation and Second Language Acquisition*, pp. 1–20. Honolulu: University of Hawaii Press.

Gardner, R.C. and Lambert, W.E. (1972). *Attitudes and Motivation in Second-Language Learning.* Rowley: Newbury House.

Gardner, R.C. and Tremblay, P.F. (1994). 'On motivation, research agendas, and theoretical frameworks', *The Modern Language Journal*, 78(3), 359–368.

Hall, J.K. (2002). *Teaching and Researching Language and Culture.* London: Longman.

Kramsch, C. (1998). *Language and Culture.* Oxford: Oxford University Press.

Kramsch, C. (2006). 'Culture in language teaching'. In Brown, K. (ed.), *Encyclopedia of Language and Linguistics (2nd edition)*, pp. 322–329. Oxford: Elsevier Science.

Lee, J. (2005). 'The native speaker: An achievable model?', *Asian EFL Journal*, 7(2), 152–163.

Little, D.G., Ó Murchú, H. and Singleton, D.M. (1985). *A Functional-Notional Syllabus for Adult Learners of Irish.* Dublin: Trinity College, Centre for Language and Communication Studies.

Littlewood, W. (1981). *Communicative Language Teaching: An Introduction.* Cambridge: Cambridge University Press.

Littlewood, W. (1984). *Foreign and Second Language Learning.* Cambridge: Cambridge University Press.

Mac Mathúna, L. (1996). 'Integrating language and cultural awareness components in Irish-language teaching programmes'. In Hickey, T. and Williams, J. (eds), *Language, Education and Society in a Changing World*, pp. 179–187. Dublin: IRAAL/Multilingual Matters.

Markus, H.R., and Nurius, P. (1986). 'Possible selves', *American Psychologist*, 41(9), 954–969.

Masny, D. (1997). 'Linguistic awareness and writing: exploring the relationship with language awareness', *Language Awareness*, 6(2), 105–118.

Morgan, D.L. (2008). 'Focus groups'. In L.M. Given (ed.), *The SAGE Encyclopedia of Qualitative Research Methods, Vol. 1*, pp. 352–354. London: SAGE.

Ó Baoill, D. (1999). 'Social cultural distance, integrational orientation and the learning of Irish'. In Chambers, A. and Ó Baoill, D. (eds), *Intercultural Communication and Language Learning*, pp. 189–200. Dublin: IRAAL.

Ó Laoire, M. (2000). 'Learning Irish for participation in the Irish language speech community outside the Gaeltacht', *Journal of Celtic Language Learning*, 5, 20–33.

Ó Laoire, M. (2004). 'Cultural awareness in the Irish language classroom: an overview'. In Smith, M. (ed.), *Readings in the Teaching of Culture*, pp. 9–15. Dublin: IRAAL.

Oyserman, D., Bybee, D., Terry, K., and Hart-Johnson, T. (2004). 'Possible selves as roadmaps', *Journal of Research in Personality*, 38(2), 130–149.

Singleton, D. (1987). 'Communicative needs: the case of Irish'. In Valdman, A. (ed.), *Proceedings from the Symposium on the Evaluation of Foreign Language Proficiency*, pp. 79–83. Bloomington, IN: Indiana University.

Tomlinson, B. and Masuhara, H. (2004). 'Developing cultural awareness', *Modern English Teacher*, 13(1), 5–11.

Williams, M. and Burden, R.L. (1997). *Psychology for Language Teachers: A Social Constructivist Approach*. Cambridge: Cambridge University Press.

LAUREN KAVANAGH AND TINA HICKEY[1]

3   An exploration of parents' experiences of
involvement in immersion schooling:
Identifying barriers to successful involvement

Introduction

A significant body of international research has demonstrated that parental
involvement in education is beneficial to children's learning (e.g. Hoover-
Dempsey & Sandler 1995; Hill & Taylor 2004). Cross-sectional studies
have consistently shown an association between higher parental involvement and greater academic success of children (e.g. Grolnick & Slowiazcek
1994), and longitudinal studies have found similar results (e.g. Miedel &
Reynolds 1999; Barnard 2004). Benefits have been shown for students'
motivation (e.g. Grolnick & Slowiaczek 1994; Gonzales-DeHass, Willems
& Doan Holbein 2005) *reading attainment* (e.g. Sénéchal & LeFevre 2002)
behaviour in school (e.g. Cotton & Wikelund 2001; Hill et al. 2004) *attendance* (Sheldon & Epstein 2002; Cotton & Wikelund 2001) and *academic
achievement* (e.g. Epstein, Coates, Salinas, Sanders & Simon 1997; Miedel
& Reynolds 1999; Hill & Taylor 2004). These benefits have been demonstrated across a wide range of ages and across a variety of contexts (Hoover-
Dempsey & Sandler 1995). Parental involvement has been found not only
to have benefits for children, but also for parents and schools themselves
(Peña 2000). As a result, the identification of ways of increasing parental
involvement in education has been a goal of many major recent educational
reforms. In order to attempt to foster successful parental involvement, it

1   Supported by COGG, An Chomhairle um Oideachas Gaeltachta & Gaelscolaíochta.

is necessary to identify how parents can be involved, why and when they choose to become involved, and also how their involvement affects their children's education.

It is also imperative that the topic of parental involvement be examined in less typical educational models such as immersion. Parental motivation and high parental support have been posited as essential features of the success of immersion programmes (Baker 2006; Branaman & Rennie 1998). While immersion students have consistently been found to achieve higher levels of proficiency in the target language than their 'drip-feed' counterparts, it is argued that the classroom by itself is insufficient to attain fluency, and that classroom teaching must also be accompanied by family commitment and community support (Hinton 2001). Research in Ireland also points to significant relationships between parent variables and immersion pupils' proficiency in Irish (Harris & Ó Laoire 2006). Out of school use of Irish has also been found to be linked to pupil proficiency (Murtagh 2007). If parents are proficient in Irish they could be expected to be equipped to provide opportunities for their children to use the language in real communicative settings outside of the classroom environment.

What is 'parental involvement'?

One criticism that has been levelled at a large proportion of previous research in the domain of parental involvement has been the lack of consistency in the definitions of 'parental involvement' operationalized by the researchers. Some have chosen to focus on particular dynamic aspects of parental participation, such as parent aspirations, or specific behaviours, such as attendance at parent-teacher meetings or volunteering activities. However, it appears that there is a wide variety of ways in which parents can be involved, which can, in turn, positively influence children's school experience. As a result, it would appear more appropriate to think of parental involvement as a multidimensional construct. Epstein and colleagues have supported this view, and have expressed concern that early work on parent involvement failed to provide insight on what schools could do to promote more extensive parental involvement (Dauber & Epstein 1993). Efforts to redress this led to the development of a typology which aimed to categorize comprehensively the variety of involvement activities in which parents could potentially engage. The 'Model of Overlapping Spheres of Influence' (Epstein 1992) identifies three major contexts within which children develop and learn: the family, the school, and the community (Epstein 1992; Epstein et al. 1997). This model, building on the ecological work of Bronfenbrenner, recognizes that there are some practices that family, school and community conduct separately, while there are others that they conduct jointly in order to influence the growth and learning of the child. Epstein (1992, 1997) argues that successful partnerships must be forged between these three spheres in order to best meet the needs of the child.

Epstein (1992) identified six types of parental involvement which she argues are important for successful partnerships between home and school. These are: parenting, communicating, volunteering, learning at home, decision making and collaborating with the community. All six of these types of involvement are necessary for successful partnerships between parents (or family), school, and community. Each type of involvement elicits many different practices of partnership, and the implementation of these practices will vary. However, Epstein argues that, if done well, all can lead to positive outcomes for students. According to advocates of this model, a successful parental involvement intervention programme will involve all six types of involvement to some degree, and will be linked to individual school goals.

Epstein's typology is taken as the guiding framework for the present research. It is a comprehensive model which addresses the weaknesses inherent in other typologies (e.g. Gordon's System's Approach 1979; Berger's Role Categories 1994) by viewing parents as important partners in the education process and emphasizing the importance of communication and collaboration between the home and school spheres. As a result, it is one of the most widely used frameworks in contemporary parental involvement research.

How and why do parents choose to become involved?

For the purpose of the present research, which examines the nature of
parental involvement in an immersion context, it is pertinent to look both at
how and *why* parents become involved in their child's schooling, to identify
the conditions that facilitate that involvement. Hoover-Dempsey, Sandler
and colleagues (1995, 1997, 2005, 2007) suggest that parents will choose
to become involved in their child's education for four main reasons: (1)
their personal construction of the parental role; (2) their personal sense of
efficacy for helping their children succeed in school; (3) their perception
of opportunities and demands for involvement presented both by their
children and their children's schools and (4) life context variables.

Several investigators have contended that if parents are to become
involved, they must first construe their role as a parent as including a role
in the involvement of their children. In other words, parents who believe
it is their role to be a co-educator of their child are more likely to adopt
an actively involved role than parents who believe the responsibility for
a child's education lies solely with the school (e.g. Eccles & Harold 1993;
Hoover-Dempsey & Sandler 1995, 1997; Walker, Wilkins, Dellaire, Hoover-
Dempsey & Sandler 2005). It has been suggested that the way in which
parents construe the parental role is learned largely from their own parents'
school-related involvement and their friends' involvement in children's
schooling, among other factors. A construction of the parental role as
including a role in their child's education is important because it enables
parents to imagine, anticipate and act on a range of educational activities
with their child (Walker et al. 2005). However, while it is argued that such
a construction is necessary, it is not a sufficient condition for the emergence
of parental involvement in education.

It is posited that when a personal construction of this kind is coupled
with a parental personal sense of efficacy for helping a child succeed in
school, then parents are likely to adopt an active role in their child's education. Hoover-Dempsey & Sandler (1995) argue that this sense of efficacy
comes from four main sources: the direct experience of being successfully
involved in other activities; the vicarious experience of the success of others
in involvement activities; persuasion that involvement is important and is

achievable by the parent; and the emotional response elicited when matters important to the parent, e.g. the success of the child, or his or her own success as a parent, are at issue. This personal sense of efficacy means that a parent believes that s/he has the knowledge and skills required to aid the child, and that s/he is able to find alternative sources of knowledge and skill if they become necessary (Hoover-Dempsey & Sandler 1995).

There is also evidence that parents' involvement is influenced by their observation of opportunities, invitations or demands to do so, either from their child, or their child's school. These may include a child asking for help with homework, or a child being eager to talk about their day in school. Opportunities or invitations from the school may include encouraging parents to volunteer in the classroom, asking them to fundraise for materials, or requiring parents to monitor their child's homework. Hoover-Dempsey and Sandler (1995) argue that *all* parent involvement activities are potentially important because they suggest that school-related activities are important to *both* the parent and the child. Since children tend to feel positively towards their parents, and view them as powerful and requiring respect, modelling theory predicts that children will choose to imitate selected behaviours of their parents. Therefore, the more time parents spend *with* or *for* their child in school-related activities, the more likely it is that children will model their parents' school-focused attitudes and behaviours.

Higher levels of involvement have also been found to be related to certain demographic characteristics of parents (Hill & Taylor 2004). Parents from higher socioeconomic groups are more likely to have higher levels of involvement (Grolnick et al. 1997). Conversely, parents from lower socioeconomic groups are likely to experience more barriers to involvement, ranging from lack of resources to transportation problems. Also, parents who have received less education themselves or who have had negative experiences of education are less likely to take an actively involved role. In such cases, parents may have worries or fears surrounding contact with their child's teacher or other school staff (Lareau 1996). Davis-Kean (2005) suggests that the amount of education the parent has received impacts on how they structure their home environment and how they interact with their child to promote academic achievement.

The role of parents in immersion education

Having a child educated through the medium of a language that is not the
first language of the parents has also been found to be a barrier to effective
parental involvement in education. So far, however, this has mainly been
researched in the context of parents of students who are being submerged
in the target language, which is the majority language of the community,
e.g. the case of Hispanic immigrant parents in the U.S. In such cases, barriers to parental involvement relating to home language, differing cultures
and expectations of education, and socioeconomic status have been studied extensively (e.g. Bermudez & Marquez 1996). It is argued here that,
although there may be some similarities, research findings from this context
cannot be generalized to the heritage immersion context of Ireland, where
parents are opting to have their children educated through a language which
is not the parents' own L1. It is expected that a variety of different psychological and socio-cultural factors may influence the nature of involvement
in this setting compared to the migrant one, and that parental involvement
in the immersion context thus merits study in its own right.

    While Hickey (1998) looked at the reciprocity between home fac-
tors and early immersion in preschool, Harris and Ó Laoire (2006)
note that it is surprising how little detailed research on parental involvement in Irish immersion schools has been conducted, given that the
Gaelscoileanna, or Irish-medium education, movement has been so par-
ent-driven. Gaelscoileanna in their current form were established from
the early 1970s in response to parental demand, rather than imposed by
government policy as in the preceding decades. Cummins (1974; as cited
in Coady & Ó Laoire 2002) found that in 1974, almost half the children
enrolled in Gaelscoileanna were from Irish-speaking homes. Also, many
of the parents who chose to send their children to these schools appeared
to use the Irish language in the work sphere, or at least need competence
in the language in order to qualify for their posts: 51 per cent of fathers of
children in Gaelscoileanna at that time were employed in government or
semi-state jobs which required Irish (Ó Riagáin & Ó Gliasáin 1979). The

number of Irish immersion schools grew throughout the 1970s, and experienced a dramatic growth spurt in the 1980s, continuing to increase steadily since then. Some of this growth has been attributed by commentators to parents perceiving advantages of all-Irish schools that were not necessarily linguistic in nature. Parents are aware of the additional points awarded to pupils who sit second-level State examinations through the medium of Irish. This is a policy which is intended to compensate for the paucity of learning resources in Irish, but which has been cited as a policy which places children from English speaking and immigrant families at a disadvantage (Holmquist, as cited in Borooah, Dineen & Lynch 2009). Smaller pupil-teacher ratios, co-education and the religious ethos of particular schools have also been cited as motivating factors in parents' choice of immersion (e.g. Ó Laoire 2005). Currently, there are 139 all-Irish primary schools outside of Gaeltacht areas in the Republic of Ireland (Gaelscoileanna 2011), a number which is expected to grow in the coming years in response to increased parental demand (Watson & Mac Ghiolla Phádraig 2011).

Harris & Ó Laoire (2006) claim that this rapid rise in the popularity of immersion schools in Ireland has likely brought with it associated changes to the profile of a 'typical' immersion parent. The traditional profile of an Irish immersion parent as someone who is highly committed to (and proficient in) Irish may no longer be adequate. Gaeilscoileanna have often been branded as elitist, and it has been argued that Irish-medium education is the preserve of children from wealthy and highly-educated families. However, as Borooah et al. (2009) note: 'allegations of the comfortable middle class ambience of Gaelscoileanna have remained at the level of anecdote' (p. 435) Indeed, there are several all-Irish schools in areas of social disadvantage (Gaelscoileanna 2011) and increasing numbers of non-Irish speaking parents choosing immersion for their children. It is reasonable to assume that there is now more diversity in terms of education, socioeconomic status and proficiency in Irish among the Gaelscoileanna parent body than ever before. It is therefore possible that there are increasing numbers of parents who experience some challenges to becoming involved in their child's education through Irish.

In the report commissioned by the National Council for Curriculum and Assessment on the literature surrounding language and literacy in

Irish-immersion primary education, Harris and Ó Laoire (2006) made a call for research on parental involvement in Gaelscoileanna. The authors argued that further research on parental profile and parental involvement is needed, as it may be useful in understanding declining standards in Irish attainment, as well as having implications for planning and policy in these schools. This study aims to address this call for further investigation of an under-researched topic in the literature. Specifically, it aims to identify factors that facilitate and obstruct parental involvement in Irish immersion schools, in the context of the psychological and educational literature on such involvement, as well as the sociolinguistic context of Irish. The presence of barriers to parental involvement may have implications for children's educational success generally, and may also have a significant impact on their learning of Irish.

The present study

A series of in-depth semi-structured interviews were conducted with ten parents. Participants were recruited through four Gaelscoileanna in the Greater Dublin area. All parents in selected classes in these schools were invited to participate, and all those who volunteered to participate were interviewed. Nine participants were female and one was male. Six parents reported low proficiency in Irish, while four parents reported higher proficiency levels. Higher proficiency parents are referred to here as HP1, HP2, etc., and low proficiency parents are referred to as LP1, LP2, etc. In order to preserve confidentiality, only these codes are used to differentiate participants, and any names given in quotes are researcher-selected pseudonyms.

The semi-structured interview schedule was developed on the basis of parental involvement theory and the research described above, and revised following a series of six pilot interviews. Interviews were between thirty and forty-five minutes in length. They were audio-recorded and transcribed verbatim. Data were submitted to content analysis, closely following the guidelines set out by Mayring (2000). Transcripts were reviewed until clear sections were identified. Participants' responses for each section were then isolated. These responses were reviewed in order to establish what they communicated. Responses were condensed into distinct themes under each section. These categories were then adapted for use as a coding frame. All ten interviews were then coded using this framework. Inter-rater reliability was carried out on 20 per cent of the data and was found to be 84.5 per cent, considered a satisfactory reliability outcome (Guerin & Hennessy 2002).

Ten sections were identified during the process of analysis. These were: reasons for school choice, attitudes towards Irish, home-school contact, progress of child, reading, use of Irish in the home, involvement activities, barriers to involvement, facilitators of involvement, and suggestions for support. Given space limitations, this chapter will focus on one area, the themes relating to the section *Barriers to Involvement*. Quotes are presented to illustrate each theme.

Low proficiency as a barrier

The most frequently reported barrier to involvement that was identified by the parents interviewed was their perceived lack of proficiency in the Irish language. They perceived their low proficiency as a barrier to helping with homework and to speaking Irish with their children. Ancillary issues such as feeling uncomfortable about being present on the school premises as a result of low proficiency, and lack of confidence when communicating with their child's teacher were also expressed. One parent recounted that it took her several years to feel confident enough to increase her involvement with her child's school. She sees her increase in confidence as directly related to her increase in proficiency in the Irish language:

> To be honest with you, I was one of them parents that just dropped them at the school and things like that. And it's an awful lot to do with confidence, 'cause straight away you're looking at another language and it's like, even though your kids are coming home speaking it and everything, you're looking at it as a different language, and it, it freezes you out straight away. You're afraid to go there. Because, I think it's more that parents, do you know what I mean, don't want other people to think they're stupid, dumb. To be honest, that's the way I felt. (LP1)

Another parent appears to echo this sentiment, stating that it is initially daunting for parents to communicate with their child's school if they do not speak Irish well. She described how she would try to speak Irish on school grounds, as it was the encouraged practice, but says: 'I was embarrassed, 'cause you don't know whether you're pronouncing it properly, or you think they're looking at you going "Huh, she's after saying that wrong" or something.' (LP6). Similarly, another participant described an incident where she noticed how significant a lack of proficiency is for other parents: 'I was standing one day waiting for a teacher's meeting and the husbands were coming up going "I'm just afraid someone's going to speak to me in Irish 'cause I don't know how to reply!" I think there is that fear, there is that barrier that, yes, you're sending your child, but we don't know how to speak it, you know?' (LP2). Other parents talked about the difficulties of being involved in their child's home learning as a direct result of their inability to speak Irish well: 'I just wouldn't know enough. I feel I'd just tell them the wrong thing, so I feel like I would just be better off leaving them to get on with it themselves. It gets frustrating always having to say to them "you'll have to ask your teacher tomorrow"'. (LP4)

Interestingly, however, some parents noted that the proficiency barrier need not be permanent. One mother found that her perception of low proficiency as a barrier changed over time. She reported that this was a result of positive experiences, such as finding the staff in her child's school to be very understanding of her low Irish proficiency and helping her to overcome her reluctance: 'Like I wrote something on an envelope in Irish yesterday and I wasn't sure if I wrote the proper thing down, and I just asked and she said "Yeah, you got that perfect." So they're very encouraging for the parents.' (LP6). Another reported that as her child went through school she learned enough from him to make it less daunting to visit the school: 'It's only now that from my young lad I picked up bits and pieces [of Irish] that I've more confidence to come' (LP2).

Lack of invitations for involvement /resistance from child

While parents' involvement is often linked to the policies of school, the data here also pointed to the role of children in shaping their parents' involvement. Some of the parents interviewed attribute their lack of involvement in particular activities to their not receiving appeals from their children to be involved. They note that the frequency of invitations for involvement seemed to decrease as a function of the child's age, with parents reporting that the older their child got, the less they expressed a need or a want for their parents help or involvement. This resulted in some parents failing to make overtures for involvement, as they believe that if their child requires their help they will ask for it. For example, one mother said that she rarely helps her daughter with learning activities in the home anymore: 'She gets on with her all her homework and that herself. She doesn't need my help at all anymore really. If she did I'm sure she'd ask me' (LP5).

A second theme in this section concerned parents' reports of having made repeated attempts at involvement which were rebuffed by their children. This particularly seems to be a barrier for parents who attempt to use Irish in the home. One parent describes this happening in her family: 'As the years went on, we tried to speak Irish with him at home, and his attitude was "I've had it all day at school. I don't want it here." So we stopped doing that' (LP2). This was supported by comments from three other parents, with similar experiences being reported: 'The ten year old, a couple of years ago, starting saying "Ah Mam, I'm not in school now. Don't be starting".' (HP3) One parent described a need to be sensitive to the child's response in terms of efforts to use Irish at home: 'There'd be days when she'd say "Oh no, just English" but then there are days [...] At home we'd often say to them "let's speak as Gaeilge", do you know that way? Just to try and bring it in, but then if after fifteen minutes she's not interested we'd just leave it like' (HP2).

Another parent talked about her son rejecting her attempts to help with reading, both in English and Irish. She felt that her son resisted her attempts at involvement due to his perception that she lacked the ability to help him: 'I don't go near the reading really. Adam would laugh at me if I tried. He's much better at reading than me' (LP1).

Practical issues

Several parents mentioned practical, logistical barriers to their involvement. These included time pressures, childcare issues, rival commitments, etc. Being a single parent, having other children, and working outside the home, were all issues mentioned by parents interviewed. These were reported as barriers to involvement generally, and also to specific aspects of involvement which parents felt to be required by immersion education, such as trying to speak Irish with the children in the home. One participant noted:

> I find that the biggest barrier to it is that you're in such a rush during the day, 'cause I've three of them, and trying to get them ... And it's not that I don't want to [speak Irish to children at home], but it's the rushing that's the biggest problem. But I've started to speak it with them, and I'm trying. (HP1)

When asked about her involvement in her child's school, another parent expressed a wish to be more involved, but felt she did not have the time to do so: 'I should be more active [...] But I'm a single mum and it's hard, you know?' (LP2).

Lack of appropriate resources

Another barrier reported by parents who would like to support their children's Irish learning is the perceived lack of suitable materials in Irish, particularly lack of appropriate books and media programmes. Parents articulated this as a lack of suitable materials, rather than a lack of awareness of materials. When asked if her child ever read non-school books in Irish, one parent explained:

> There's nothing there for them in Irish. Everything's in English, you know? And yes, I could go out and buy him a book that's in Irish, but I don't know how I'd ... But if it were a newspaper or something maybe I could throw it at him and say 'here, have a read of that'. But there isn't actually anything on a daily basis that you would read, because there's nothing around. (LP2)

Another parent reported a similar experience:

> There isn't a lot in Irish [...] And, as I say, back to John again, because he loves to read and you if could go out there and get some of the really interesting books that you can get in English. Like, he loved all the Harry Potter books and different things like that. But if they were more, like if there was a lot more Irish displayed, he would be able to get out there and get them. (LP1)

Inappropriate supports offered

Given the proficiency issues noted above, it is not surprising that the most common way in which schools attempted to support parents to be involved in their child's schooling was to make Irish classes available to parents. However, this appears not to guarantee success. Several of the parents interviewed had attended Irish classes at some stage in their child's school career in an effort to enable themselves to be more involved, yet most found the experience very unsatisfactory. One parent, for example, found she did not reap much benefit from the class, as she did not receive any one-on-one interaction with the teacher, and thus felt she was unable to keep up:

> I did go to class, but I had the little one with me and it was a very full class, and it was going over my head like [...] I mean, I think some people don't grasp it quite as quick. They need a bit more one-on-one time. Or, I'd need one-on-one time I should say, to understand it more, or to ask questions. When there's a big group of people it's hard to put questions across. (LP6)

Another parent explains how she lost interest very quickly in the Irish class she attended, as the agenda of the teacher did not marry with her own personal goals for attending:

> Well the one thing that I found when I was doing the night course was that the person who was doing it, he was from Donegal [...] and that turned me off, because they have a different accent, and I kind of got disinterested. You see I just want to learn the basics. I just want to learn how to say 'Hello! Goodbye!' and help with the homework a little bit, and that's all I'm interested in. Whereas this was a whole big conversation, and he was giving us poems and everything, and I thought: 'Not interested'. (LP2)

Several parents appeared to agree with this view, stating that they are only interested in learning basic Irish and feeling that any Irish night courses for parents should focus on this. More than one parent mentioned that they would just like to learn some more 'little phrases' and to be able to understand their children's homework.

However, one parent expressed a contrary view. She argued that to learn Irish to just this basic level is insufficient if a parent truly wants to support their child's education effectively:

> Yeah, if you're doing it in a basic sense, yes, 'Dún an doras. Téigh go dtí do leaba.' [Close the door. Go to bed], you know, all the small phrases. But if you're doing it to help your child with homework you actually would need to write an essay, or learn poetry, because that's what the child is going to learn. If your child is coming home and they have a six-page book and they need to learn the grammar from the book, what are you going to do? Say 'Oh well, dún an doras' [close the door]? (HP4)

Some parents seemed to be aware of this view but saw it as impossible, saying that parents do not have the time to commit to learning Irish to this degree: 'Parents are busy. They don't have time really to be going to a class every week.' (LP5) However, this high proficiency parent felt that other parents should be willing to make this effort to do their very best to support their children, since their children are receiving huge benefits from receiving all-Irish education:

> 'It's a big ask. But as I see it, if you're thinking of putting your child into anything, there's always something that's asked. Like, if you're putting your child into an English school, you know they're going to be speaking English, and you have the basic concepts for them. So, if you're putting them into an Irish school, it's the same commitment. You need to, you know? And I think there are a lot of rewards that come from sending your child to an all-Irish school – the culture, the dance, the sports side of it. There's an awful lot.' (HP4)

It appears that parents differ in their beliefs in what is required for them to be active and effective partners in their children's education, and this divergence of opinion in terms of attitude and practice is itself very relevant to understanding and addressing the needs of this heterogeneous group.

Discussion

This extract from the findings of this qualitative study indicate that Irish-immersion parents do experience barriers to involvement in their children's education. Several of the parents interviewed talk about their wish to be more involved, and several expressed feelings of guilt about their perceived lack of involvement. Their reasons for not being as involved as they would like thus could not be said to be based on a failure to construe a role in their children's education. Instead, they might indicate that their construction of the parental role is one that has not adapted to an educational model that does not use the mother-tongue as the medium of instruction. The barriers they acknowledge seem to have more to do with their sense of efficacy for involvement and also their perception of invitations for involvement, as well as due to a range of practical or logistical barriers. Parents report feelings of frustration because they find it difficult to help their children with their homework and their reading. They also express feelings of anxiety and inadequacy in relation to their contact with their children's teachers and other school staff.

The most frequently reported barriers relate to low parental proficiency in Irish. Low proficiency was reported as being a barrier to parents helping with their child's home learning, their contact with their child's school and also creating out-of-school opportunities for their children to use Irish. It is thus perhaps tempting to think that simply teaching parents Irish is the solution to increasing their involvement. Indeed, offering Irish classes to parents is the most commonly reported way in which schools attempt to involve parents, though this is clearly not a panacea, given the reservations of some of these participants. Indeed, this type of 'deficit' approach to increasing involvement, whereby parents are seen as lacking the necessary skills for partnership and where parental training is seen as a major component of parental involvement interventions, is now heavily criticized. Instead, 'empowerment models' (e.g. Shepard & Rose 1995) have been found to be more effective: it is now widely believed that educators should see parents as valuable partners in the education process and should attempt to increase their participation by utilizing the skills they *do* have rather than focusing on the skills that they are potentially lacking. Parents in this study did not seem to value their contribution to supporting their children's English oral and literacy skills and had not constructed a shared role with the school wherein they felt that such support was valued. Instead they tended to focus on their deficiency and yet did not seem to see learning Irish as a realistic solution to address this. They reported 'not bothering' to avail of the classes made available, or talked about not having the time to commit to learning Irish. Those who had attended classes all reported having negative experiences of them because they had not matched their own expectations or needs. It is clear that while providing parents with opportunities to improve their Irish may have merit, other methods of supporting parents are also needed, including some exploration of what their aims are, as well as their emotional baggage regarding their feelings of low efficacy as learners of Irish who have previously failed signally to acquire the language.

These findings also indicate the importance of recognizing the role of all of the players in the home-school context, including the children. Experiencing resistance from children when overtures to involvement are made by parents was also a recurring theme, and one that was reported by parents regardless of their Irish proficiency. Higher proficiency parents in particular reported their child's unwillingness to use Irish with them in the home. This may be linked in some way to the finding that parents perceive a lack of developmentally appropriate and engaging resources in Irish that they could make use of with their children. Raising parents' awareness of suitable existing materials may be a step in supporting them to overcome this barrier.

Parents reported having very favourable attitudes towards Irish. While this is an encouraging finding, it is important to note that positive attitudes towards Irish are not necessarily predictive of an inclination or and ability for parents to actively support their child's Irish-language learning. In fact, favourable attitudes towards Irish and the teaching of Irish have also been found among parents in English-medium schools, but in practice 'many have a lukewarm, hands-off attitude to the actual *enterprise* of their children learning Irish' (Harris 2005: 969). The present study found that although all parents described themselves as positively disposed towards supporting their child's Irish learning, they differed considerably in their actual practices of involvement.

It must also be noted that, in line with existing research on parental involvement in general (see Byrne & Smyth 2011), parents reported less frequent involvement as their child progressed through the school. Invitations for involvement were reported to dry up, and increased resistance to attempts at involvement was reported by parents. In addition to this, parents reported feeling less able to help with learning in the home as their children's proficiency in Irish surpassed their own and as the difficulty of the material to be covered increased. There is an argument to be made that support for parents should adapt to and span the length of their child's career, and perhaps that the type of support offered may be different as the child progresses through school.

Conclusions and future research

Parental involvement in education is complex, and may be construed differently by parents, children, teachers and schools. What is clear is that it can encompass a wide variety of practices that can positively impact children's educational outcomes. This is true both for general academic outcomes and for second language attainment. However, the reasons why parents choose to become actively involved in their child's education are multifaceted, and involve both individual psychological aspects and socio-cultural factors, and can also be heavily influenced by the practices of the school and by the responses of the children themselves.

This study showed that parents are keen for their children to succeed in school and to achieve high proficiency in Irish, but that they do not always feel able to do support them in this endeavour. Ways of supporting parents to construct a more feasible and adaptable model of parental involvement in order to become more active partners in the education process is thus necessary. The present study represents the first phase of an investigation of immersion parents' experiences of involvement, and the barriers to involvement identified by these parents. Given the finding that children play an active role in shaping their parents' involvement, as well as the more generally accepted role by teachers and schools, however, means it is inappropriate to examine parental involvement by looking at parents in isolation. Planned future studies will thus also use qualitative and quantitative methods to explore the perceptions and practices of teachers and principals in relation to parents, as well as those of children in Gaelscoileanna. It is hoped that consultation with all of the primary stakeholders will lead to the development of a comprehensive picture of the nature and extent of parental involvement in Irish-immersion schools. Recommendations for practice will also be made so that the invaluable resources that parents can provide can be best utilized to bring about the most positive outcomes for children, parents and schools.

References

Baker, C. (2006). *Foundations of Bilingual Education and Bilingualism* (4th Ed.). Clevedon: Multilingual Matters.

Barnard, W.M. (2004). 'Parent Involvement in Elementary School and Educational Attainment', *Children and Youth Services Review*, 26 (1), 39–62.

Berger, E.H. (1991). *Parents as Partners in Education*. New York: Macmillan Publishing Company.

Bermudez, A.B. and Marquez, J.A. (1996). 'An Examination of a Four-Way Collaborative to Increase Parental Involvement in the Schools', *The Journal of Educational Issues of Language Minority Students*, 16 (3), 1–16.

Borooah, V.K., Dineen, D.A., and Lynch, N. (2009). 'Language and Occupational Status: Linguistic Elitism in the Irish Labour Market', *The Economic and Social Review*, 40 (4), 435–460.

Branaman, L. and Rennie, R. (1998). 'Many Ways to Learn: Elementary School Foreign Language Program Models', *ERIC Review*, 6 (1), 14–23.

Byrne, D. and Smyth, E. (2011). *Behind the Scenes: A Study of Parental Involvement in Post-Primary Education*. Joint publication of the ESRI, NCCA and DES. Dublin: Liffey Press.

Coady, M. and Ó Laoire M. (2002). 'Mismatches in Language Policy and Practice in Education: The Case of Gaelscoileanna in the Republic of Ireland', *Language Policy*, 1 (2), 143–158.

Cotton, K. and Wikelund, K.R. (2001). 'Parent involvement in Education'. <http:// educationnorthwest.org/webfm_send/567>, accessed 18 August 2010.

Dauber, S.L. and Epstein, J.L. (1993). 'Parents' Attitudes and Practices of Involvement of Inner-City Elementary and Middle Schools.' In N.F. Chavkin (ed.), *Families and schools in a pluralistic society*, pp. 53–72. New York: State University of New York Press.

Davis-Kean, P.E. (2005). 'The Influence of Parent Education and Family Income on Child Achievement: The Indirect Role of Parental Expectations and the Home Environment', *Journal of Family Psychology*, 19 (2), 294–304.

Eccles, J.S., and Harold, R.D. (1993). 'Parent-School Involvement during the Early Adolescent Years', *Teachers College Record*, 94 (3), 568–587.

Epstein, J.L. (1992). 'School and Family Partnerships.' In M. Atkin (ed.) *Encyclopedia of Educational Research*, pp. 1139–51. New York: Macmillan.

Epstein, J.L., Coates, L., Salinas, K.C., Sanders, M.G., and Simon, B.S. (1997). *School, Family, and Community Partnerships: Your Handbook for Action*. Thousand Oaks, CA: Corwin Press.

Epstein, J.L. and Sheldon, S.S. (2001). 'Present and Accounted for: Improving Student Attendance through Family and Community Involvement', *The Journal of Educational Research*, 95 (5), 308–318.

Gaelscoileanna (2011). 'Statistics'. <http://www.gaelscoileanna.ie/about/statistics /?lang=ie> accessed 12 January 2011.

Gonzales-DeHass, A.R., Willems, P.P., and Doan Holbein, M.F. (2005). 'Examining the Relationship between Parental Involvement and Student Motivation', *Educational Psychology Review*, 17 (2), 99–123.

Gordon, I. (1979). 'The Effects of Parent Involvement in Schooling'. In R.S. Brandt (ed.), *Partners: Parents and Schools*, pp. 4–25. Alexandria, VA: Association for Supervision and Curriculum Development.

Green, C.L., Walker, J.M.T., Hoover-Dempsey, K.V. and Sandler, H.M. (2007). 'Parents' Motivations for Involvement in Children's Education: An Empirical test of a Theoretical Model of Parental Involvement', *Journal of Educational Psychology*, 99 (3), 532–544.

Grolnick, W.S., Benjet, C., Kurowski, C.O. and Apostoleris, N.H. (1997). 'Predictors of Parent Involvement in Children's Schooling', *Journal of Educational Psychology*, 89 (3), 538–548.

Grolnick, W.S. and Slowiaczek, M.I. (1994). 'Parents' Involvement in Children's Education: A Multidimensional Conceptualization and Motivation Model', *Child Development*, 65 (1), 237–252.

Guerin, S., and Hennessy, E. (2002). 'Pupils' Definitions of Bullying', *European Journal of Psychology of Education*, 17 (3), 249–261.

Harris, J. (2005). 'The Role of Ordinary Primary Schools in the Maintenance and Revival of Irish'. In J. Cohen, K. McAlister, K. Rolstad and J. MacSwan (eds), *ISB 4: Proceedings of the 4th International Symposium on Bilingualism*, pp. 964–977. Somerville, MA: Cascadilla Press.

Hickey, T. (1999). 'Parents and Early Immersion: Reciprocity between Home and Immersion Preschool', *Journal of Bilingual Education and Bilingualism*, 2, (2), 94–113.

Hill, N.E., Domini, R., Castellino, J.E., Nowlin, P., Dodge, K.A., Bates, J.E. and Pettit, G.S. (2004). 'Parent Academic Involvement as related to School Behaviour, Achievement, and Aspirations: Demographic Variations across Adolescence', *Child Development*, 75 (5), 1492–1509.

Hill, N.E. and Taylor, L.C. (2004). 'Parental Involvement and Children's Academic Achievement: Pragmatics and Issues', *Current Directions in Psychological Science*, 13 (4), 161–4.

Hinton, L. (2001). 'Language Revitalization: An Overview' in L. Hinton and K. Hale (eds), *The Green Book of Language Revitalization in Practice*. San Diego, CA: Academic Press, 3–19.

Hoover-Dempsey, K.V. and Sandler, H.M. (1995). 'Parental Involvement in Children's Education: Why does it Make a Difference?', *Teachers College Record*, 97 (2), 311–331.

Hoover-Dempsey, K.V. and Sandler, H.M. (1997). 'Why do Parents become Involved in their Children's Education?', *Review of Educational Research*, 67 (1), 3–42.

Lareau, A. (1996). 'The Problem of Individualism in Family-School Policies', *Sociology of Education*, 69, 24–39.

Mayring, P. (2000). 'Qualitative Content Analysis', *Forum: Qualitative Social Research*, 1 (2), <http://www.qualitative-research.net/index.php/fqs/article/view/1089/2385>, accessed 15 September 2010.

Miedel, W.T. and Reynolds, A.J. (1999). 'Parent Involvement in Early Intervention for Disadvantaged Children: Does it Matter?', *Journal of School Psychology*, 37, 370–402.

Murtagh, L. (2007). 'Out-of-School Use of Irish, Motivation to Learn the Language and Proficiency in Immersion and Subject-Only Post-Primary Programmes', *International Journal of Bilingualism and Bilingual Education*, 10 (4), 428–453.

Ó Laoire, M. (2005). 'The Language Situation in Ireland'. In R.B. Kaplan and R.B. Baldauf Jnr. (eds), *Language Planning and Policy in Europe: The Baltic States, Ireland and Italy*, pp. 193–255. Clevedon: Multilingual Matters.

Ó Riagáin, P. and Ó Gliasáin, M. (1979). *All-Irish Primary Schools in the Dublin Area. Report of a Sociological and Spatial Study of All-Irish-Medium Schools in the Greater Dublin Area, with Special Reference to Their Impact on Home and Social Network Use of Irish*. Dublin: Institiúid Teangeolaíochta Éireann.

Peña, D.C. (2000). 'Parent Involvement: Influencing Factors and Implications', *Journal of Educational Research*, 94 (1) 42–54.

Rasinski, T.V. and Fredericks, A.D. (1989). 'Working with Parents: Dimensions of Parent Involvement', *The Reader Teacher*, 43 (2), 180–182.

Sénéchal, M. and LeFevre, J. (2002). 'Parental Involvement in the Development of Children's Reading Skill: A Five-Year Longitudinal Study', *Child Development*, 73 (2), 445–460.

Sheldon, S. and Epstein, J. (2002). 'Improving Student Behaviour and Discipline with Family and Community Involvement', *Education and Urban Society*, 35 (1), 4–26.

Shepard, R. and Rose, H. (1995). 'The Power of Parents: An Empowerment Model for Increasing Parental Involvement', *Education*, 115 (3), 373–377.

Walker, J.M.T., Wilkins, A.S., Dallaire, J.R., Sandler, H.M., and Hoover-Dempsey, K.V. (2005). 'Model Revision through Scale Development', *The Elementary School Journal*, 106 (2), 85–104.

Watson, I. and Mac Ghiolla Phádraig, M. (2011). 'Linguistic Elitism: The Advantage of Speaking Irish Rather than the Irish-Speaker Advantage', *The Economic and Social Review*, 42 (4), 437–454.

4 A language socialization perspective on knowledge and identity construction in Irish post-primary education

Introduction

As education is a significant domain in which the integration of immigrant groups (in terms of assimilation versus multiculturalism) takes place, cultural and linguistic diversity has become one of the most urgent challenges for educators in Ireland. More generally, educational institutions have long been perceived as one of the primary sites through which individuals are socialized to take particular roles in the society in which they live (Oakes 1985; Olneck 1995; and Bayley & Schecter 2003: 84). The educational system has always played a major role in the socialization process, and language socialization (LS) has functioned as both the symbolic notion of cultural and social structures and as a tool for establishing these structures (Schieffelin and Ochs 1986). From this perspective, LS in formal settings (such as educational contexts) plays a primary role in the complex process of becoming part of a given society, and 'schools are also significant sites of "secondary" socialization' (L2 socialization) for immigrant students (Cole and Zuengler 2003: 98). Immigrant adolescents are often socialized through the educational system to take particular roles in the society in which they live. As experience elsewhere demonstrates, however, majority groups often make strong demands on immigrant minority groups for integration in terms of assimilation (Duff 2009).

The broad purpose of this paper is to bring the aforementioned perspective to bear on the example of Polish students themselves as they reflect on their experiences of engaging with their new sociolinguistic situation in

Ireland. The paper investigates LS processes among two groups of Polish adolescent immigrant students attending different post-primary schools in Ireland. One of the groups also attends a weekend Polish school (Polish government or community-sponsored Polish medium schools in Dublin, Cavan, and Newry, where the Polish language, Polish history, geography, mathematics and religion are taught). The second group consists of the Polish students from the same regional area who are learning exclusively in a second language (L2, in this case English), and are therefore attending regular secondary schools in Ireland.

The theoretical background of the present paper is grounded in both first- and second-language socialization. It also draws on some contributions from bilingual education research. Knowledge and identity construction are discussed in terms of the experiences of Polish immigrant adolescents in Irish educational contexts. The process of L2 development and socialization is examined in relation to concepts of basic interpersonal communicative skills (BICS) and cognitive academic language proficiency (CALP). The paper highlights that the continuous development of bilingual skills (literacy skills included) among immigrant students impacts positively on their psychological and cognitive development.

Section two of the paper deals with the theoretical framework of LS research. It provides definitions of L1 and L2 socialization and the theoretical orientations that inform LS research today, particularly in the context of immigration. In section three, it is argued that immigrant students encounter an exceptional situation of managing shifting identities and come to terms with the power relations inherent in them. This section also locates adolescents within hierarchical (coercive and collaborative) relations of power. Particular reference is made to educational structures in a broad sense, and to the micro- and macro- relations within these educational structures.

Section four investigates knowledge construction in educational settings. It examines how macro factors (such as policy and curriculum) influence micro-interactions between students, educators and communities and in what ways this impacts on students' identities and learning. In this way, the paper sheds light on the coercive and collaborative power relations outlined by Cummins (2002) which are inherent in the educational system. In section five, critical approaches to education are proposed and factors contributing to good pedagogical practice in culturally and linguistically diverse classrooms are identified and discussed. Attention is drawn to the importance of both mother tongue provision and language support for immigrant students (ESL students). The context for the present research is also described, with particular attention being paid to the Irish post-primary education system. Section six describes the research questions, procedures and methodology employed in the data collection process for the study. This is followed by a description of the preliminary results, a discussion of the findings and a conclusion.

Language socialization: theoretical framework

It has been broadly highlighted in the LS literature that LS is a continuous process (Duff 2009; Garett & Baquedano-Lopez 2002; Bayley & Schecter 2003). LS is experienced throughout different stages of human life; for example, in childhood when we are entering a new playground, then in primary and secondary schools, universities, or professional/vocational sites. It may also happen that an individual goes to live in a different country, in which case LS must take place again, and is referred to as second or L2 language socialization.

Therefore, it became widely acknowledged in the literature that 'Language Socialization is experienced throughout one's lifespan' through social interactions between 'experts' (those who have more proficiency in for example, language, literacy, culture, etc.) and 'novices' (those with less proficiency). One definition of LS states:

> Language Socialization (LS) is the lifelong process by which individuals – typically novices – are inducted into specific domains of knowledge [such as knowledge of language and literacy], beliefs, affect, roles, identities, and social representations, which they access and construct through language practices and social interaction. (Duff 1995: 508)

This occurs as an individual enters new communities such as schools or the workplace (Lave & Wenger 1991).

Duff (2009: 2) notes that L2 socialization is a process by which an individual (a non-native speaker of a given language) seeks competence in a second language and membership in a certain social group or community, with the aim of gaining inclusion and the ability to actively participate in the practices of this community. L2 socialization processes are often experienced by people, such as immigrants, who seek competence in the language of the new community, or by people returning to a language they have once used but in which they may since have lost proficiency. It can take place in a variety of language contact settings, such as a place where an L2 is the dominant language of a society, or in restricted and more isolated contexts, as in case of foreign language classrooms or among diaspora communities (Duff 2009).

As indicated by Ochs, 'novices' (newcomers) are 'socialized into using language and socialized through language into local theories and preferences for acting, feeling, and knowing in a social group' (Ochs 1993: 110). Thus, LS is the process by which individuals learn how to take part in activities of everyday life, such as speech events (greetings, narratives, jokes, essay- or memo-writing, texting, expressing emotional states, responding with culturally and socially accepted norms), and also the different values that lie beneath those practices. Appropriate participation in language practices, according to local norms and expectations, allows individuals to function well in a given society (Duff 2009).

> L2 socialization of immigrants shares many of the principles and objectives of first language socialization but with the added complexity of dealing with children or adults who already possess a repertoire of linguistic, discursive, and cultural traditions and community affiliations when encountering new ones [however they] may not experience the same degrees of access, acceptance, or accommodation within the new discourse communities as their L1 counterparts do. (Duff 2007: 310)

For example, they may not share the same discourses in use because they may lack the background knowledge about pop culture or current events in a given country. In this way, they may become silent and feel detached from and rejected by the social group they are trying to access (see Duff 2003: 324–326).

What is more, L2 novices such as immigrants often experience emotional chaos and feelings of anxiety while their, often contradictory, goals develop. As evidence elsewhere suggests, immigrants remain involved in their primary communities (family and friends they have left); in turn, this requires more and more compromises to be made on logistical and ideological grounds (Duff 2009). Language acquisition in this context, therefore, is not only a matter of a child or an adult learning to produce well-formed, referential utterances but it also involves learning 'how to co-construct meaningful contexts and how to engage with others in culturally relevant meaning-making activities' (Garrett & Baquedano-Lopez 2002: 342).

Identity construction in an educational context

Cummins (1981: 14) argues that the negotiation of identity that takes place in the case of immigrant students is a task complicated by the fact that the immigrants grow up in two cultural and language settings, which often represent different values. That is why the immigrant students often face cultural conflicts when constructing their identity. In the process of resolving these conflicts and negotiating their identity, the students might undergo certain stages involving more than one of the aforementioned tendencies. For example, a child may initially reject the home culture and language in favor of target culture, but, finally, the same child may realize that it is possible to belong to both cultures.

According to Miller (2003), immigrant adolescents, like adults, possess a personal identity (a sense of self that is constantly being negotiated) that is manifested through their primary communicative and sense-making resource, namely one's first language (L1). Therefore, being deprived of that essential resource due to immigration to another country, immigrant students are unable to meaningfully represent their sense of self to others (Miller 2003: 8); or, alternatively, their representation of who they are is limited to a somewhat restricted L2 repertoire. This makes the negotiation and re-construction of new emerging social identities at the very least extremely difficult. In the above situation, as Miller (ibid.) points out, a great amount of goodwill from both sides is needed in order to communicate, or '[the immigrant students] may be assumed somehow deficient, or worse'. That is why being audible to others is essential if one is to belong to a group and actively engage in both the negotiation of identities and the language socialization process.

Identity and power relations

Many researchers, such as Cummins (2000), Norton (2000) and Pavlenko & Blackledge (2004), highlight the fact that languages and identities are embedded within power relations. As Pavlenko & Blackledge (2004: 21) point out:

> the fact that languages – and language ideologies – are anything but neutral is especially visible in multilingual societies where some languages and identity options are, in unforgettable Orwellian words, 'more equal than others'.

For instance, those who speak with the 'appropriate' accent or possess good syntax are perceived as more authoritative speakers (Bourdieu 1977). In this way they possess a sort of symbolic power over those who do not have 'right accent' and may possess 'faulty syntax'. As Miller's research (2003: 36) suggests, this has some serious consequences for immigrant students subjected to a dominant language. As a result, these students may lack credibility or may not fulfil that affirmatory role of the believing listeners. She presents the school situation as an excellent example of such unequal power relations. School settings are perceived as markets that have the power to reward language which is approved or legitimated, or sanction and censor that which does not conform to the norms. School sets the values of different linguistic products for the purposes of assessment and certification. If schools value and authorize particular students, they disempower and disadvantage others (Miller 2003: 37–40).

Critical approaches to education are proposed by Cummins (2009). Cummins refers to the relations of power inherent in the education system as coercive. Acts of exercising power by a dominant individual, group, or country to the loss of a subordinated individual, group or country are referred to as 'coercive relations of power'. Given the centrality of power in the social structures and policies that exist within schools, critical approaches to education aim to challenge the 'coercive relations of power' (2009: 262) present in the educational system. Alternatively, Cummins (2009: 263) proposes 'collaborative relations of power' that are referred to as 'being enabled, empowered' to achieve more. The more empowered an individual or group becomes, the more is generated for others to share. Cummins (ibid.) highlights that relations of power in the wider society influence the ways in which educators define their roles, and the types of structures that are established in the educational system. The macro-education structures (policies, programs, curriculum and assessment), along with educators (who bring their own expectations, assumptions and goals to the task of educating culturally diverse students), shape the 'micro-interactions' between educators, students and communities and in this way may impact on students' academic achievement at both the macro level (such as national policies, national curriculum) and micro level (such as school-based language policies, classroom pedagogical practices).

Knowledge construction in an educational context

According to Cummins (2005), affirmation of students' identities in multilingual classrooms is essential in order to construct new knowledge. This is because effective learning involves three major conditions: (i) engaging prior understandings and background knowledge (ii) integrating factual knowledge with conceptual frameworks (iii) taking active control over the learning process through meta-cognitive strategies (Cummins 2009: 266).

Cummins (2000) emphasizes that engagement of prior knowledge is particularly important for cross-linguistic transfer to happen, as immigrant students' knowledge is encoded in their L1, and is therefore mediated through the L1. Prior knowledge refers not only to knowledge gained through formal instruction, it also entails all the experiences that have shaped students' identity and cognitive functioning; this is because students' own perspectives or ways in which they perceive the surrounding world reflect their cultural and linguistic heritage. Moreover, when students invest those prior identities and knowledge, an active construction of new knowledge and new emerging identities may occur. As previous experiences show, 'human relationships are important in children's adjustment to schooling [and their] engagement in learning' (Cummins 2000). Although research (cf. Cummins 1979; 1996; 2000) supports the above findings, there is considerable discrepancy between school policies on language teaching and immigrant students' needs to express themselves linguistically and culturally. There are still false assumptions, such as the irrelevance of ESL students' L1, or even its impediment to literacy development and academic achievement in an L2 in the future. Furthermore, ESL students' cultural and linguistic knowledge have been considered of little relevance for teachers.

Cummins (2009: 265–267) suggests alternative solutions, which would entail acknowledging that students' L1 and home culture are an important resource for learning, and as ensuring that formal instruction affirms students' identities and allows for investment of those identities into learning. This would not only facilitate students' personal development in terms of identity construction, but would also enable cross–lingual transfer of conceptual elements, metacognitive and metalinguistic strategies, pragmatic aspects of language and phonological awareness, thereby contributing to the development of bilingual LS. Cummins's theory (1981) of the interdependence of literacy skills and knowledge is supported by extensive empirical research such as that undertaken by Baker 2000; Cummins 2001; Genesee, Lindholm-Leary et al. 2006. Moreover, Thomas and Collier (2002) have demonstrated that students' proficiency in their L1 at the moment of arrival in the US was the strongest predictor of their future academic success or failure.

As a practical example of teaching for transfer to occur, one specific strategy suggested by Cummins (2009) is the identity text. An identity text is a dual-language text in which a student's identity is reflected. It can be written or spoken, visual or musical, depending on the student's creativity (Cummins 2009a).

The image of an incoming student who differs culturally and linguistically from his/her peers can change dramatically, from being perceived as somehow deficient to being regarded as a valuable member of new groups (communities of practice such as peer groups or classrooms). Further negotiation of identities and construction of knowledge can take place between the students themselves as the teachers begin to develop and share common/ mutual discourses. In this way, schools can become sites of intercultural communication and prepare students for future intercultural contacts that are inevitable in contemporary multicultural Europe. Thus, employing bilingual instructional strategies can promote 'identity investment' both for majority-language and minority-language students.

Pedagogical practices in culturally and linguistically diverse classrooms

A review of research and theory in the area of bilingualism highlights some strategies and practices that promote continuous development of L1 and L2 language socialization among students from different linguistic and cultural minorities.

An ample amount of research has been undertaken that shows the relationship between ethnic identities, cultural continuities and educational achievement (see, for example, Archer and Francis 2007; Creese 2000; Markose and Hellsten 2009). It is therefore reasonable to conclude that the mainstream curriculum should reflect cultural and linguistic diversity as well as promote the cultural and linguistic potential within the school and in the broader community (Cummins 2000). There are then some choices for educators. Regardless of institutional constraints, educators have options with regard to how they choose to deal with the issue of identity negotiation with students and communities. As Cummins (2009: 267) argues, these choices are expressed in how: educators interact with students; engage them cognitively; they activate their prior knowledge;

they use technology to amplify imagination; they involve parents in their children's education and in what and how they communicate to students regarding their home language and culture.

Cummins (2009) points to the need for the re-examination of normalized assumptions regarding the above choices, as well for consideration of assessment and instruction issues in culturally diverse classrooms. He identifies several 'normalized assumptions' that are in fact misconceptions which have given way to 'benign neglect' – that is, a 'less obvious but equally effective conduit for coercive relations of power' (Cummins 2009: 262). Among the most important of such assumptions are: that the development of literacy refers to students' dominant language only; that literacy abilities in languages other than English and in modalities other than the written modality are ignored; that the cultural knowledge and first language linguistic abilities of the bilingual students have little or no instructional relevance; and that the fact that culturally and linguistically diverse parents whose English is often limited do not have linguistic skills/ resources to contribute to their children's literacy development.

Nowlan (2008: 254–263) argues that principles such as inclusion, differentiation and the individualization of teaching methods should become the norm in our classrooms, in order for students from linguistic minority backgrounds to benefit. It is because 'continued development of the bilingual student's skills in his or her mother tongue is considered extremely important both in terms of the student's linguistic, cognitive and social development and from the perspective of providing equal status for minority languages and cultures' (Cummins 2000; OECD 2004; NCCA 2005; Ofsted 2005b; Nowlan 2008: 257). Moreover, Cummins (2009) calls for recognition of the role of societal power relations in determining academic achievement, and for basing school-based language policies and educational policy in general on a 'firm foundation' of what the research says about the influence of students' L1 on L2 literacy development (ibid: 263).

Furthermore, Nowlan (2009) notes that in order to develop strategies that tend to the needs of bilingual students, balance should be reached between schools to flexibly adapt solutions to the particular needs of individual students and communities. Communication between schools should be improved, particularly with regard to the coordination of services in order to facilitate the sharing of good practices. The school should also be actively engaged in promoting intercultural awareness and language and literacy development (Cummins 2000; OECD 2004). Moreover this 'whole-school approach' should be well coordinated and planned. Teachers, students, parents and minority communities should be involved in the process (Blair 2002; Devine 2005). According to Cummins (2009), new strategies are also needed to prepare teachers and educators to teach the new linguistically and culturally diverse populations of students. As Lewis and Wray (2000) note, intercultural and language awareness should be part of teacher education and in-service training. Moreover, communication between teachers and cultural and linguistic minority parents and students can be facilitated by the use of bilingual assistants, interpreters and cultural mediators (ibid.).

It is also necessary to differentiate between CALP and BICS. As Cummins (2000) and Lyons and Little (2009) point out, CALP grows out of BICS, which means in practice that English language support at post-primary level needs to give as much attention to BICS (especially in early stages of language learning) as it does to CALP. In other words, the more integrated the students are and the more they engage in extra-curricular activities, the greater the chance of their academic success. CALP is never, however, developed automatically, especially in the case of adolescents who arrive in a host country aged between twelve and fifteen. Collier (1987) and Cummins (2000), among others, have reported that immigrant students need between five and eight years to catch up with national native speakers of a given language. That is why specific language support should be provided to those students. Such support should be based on a thorough initial assessment of individual oral and written language skills. It should also take into consideration educational background and literacy skills in the student's mother tongue (Cummins 2000, 2001; Miller 1999).

There is extensive evidence suggesting a necessity for long-term scaffolding strategies and support provision beyond the achievement of an initial level of fluency [BICS] (Cummins 2000; 2001). It is also highlighted in the literature and in empirical research that bilingual students should not be viewed in 'deficit terms'. On the contrary, their bilingual potential – both linguistically and culturally – should be valued by schools and promoted at all levels of society (Cummins 2000; Lyons and Little 2009; Council of Europe 2001). Moreover, language ability should not be associated with academic ability and should not result in the placement of ESL students into inappropriate age or ability groupings. Therefore a clear distinction should be made between special educational needs (SEN) provision and language support provision for linguistically diverse students (Troyna and Siraj-Blatchford 1993; Tomlinson and Craft 1995).

Context for the present research

In recent years, Ireland has been experiencing a dramatic increase in the immigration of adolescents and young speakers of languages other than English. Young Polish immigrants constitute a significant group within this immigrant population. It is estimated that there are about 25,000 Poles under nineteen years of age living in Ireland (CSO 2006). Furthermore, according to Census 2006 figures, 10.2 per cent (117,600) of all 0–19 year olds living in Ireland were born outside Ireland. Approximately 5,900 (0–19 year olds) of these were born in Poland. This places the Polish group in third place after immigrant children born in the UK (who may actually have Irish parents or parents of Irish origins) and in the US.

Due to this dramatic increase in the population of immigrants in Ireland, the sociolinguistic dynamics of classrooms has changed considerably. Schools are faced with the educational, linguistic and cultural challenges of adapting their curricula to this trend/development. As Guidera (2007) reported, one out of five immigrant students in post-primary schools in Dublin had little English or no English at the time of their arrival in Ireland. Going to school was reported as being a vital part of their socialization experience in Ireland (Ní Laoire et al. 2009).

English Language Support (ELS), as well as the maintenance of the native language, are considered to be crucial for the well-being of these children. As the study by Ní Laoire et al. (2009) reports, parents of immigrant students often emphasize that it is essential for their children to 'keep up' with the education system in their home country and maintain the language of that country, even if they were not intending to return there in the near future.

In Ireland, however, as Lyons and Little (2009) state, there is much room for improvement in the areas of both language support and home language provision. Previous research in Ireland has identified many problems with levels of funding, the scale and nature of support and home language provision, coordination and planning, teacher allocation and training, the culture-specific nature of the post-primary curriculum, and the training and resources available to educators (Keogh and Whyte 2003; Lodge and Lynch 2004; Ward 2004; Devine 2005; Lyons and Little 2009). Furthermore, as Lyons and Little (2009: 74–82) indicate, the policy response of the Department of Education and Science (DES) to the English language needs of newcomer students reflects little knowledge of the realities of language learning. In particular, Lyons and Little (2009) note that the DES fails to take into account the distinction between BICS and CALP, which has serious consequences for immigrant students.

In addition, home language teaching for immigrant students can only take place outside school hours, mainly at weekends. In order to maintain the minority language of Polish immigrants (Polonia) living outside the state, the government of Poland (through the Ministersto Edukacji Narodowej (MEN)) sponsors a certain number of institutions that support the maintenance of Polish language and culture. MEN develops curricula and methodology guides for teaching Polish abroad and equips teachers with textbooks and teaching aids. The Polish primary and secondary level mainstream education programmes are implemented in areas absent from the Irish curricula (e.g. Polish language, history and geography). As a form of complementary education, classes take place on Saturday and Sunday, the two days on which children are free from school in Ireland.

Moreover, the study conducted by Lyons and Little (2009) identified several deficits in the Irish education system with regard to newcomer students' first languages. Among the most prominent were: (i) the culture-specific nature of the Irish curriculum, which is a barrier to equality of access and outcomes; (ii) the failure to recognize native language maintenance as an academic resource; (iii) lack of skills on the part of teachers to capitalize on the cognitive, linguistic and emotional resources that comes with students' L1 proficiency.

Research questions and methodology

This paper aims to provide preliminary exploration of how and to what extent each educational context promotes different approaches to identity and knowledge construction, and whether each educational context predisposes students to adopt different language strategies at home and in school, including different literacy practices. The extent to which macro factors (such as DES policy for immigrant students, curriculum) may influence micro-interactions between students, educators and communities is examined.

This paper also focuses on how Polish students engage with issues of conflicting identities and competing language learning (English) and language maintenance (Polish) goals as they grow up and try to find their place in a new country and society. How the students' current socialization goals and practices in the host community are reconciled with the maintenance of connections to their personal past, to their family in Ireland, and to their extended family in Poland, as well as to their ethnic heritage more generally, is considered.

Preliminary investigation of the educational (national) programmes available to Polish immigrant students in Ireland revealed two broad educational contexts (labelled here as EC1 and EC2). First, in order to examine what bilingual/language/educational programmes are available to Polish students in Ireland, existing educational programmes for immigrant students in Ireland were placed in the spectrum of bilingual and monolingual education. The different language programmes offered by schools and the pedagogical approaches represented by different educational contexts were considered. The national policy for immigrant students in Ireland was also examined. The school curriculum for post-primary level (National Council for Curriculum and Assessment), with the inclusion of a graded curriculum for language support set out in the English Language Proficiency Benchmarks for non-English speaking pupils at Post-Primary Level (2003) (available at <http://www.iilt.ie>), was also taken into consideration. Polish homeland policies and institutional support for Polish immigrants living in Ireland, as noted above, were also examined.

On this basis, it was estimated that Polish students living in Ireland are engaging in two broad educational contexts: EC1 is where the Polish students are learning both English and Polish languages in schools; L1 at Polish weekend school partially sponsored by the Polish government and L2 at a regular Irish secondary school. EC 2 applies to the Polish students who are being educated solely through the L2 (English) and are therefore attending regular secondary schools only. This led the researcher to two main groups of participants. Those who attend Polish weekend schools were identified with the help of principals of Polish schools. The second group of participants was identified with the help of the teachers and parents earlier engaged in the pilot project of the ongoing study of LS. The students' parents and their teachers of subjects such as English, Polish, History and Mathematics also took part in this study.

Study design

This study is designed in a way to accommodate the broad focus of the project, and to provide the meaningful contexts that would reflect the complex reality of Polish adolescents' lives as they engage with the EC1 and EC2 contexts. For that reason, a case study design applying child-centred methods is employed. In addition, the study draws on ethnographic approaches such as extended observations of an engagement with participants and the collection of artefacts and documents (test scores, notes, students' notebooks; field notes). Thus, the design of the study can be summarized as follows: it is an instrumental (illuminating particular issues involved in identity and knowledge construction), multiple (more than one case is investigated), comparative (two cases [EC1 and EC2] are compared) case study of two groups of Polish adolescents situated in two different educational contexts, having two students (a fourteen year old girl and a twelve year old boy) in EC1 and two students (a fourteen year old girl and a twelve year old boy) in EC2.

Child-centred approach

The methodology for this project attempts to incorporate the students' own perspectives, to reveal their hopes and needs for the future. This is best achieved by using children-centred methods grounded in a common theoretical perspective on adolescents and their psychological develop-ment, which recognizes that adolescents are active socio-cultural producers in their own right, thus 'recognizing children as people with abilities and capabilities different from, rather than simply less than adults' (Greene 2005: 154). The child-cantered methods employed in the present study include empowering children by constructing 'ground rules' with the stu-dents themselves prior to their interviews, in order to co-construct the meaning between the interviewer and each participant and so to share the discursive framework of the open-ended interviews (Greene 2005: 144–54). This approach involved spending time with young participants in their homes and school settings, building up relations of trust and get-ting to know them.

Empirical data for the present project

The research tools for this study include: classroom observations; structured but open-ended, in-depth interviews; focus groups; analysis of different sorts of documents; students' self-assessment grids; review of literacy mate-rials; completion of a research journal; and memos. The data collected through interviews come from three major sources of informants: (i) four Polish students themselves, (ii) their parents, (iii) their teachers. Two types of triangulation are used for the purposes of this study: (i) triangulation within methods to obtain a more holistic perspective (in this way, findings can also be confirmed or questioned) and (ii) informant triangulation to check the validity of the findings. The preliminary data come from both the pilot study and an ongoing study of LS processes among Polish stu-dents in Ireland.

Preliminary findings

A preliminary examination of the limited data collected so far revealed that in EC1, the Polish students' experience in Ireland is facilitated by a weak form of bilingual education experience. Language socialization is enhanced by maintaining a lived connection to the Polish language, culture and native traditions in and through a school context (Polish weekend school). Students' ethnic identity is in a way confirmed and recognized in this context by their teachers and classmates. As the students have access to some literacy materials that are used in Polish schools in Poland, their learning experience is in some ways comparable to what it might be in their original home school. Consider the example of Marysia (aged fourteen, attending 1st class in junior high school), presented in Figure 4.1. She arrived in Ireland three years ago. She spends about five hours in Polish school every Saturday of the school year. She uses Polish outside home with her friends and with Polish teachers in Polish schools. Her literacy skills in Polish are developed both at home and in the school context. She knows a lot about Polish culture and traditions. She has reached the level of B1 (Council of Europe 2001) in English according to her ESL teacher.

Excerpt 61
I really like it here [in Ireland] and I do not know if we'll ever go back to Poland, but I think going to the Polish school is important ... Even though I go to the Polish school I think I read and write much more in English, so whenever I'm in Poland I bring some girls' magazines from Poland ... I also celebrate all Polish holidays here, and I really like some Irish holidays like St. Patrick's Day and Halloween too. I really like learning English and would like to be fluent in English as soon as possible. It would be great if other kids would not recognize me by my foreign accent ...
Excerpt 62
I have so many non-Polish friends here. One of my best friends is Lithuanian, but we hang around with another girl too. She's Polish. There is actually another Polish friend with us. When we spend time together we speak mainly English so that the other girls do not feel left out. I also have some Irish friends and I use 'Bebo' so I know what's going on here. I also use Polish 'GaduGadu'[1] in order to communicate with my Polish friends.

1   GaduGadu is a Polish instant messaging service.

Figure 4.1 Excerpts from Marysia

Analysis of the curriculum used in Polish weekend schools in Ireland (MEN coordinated) revealed that the scope is limited and does not provide an opportunity to relate and explore the fact of being an 'immigrant student'. In addition, most of the students' learning experience is L2 mediated (about 80 per cent ELT programme included), as their English-medium mainstream education takes place in contexts of Irish secondary schools. The students' cultural and social identity, their cultural background and experiences as immigrants are not fully reflected in the available materials and educational programme. Preliminary analysis (through comparing and examining the curriculum of the Polish weekend schools and the Irish national curriculum at both primary and post-primary levels) also revealed some cultural and pedagogical discontinuities between Polish weekend school practices and those of Irish schools.

In the EC2, the Polish students' experience in Ireland does not include attending a Polish weekend school. Therefore, their learning experience is very different from that of Polish students in EC1 as well as from the experience of their formal classmates back in Poland. Their school experience is exclusively L2 mediated as they are educated through English in Irish secondary schools, with the inclusion of an ELT programme that does not provide a distinguishing 'Polish' context for learning (for the very limited time it is in operation). The ELS programme is delivered by the teacher of English to immigrant students who are below B2 level in mixed nationality groups. Students in EC2 often adopt different linguistic acculturation strategies from the students in EC1. Consider the following example (from the pilot study) of Zosia (aged thirteen, 1st class in junior high school). Zosia has been living in Ireland for three years. She does not attend Polish school or learn Polish in any formal way. She uses Polish only when speaking to her parents and baby sister. She does not use any Polish communication medium or websites. She prefers spending time with English-speaking friends (her mother reported that she never uses Polish when she is with her friends); she does not remember Polish holidays and thinks that she does not need Polish or Polish friends.

> Excerpt 71
>
> I don't have Polish friends. I think I have nothing in common with them ... I have many Irish friends. They say, you know, that when I speak English they are unable to recognize me by the accent ... I don't learn Polish; I don't think I will ever need it. We're not going back there ... People are so different here; they don't look at you as if they were going to kill you or something.

Figure 4.2 Excerpt from Zosia

Although both the EC1 and EC2 participants have Polish schoolmates, classmates or friends, the students' personal experiences and identities are not fully echoed and affirmed in the available materials and pedagogical strategies used by the schools. However, to some extent, educational context EC1 acknowledges and celebrates students' identities in a way the EC2 context does not.

The preliminary interviews with the parents and the teachers (ESL teachers not included) revealed that most of them do not know how to support their children's or students' bilingualism. Support for bilingual development is great at attitudinal level; however, there are degrees of confusion and misinformation among parents and teachers alike. The teachers' interviews revealed lack of resources and funding needed to provide support for the linguistically diverse students in their classrooms.

Discussion and preliminary conclusions

Primary investigation of the EC1 and EC2 revealed that they promote use of English and Polish differently, and because of this they impact on Polish students' choice of linguistic and cultural strategies. Thus, languages (Polish and English) are socialized differently in EC1 and EC2. Preliminary results from the current study shed light on different identity construction strategies adopted by the Polish students, which vary a lot and may be related to the fact that the students attend certain school settings. The present study revealed that micro-interactions between Polish students and their educators and communities are partially shaped by the macro-structures like DES policy which is characterized by its very limited ESL provision.

The patterns of bilingualism which participants in this study develop are very closely tied to their attitudes towards their two languages, and also to the two cultural groups that speak these languages. As Cummins (2000) states, these attitudes are often shaped in and through educational contexts where relations of power are embedded. Thus, the assumption of different 'personal identities' may be perceived as the assumption of different 'personal strategies'. In turn, this impacts on the choice of linguistic and acculturation strategies adopted, as language holds a strong identity marker for the community (Fasold 1984: 77). Some strategies may facilitate integration with the host country, along with self-development and language learning, whereas some can lead to adjustment problems and academic difficulties.

Lambert (1975) and Cummins (2000, 2001, 2009) underline the importance of promotion/encouragement (from as many sources as possible) to maintain immigrant students' dual heritage, as doing so contributes significantly to the students' personal development as well as to L2 learning success. Lambert (ibid.) concludes:

> I do not think they [immigrant students] will be able to be fully North American unless they are given every possibility of being fully French, Portuguese, Spanish, or whatever as well.

Cummins (1981: 15) sums up that it is absolutely necessary to be sensitive to immigrant students' identities (and to the stages in negotiation of these identities), as in the past, insensitivity has led to many problems and academic failures. 'Regardless of institutional constraints, educators have individual and collective choices in how they negotiate identities with students and communities' (ibid: 262). This is so because there is always variation among individuals, variation which is socially structured and is at the same time a 'wellspring of ongoing social dynamics' (Schieffelin 1990: 87). Therefore, further research of the kind presented in the present study has unique potential in revealing students' own educational and linguistic experiences, due to its ability to emphasize the complexity of immigrant students' real lives.

References

Archer, L., and Francis, B. (2007). *Understanding minority ethnic achievement.* Abingdon: Routledge.

Baker, C. (2000). *Foundations of bilingual education and bilingualism.* Clevedon: Multilingual Matters.

Baquedano-López, P. (2000). 'Narrating community in Doctrina classes', *Narration Inquiry*, 10 (2), 1–24.

Bayley, R., and Schecter, S. (eds) (2003). *Language socialization in bilingual and multilingual societies.* UK: Clevledon, Multilingual Matters.

Blair, D. (2002). 'Effective school leadership: The multi-ethnic context', *British Journal of Sociology of Education*, 23 (2), 171–191.

Bourdieu, P. (1977). *Outline of a theory of practice.* Cambridge: Cambridge University Press.

Central Statistics Office Ireland (2008): *Census 2006 Results.* <http://www.cso.ie/census/census2006results/volume_5/vol_5_2006_complete.pdf> accessed 17 January 2011.

Cole, K., and Zuengler, J. (2003). 'Engaging in an Authentic Science Project: Appropriating, Resisting, and Denying Scientific Identities'. In R. Bayley and S. Schecter (ed.), *Language socialization in bilingual and multilingual societies*, pp. 67–74. Clevedon, UK: Multilingual Matters.

Collier, V. (1987). 'Age and rate of acquisition of second language for academic purposes'. *TESOL Quarterly*, 21(4), 617–641.

Council of Europe (2001). *Common European Framework of Reference for Languages: Learning, teaching, assessment.* Cambridge: Cambridge University Press.

Creese, A. (2000). 'The Role of the Language Specialist in Disciplinary Teaching', *Journal of Multilingual and Multicultural Development*, 21 (6), 451–470.

Cummins, J. (1979). 'Linguistic interdependence and the educational development of bilingual children', *Review of Educational Research*, 49 (1), 222–251.

Cummins, J. (2000). *Language, power and pedagogy: Bilingual children in the crossfire.* Clevedon, UK: Multilingual Matters.

Cummins, J. (2001). *Negotiating identities: Education for empowerment in a diverse society.* Los Angeles: California Association for Bilingual Education.

Cummins, J. (2002). 'Rights and responsibilities of educators of bilingual-bicultural children'. In L.D. Soto (ed.), *Making a difference in the lives of bilingual-bicultural learners.* New York: Peter Lang.

Cummins, J. (2009). 'Foreword: Pedagogies of choice: Challenging coercive relations of power in classrooms and communities'. *International Journal of Bilingual Education and Bilingualism*, 12 (3), 261–271.

Cummins, J., Chow, V., Cohen, S., Giampapa, F., Leoni, L., Sandhu, P. and Sastri, P. (2005). 'Affirming identity in multilingual classrooms'. *Educational Leadership*, 6 (1), 38–43.

Department of Education and Science (DES) (2007). *Meeting the needs of pupils for whom English is a second language.* Circular 0053/2007. Dublin: Department of Education and Science. <http://www.into.ie/ROI/WhatsNew/Children-withEnglishasanAddition alLanguage/filedownload5849,en.doc > accessed 14 August 2008.

Devine, D. (2005). 'Children, power and schooling: How childhood is structured in the primary school 2005. Welcome to the Celtic tiger? Teacher responses to immigration and increasing ethnic diversity in Irish schools', *International Studies in Sociology of Education*, 15 (1), 49–70.

Duff, P.A. (1995). 'An ethnography of communication in immersion classrooms in Hungary', *TESOL Quarterly* (29), 505–537.

Duff, P.A. (2003). 'New directions in second language socialization research', *Korean Journal of English Language and Linguistics* (3), 309–339.

Duff, P.A. (2007). 'Second language socialization as sociocultural theory: Insights and issues', *Language Teaching* (40), 309–319.

Duff, P.A. (2009). *Second Language Socialization.* <http://www.lerc.educ.ubc.ca/fac/duff/personal_website/Publications/Duff_SEcond_Language_Socialization_Oct_15_2009.pdf> accessed 17 December 2009.

Duff, P.A., and Hornberger, N.H. (eds) (2008). *Encyclopaedia of language and education, Vol. 8: Language socialization*, pp. 43–56. New York: Springer.

Fasold, R. (1984). *The sociolinguistics of society.* Oxford: Blackwell.

Garrett, P.B. and Baquedano-Lopez, P. (2002). 'Language socialization: Reproduction and continuity, transformation and change', *Annual Review of Anthropology*, Vol. 31, 339–361.

Genesee, F. Lindholm-Leary, Saunders, K. and Christian, D. (eds) (2006). *Educating English Language Learners: A Synthesis of Research Evidence.* Cambridge: Cambridge University Press.

Goodwin, M.H. (1990). *He-Said-She-Said: Talk as Social Organization Among Black Children.* Bloomington: Indiana University Press.

Greene, S. and Hogan, D. (2005). *Researching children's experience: methods and approaches.* London: Sage Publications Ltd.

Guidera, A. (2007). 'Non-native speaking pupils are being left behind', *The Irish Independent*, 13 April.

Keogh, A.F., and Whyte, J. (eds) (2003). *Getting on: The experiences of immigrant students in second level schools linked to the Trinity access programmes*. Dublin: Children's Research Centre, Trinity College Dublin.

Lambert, W.E. (1975). *Culture and Language as Factors in Learning and Education*. <http://www.eric.ed.gov/PDFS/ED096820.pdf> accessed 16 June 2009.

Lave, J. and Wenger, E. (eds) (1991). *Situated learning: Legitimate peripheral participation*. Cambridge: Cambridge University Press.

Lewis, M., and Wray, D. (eds) (2000). *Literacy in the secondary school*. London: David Fulton.

Lodge, A., and Lynch, K. (2004). *Diversity at school*. Dublin: Institute of Public Administration.

Lynch, K., and Lodge. A. (2002). *Equality and power in schools: Redistribution, recognition and representation*. London and New York: Routledge.

Lyons, Z. and Little, D. (2009). *English Language Support in Irish Post-Primary Schools Policy, challenges and deficits:* Dublin: Trinity College Dublin.

Markose, S. and Hellsten, M. (2009). 'Explaining success and failure in mainstream schooling through the lens of cultural continuities and discontinuities: two case studies'. *Language and Education*, 23 (1), 59–77.

Miller, P. (1994). 'Narrative practices: their role in socialization and self-construction'. In U. Neisser, and R. Fivush (eds), *The Remembering Self: Construction and Accuracy in the Self-Narrative*, pp. 158–79. Cambridge: Cambridge University Press.

Miller, P. (1999). 'Becoming audible: social identity and second language use', *Journal of Intercultural Studies*, 20 (2), 149–165.

Miller, P. (2003). *Audible Difference: ESL and social identity in schools*. Clevedon: Multilingual Matters.

Ni Laoire, C., Bushin, N., Carpena-Mendez, F. and White, A. (2009). 'Tell me about yourself migrant children's experiences of moving to and living in Ireland'. <http://www.educatetogether.ie/wordpress/wp-content/uploads/2010/03> accessed 7 January 2011.

Norton, B. (2000). *Identity and Language Learning*. New York: Pearson.

Nowlan, E. (2008). 'Educate Together Second-level'. *Newsletter, 1(6)* <http://www.educatetogether.ie/wordpress/wp-content/uploads/2010/03/Newsletter-Vol.-1-Issue-6-September-2008.pdf> accessed 15 April 2009.

Nowlan, E. (2009). 'Underneath the Band-Aid: supporting bilingual students in Irish schools'. *Irish Educational Studies*, 27 (3), 253–266.

Oakes, J. (1985). *Keeping Track: How School Structure Inequality*. New Haven: Yale University Press.

Ochs, E. (1993). 'Constructing social identity: a language socialization perspective.' *Research on Language and Social Interaction*, 26 (3), 287–306.

Office for Standards in Education (Ofsted). (2005a). *Race equality in education: Good practice in schools and local authorities*. <http://www.oecd.org/document/7/o ,3746,en_2649_39263238_33712135_1_1_1_1,00.html> accessed 13 May 2009.

Office for Standards in Education (Ofsted). (2005b). 'Raising the achievement of bilingual learners.' London: Ofsted.

Olneck, M.R. 1995. Immigrants and education, in Bayley, R. and Schecter, S.R., 2003, Language Socialization in Bilingual and Multilingual Societies. Clevedon: Multilingual Matters. Pavlenko, A. and Blackledge, A. (2004). *Negotiation of Identities in Multilingual Contexts*. United Kingdom: Multilingual Matters Ltd.

Rampton, B. (1995). *Crossings: Language and Ethnicity among Adolescents*, Longman, London.

Schieffelin, B.B. (1990). *The Give and Take of Everyday Life: Language Socialization of Kaluli Children*. NewYork: Cambridge University Press.

Schieffelin, B.B. and Ochs, Elinor. (eds) (1986). *Language socialization across cultures*. Cambridge: Cambridge University Press.

Thomas, W.P., and Collier, V.P. (2002). 'A national study of school effectiveness for language minority students' long-term academic achievement'. Santa Cruz, CA: Centre for Research on Education, Diversity and Excellence, University of California-Santa Cruz. <http://repositories.cdlib.org/crede/finalrpts/1_1_final or http://crede.berkeley.edu/research/crede/research/llaa/1.1_final.html> accessed 14 May 2008.

Tomlinson, S. and Craft, M. (1995). *Education for all in the 1990s. In Ethnic relations and schooling*: London: Athlone Press.

Troyna, B. and I. Siraj-Blatchford. (1993). 'Providing support or denying access? The experiences of students designated as 'ESL' and 'SN' in a multi-ethnic secondary school'. *Educational Review* 45 (1), 3–11.

Ward, T. (2004). 'Education and language needs of separated children'. Dublin: City of Dublin Vocational Education Committee (VEC), County Dublin VEC. <http://www.cdvec.ie/uploads/publications/LanguageNeedsChildren.pdf> accessed 18 November 2009.

Exploring Language and Discourses

JOANNA BAUMGART[1]

5   Looking at multicultural classrooms in Ireland: Teacher educators' perspectives

'Good intercultural teacher education is one of the greater challenges we face in the European Union.'

— GUNDARA 2000: 124

Introduction

The face of Ireland has changed dramatically over the last thirty years, with economic and social transformations taking the country through the recession of the 1980s, the boom of the Celtic Tiger in the mid-1990s, and back to the current economic downturn. With its competitive economy, Ireland became an attractive destination, during certain periods, and immigration numbers grew extensively, albeit not consistently. However, it was not until the biggest enlargement of the EU to date in May 2004 that Ireland was faced with mass net migration, especially from the newly admitted states. According to Central Statistics Office data (<http://www.cso.ie>) immigration to Ireland peaked in 2006 and 2007 with numbers as high as 107,800 and 109,500 respectively and, based on statistical data, it is possible to assume that a majority of immigrants to Ireland did not have English as their first language. Due to recent economic trends inward migration has

1   Joanna Baumgart wishes to acknowledge the support of Irish Research Council for the Humanities and Social Sciences which provided a doctoral Scholarship for her research.

certainly levelled out (57,300 in 2009 and 30,800 in 2010)[2] yet Irish society remained highly multicultural[3] with many immigrants choosing to stay (Barrett 2009, DES[4] and OMI[5] 2010: 9–13) despite mass exodus forecasts.

A multicultural society can create an opportunity to better understand other people, thereby minimizing cultural ignorance and racism; however, it can also present many new challenges as various aspects of the functioning of that society are influenced, with language playing a major part in the equation. One of the main issues Ireland has faced so far seems to be the impact immigration has had directly on first and second level education, and indirectly, on teacher education. Many of the young migrant students who have been arriving in Ireland have very limited or no knowledge of English but still need to cope with the new academic demands that face them. The dynamic of Irish classrooms was thus transformed, from largely homogenous to multicultural and multilingual contexts. Demand for new approaches, and possibly curricula, aiming to better accommodate students' needs arose and this in turn would also suggest a desired impact on teacher education programmes.

Embracing cultural diversity

The following sections briefly summarize some important documents concerning the various issues surrounding multiculturalism which are relevant to this research. The list presented below is, however, by no means finite due to the constraints of this chapter.

---

2   CSO data for 2007 to 2010 is preliminary.
3   Throughout this chapter terms 'interculturalism' and 'multiculturalism' are used interchangeably.
4   DES – Department of Education and Skills, previously Department of Education and Science.
5   OMI – Office of the Minister for Integration.

Examples of policy: The United Nations and the EU

The *Universal Declaration of Human Rights*, presented by the United Nations in 1948, refers to education as an indispensable human right and it emphasizes its role in encouraging acceptance and appreciation of other people. It was followed by the Council of Europe's publication of the *European Convention on Human Right* in 1950. These two documents were further augmented by the *Convention on the Rights Of The Child* (United Nations 1989). More recently two policy statements were issued – the Council of Europe's *Framework Convention for the Protection Of National Minorities* (1995) and the *Charter Of The Fundamental Rights Of The EU* (EU 2000).

Apart form these fundamental texts a number of other publications important to the context of this study need to be mentioned. In 2004 Council of the European Union published a press release from its 2,618th meeting where it presents its conclusions regarding immigrant integration policy in the EU (Council of the European Union 2004: 15–25). The most significant message of this document was an acknowledgement that inward migration is a permanent feature of the EU and, furthermore, that it is a 'dynamic, two-way process of mutual accommodation' (EU Council 2004: 17). The value of cultural diversity is further discussed in the Council of Europe's White Paper on Intercultural Dialogue (2008). The recent scale of migration within the EU has presented many challenges to the educational systems of the member states hence the following were published: EU Commission: Green Paper *Migration And Mobility: Challenges And Opportunities For EU Education Systems* (2008) where the emphasis is placed on schools as leaders in creating an inclusive society, and the Council of Europe's 'Policies and Practices for Teaching Socio-Cultural Diversity – *A Framework Of Teacher Competencies For Engaging With Diversity* (2009). The latter is intended for initial teacher educators as well as student teachers. By focusing on reflective practice it aims at assisting future teachers who find themselves in culturally diverse classrooms.

The international context

Although a relatively recent phenomenon in Ireland, multicultural and multilingual education has long been the experience of countries such as England, Australia (Burns 2003, Carder 2008, Davison 2001) or Canada (Ashworth 2001, Carder 2008, Cummins and Swain 1986). Bearing in mind constraints of this chapter as well as specific features of the educational systems in the nation states mentioned above, this section will briefly present the integration of EAL issues into the school curriculum and teacher education in England.

The approach to teaching EAL students underwent a significant change between 1950s and mid-1980s, from four different types of language support – full time/part time language centres, full time language classes/ part time language classes within ordinary schools – to mainstreaming, which involves placing EAL learners in an age appropriate class where he/she follows the National Curriculum (Leung and Franson 2001: 153–176). The current model of teaching in multicultural schools supported by policy is that of Partnership Teaching where the subject and EAL teacher develop the curriculum together (Leung 2005: 97, see also Creese 2000, Franson 2007).

Similarly to the Irish context, the question of EAL and initial teacher education has sparked a considerable debate. As Leung points out EAL is not an available main subject specialism for student teachers and pre-service EAL teacher training courses were withdrawn from third level institutions in the early 1990s (Leung 2005: 98, Leung 2001: 45). Despite presenting teaching English to EAL pupils as the responsibility of all teachers (SCAA 1996 in Leung 2005: 97), specialist teacher training is limited mainly to in-service programmes which are 'non-qualificatory, voluntary and localised' (Leung 2005: 98). Although the current approach to EAL practice has resulted in the integration of students into the mainstream schooling, the 'lack of systemic attention to EAL [...] has served to reduce the expertise base in the school system' (Leung 2005: 108, see also Creese and Leung 2003), while limiting the discussion mainly to classroom strategies (Leung 2001: 45). Therefore Leung postulates not only a formalized discipline-specific training but also rigorous professional development (2001: 46).

The Irish context

One of the first and most fundamental policy documents in Ireland to acknowledge cultural diversity and the role of education in the new society is The 1998 Education Act (Office of the Attorney General 51 of 1998), which states that the education system should respect 'the diversity of values, beliefs, languages and traditions in Irish society'. In terms of other documents relating to teaching and learning in multicultural settings, three publications produced by the DES have been of significant interest for this research. Firstly, the White Paper in Adult Education *Learning For Life* (DES 2000) which emphasizes that an intercultural education system 'must work towards a view of difference as something to be celebrated and which is enriching to the totality of the society rather than as the basis for enmity' (p. 34). In 2003, the DES, in conjunction with the Equality Authority, published *Schools And The Equal Status Act* where characteristics of an inclusive school as one which '(...) respects, values, and accommodates diversity' (p. 1) were further highlighted. Finally, in 2008, the DES brought out its strategy for the years 2008–2010 where the main objective was defined as the provision of high quality education for all individuals which, in turn, would result in Ireland's social, cultural and economic development.

In 2005 and 2006 the National Council for Curriculum and Assessment (NCCA) published intercultural education guidelines for primary and post-primary level which are one of the major steps taken in order to respond to cultural diversity in schools. The guidelines provide practical advice for teachers in areas such as classroom planning, approaches, methodologies and assessment. As Gundara (2000: 65) points out, intercultural education should be embedded in the mainstream curriculum to prevent, as far as possible, the development of racist reactions. Therefore, both primary and post-primary level guidelines suggest how intercultural education can be integrated into the curriculum. Intercultural education for all learners, as expressed in the guidelines, pays special attention to increasing pupils' awareness of linguistic and cultural diversity currently existing in Ireland. This idea was further emphasized in the report prepared by the DES in cooperation with the Council of Europe (2008). Unfortunately, despite the publicity those publications received, many teachers still have them on their 'ever increasing pile of stuff' to be implemented (DICE[6] 2006: 29), or are simply not aware of their existence.

Finally, two research projects published by the ESRI[7] (Byrne et al. 2009) and the OECD (2009) should be mentioned with respect to this chapter. 'Adapting to Diversity: Irish Schools and Newcomer Students' (Byrne et al. 2009) focuses on the integration of newcomer students in primary and secondary schools. Results of the ESRI study indicate that the largest group of teachers working in language support for English as an Additional Language EAL students are mainstream teachers and only a minority holds formal ELT (English Language Teaching) qualifications. Furthermore, the survey also shows existing dissatisfaction with the amount of time allocated to EAL students, which ranges from 30 to 45 minutes per student or group. Considering how little time a Language Support Teacher has at his/her disposal, it becomes clear that effective English language learning in multicultural educational systems cannot be the exclusive task of these teachers, but is best achieved by efforts from all educators across the curriculum (Corson 1998, Leung 2001 and 2005, IES[8] 2010). The report on migrant education prepared by the OECD (2009) examines policy and practice at all educational levels in Ireland. The main suggestions arising from the OECD work, which are important for this research, include the following: prioritizing initial education and in-service development opportunities for all teachers in the area of EAL and interculturalism; developing one point of contact for teachers, educational managers, researchers and policy makers for bilateral information exchange; determining whether the current school patronage model is appropriately responding to cultural diversity among children and, lastly, supporting a whole school approach to multicultural education.

---

6   DICE – Development and InterCultural Education.
7   ESRI – Economic and Social Research Institute.
8   IES – *Intercultural Education Strategy 2010–2015* published by the Department of Education and Skills and the Office of the Minister for Integration in October 2010.

One of the central issues in research and literature discussed is the provision of EAL. According to 'Migration Nation', a document launched by the Office of the Minister for Integration (May 2008), there were, at the time, almost 2,000 posts for language support teachers allocated across primary and secondary level, subject to the requisite number of EAL learners being in a school. However, budget cuts were introduced in the final months of 2008 and the DES Circular 0015/2009 reads as follows 'the level of EAL support will generally be reduced to maximum of two teachers per school as was the case before 2007'. Table 5.1 presents a comparison between level of EAL support in 2007 and 2009 (Circular 0053/2007 and Circular 0015/2009).

Table 5.1 English as an Additional Language Support in Ireland, 2007–2009

English as an Additional Language Support			
Circular 0053/2007		Circular 0015/2009	
No of teachers	No of EAL learners	No of teachers	No of EAL learners
1	14–27	1	14–30
2	28–41	2	31–90
3	42–64	3	91–120
4	65–90	4	120 and more
5	91–120		
6	120 and more		

The two-year cap on language support provision has been objected to by a number of teachers (DICE 2006) because 'many children acquire only a functional knowledge of English in this time' (p. 35). The mention of functional knowledge hints at a common linguistic distinction which is appropriate here, that is, the difference between conversational fluency and academic fluency, the former being achieved earlier in most cases (Cummins 2008). Ideally, this division should be reflected in policy, pedagogy and assessment. Although in the English context, Leung suggests a differentiated EAL curriculum focusing on teaching of lexicogrammar, pragmatics and academic genres in the context of the main curricular subject areas (2005: 108).

There are certain initial conclusions stemming from the short review of literature and research in the area presented in this section. First of all, in the context of multicultural and multilingual classrooms, all teachers, apart from being subject specialists, also become language tutors as well and, as such, play a vital role in the linguistic development of EAL learners (Council of Europe 2009; ESRI 2009; OECD 2009), hence appropriate English Language Teaching (ELT) education should be offered to teachers of all subjects and levels. Furthermore, knowledge and skills in the areas of EAL, cultural diversity and intercultural education should be developed comprehensively across all the stages of teacher education (OECD 2009). Finally, immigrants' entry into the teaching profession should be supported at all educational levels (OECD 2009). Having briefly presented main research in the area of EAL both internationally and in Ireland, the next sections will focus on the methodology of data collection and theoretical frameworks respectively, thus providing further context for this research.

Data and methodology

The research described in this paper aims to investigate teacher educators' perspectives on cultural diversity in Irish education. This study is a part of a larger project looking at the discourse of educational multiculturalism among key stakeholders (teachers, teacher educators and representatives of professional organizations) and the influence of multiculturalism and multilingualism on classroom practice.

Interview as a research tool

The data presented in this chapter was collected with the use of individual interviews (see *Data* sub-section for details). There is a great variety in classifications of interview as a research method, for example, Patton (1980), LeCompte and Preissle (1993) and Bogdan and Biklen (2007) to name just a few. Interviews conducted for the purpose of this research fall into the qualitative category thus bearing the following characteristics (as outlined by Kvale and Brinkmann 2009: 29) 'life world, meaning, qualitative aspect, specificity, deliberate naivete, focused, ambiguity, change, sensitivity, interpersonal situation and, finally, positive experience'. However, constituting a part of a larger study, the interviews conducted to date also function as a source of quantitative data as the answers obtained are used to establish regularities, gain description of the context and for comparison (Cohen et al. 2000: 272). As such, interviews used for this research can be classified as standardized open-ended interviews (Patton 1980: 206) where questions were predetermined and asked in the same order. This allowed for increased comparability of data and aimed at reducing bias. Standardized open-ended interviews, however, allow for little flexibility thus the researcher allowed for basic questions to be expanded and enhanced by probes if deemed necessary, therefore, qualifying the process as a semi-structured interview (Schensul, Schensul and LeCompte 1999: 149). Interview data was analysed with content analysis techniques (Kvale and Brinkmann 2009: 203) and further presented as re-occurring themes. The majority of themes discussed stem from interview questions, however, some developed spontaneously in the course of the interviews.

Data

The data presented in this chapter was collected over the course of individual interviews with six teacher educators. Each of the interviews took approximately 30 minutes and the following topics were discussed: the impact of multiculturalism on teacher education, the response of the education system to cultural and linguistic diversity, EAL learners and teacher education, student teachers' attitudes towards working in multicultural environments, continuous professional development of teachers and, finally, policy issues (see Appendix 1 for guiding interview questions used).

Table 5.2 summarizes profile information of the participants. In the interest of confidentiality all interviewees have been assigned pseudonyms.

Table 5.2 Participants' profile information

Pseudonym	Gender	Experience	Areas	Primary/ Post-Primary Education
Diane	F	3 years	Intercultural education, development education, TP supervision	Primary level teacher education
Alice	F	10 years	Mathematics education	Primary level teacher education
Tracy	F	19 years	Religious education, theology	Primary level teacher education
Charlotte	F	11 years	SPHE[1] education and health promotion	Primary level teacher education
Mia	F	10 years	History of education	Post-primary level teacher education
James	M	19 years	General Pedagogy, science pedagogy, TP supervision	Post-primary level teacher education

1   SPHE – Social, Personal and Health Education.

This table shows that both professional experience and teaching areas are hugely varied, which might allow an assumption that a broader spectrum of views was expresses. Given the complex nature of issues examined, all participants received the interview questions in advance. It should be emphasized that participants were made aware that questions were in no way limiting and any additional comments and reflections were welcomed throughout the interviews. Furthermore, the following study is work in progress and the analysis of the interviews, which is presented in the following sections, is theme-based as the size of the data set does not allow for quantitative investigation at present.

Theoretical frameworks

The following sections present theoretical frameworks used to conduct the research. The first subsection discusses the issue of reflective practice and its place in modern teacher education. The second subsection focuses on the notion of linguistic face and its importance in multicultural classrooms.

Reflective practice

One of the issues embedded in all the interviews was that of reflective practice for teachers working in multicultural contexts. Modern education systems aim to implement the Reflective Model of teacher education (Banfi 1997, Wallace 1991) where practitioners possess two types of knowledge – received and experiential. Received knowledge is part of the official educational curriculum while experiential knowledge results from everyday practice and reflection on it. As data collected in this research indicates, it is especially a space for reflection that is needed by teachers. However as Head and Taylor (1997: 9) suggest, there is a clear distinction between teacher training and teacher development with the following features, among others, being juxtaposed: competency based vs holistic, short term vs long term, one off vs ongoing, top-down vs bottom up. For the Reflective Model of teacher education to be fully implemented there is, therefore, a need for teacher training and further professional development to form a continuum with reflective practice constituting an integral part throughout the process. Although reflective practice is underlying modern teacher education, there is also a requisite for it to become an integral part of classroom teaching. In the context of this research, reflective practice allows practitioners critically consider their pedagogical approaches in the light of a particular learning situation and thus identify potential areas for development as well as good practice.

Face

The second issue which was prominent and connected to general discourse of multiculturalism was that of *face*. As a linguistic concept *face* was defined by Goffman as the 'the positive social value a person effectively claims for himself by the line others assume he has taken during a particular contact' (2006: 299). Goffman's notion of face is therefore constrained by the line others think he/ she is taking and thus as a social value it is dependent on others and can change from one moment to another (Watts 2003: 103). Brown and Levinson further develop concept of face as 'public self-image that every member wants to claim for himself. [...] something that is emotionally invested, and that can be lost, maintained, or enhanced, and must be constantly attended to in interaction' (2006: 311). Apart from introducing a dualistic distinction between positive face (self-image to be appreciated and approved) and negative face (claim to non-distraction), Brown and Levinson also differ from Goffman in their assumption that face is constructed prior to interaction and is desired to be upheld by society (Watts 2003: 103–107). Although this conceptualization of face does not exclude change, it indicates less room for interactional negotiations than originally suggested by Goffman (Watts 2003: 103–107). It is then the face as presented by Brown and Levinson that comes into play in multicultural educational contexts as a conflict between professional image assumed by teachers and classroom reality presenting difficult challenges. Mainstream teachers working in multicultural and multilingual contexts may feel their professional face of authority within their subject area to be threatened by their limited pedagogical knowledge of EAL teaching. This in turn might have a negative impact on their classroom practice and, as a result, on the teaching/learning process. This issue is further exemplified and discussed in the results section later.

Results

This section presents the outcomes of the study described above with findings being divided into seven subsections according to interview themes. In addition, some initial thoughts on the discourse of multiculturalism will be presented in the second part of this section.

Multiculturalism and teacher education

Considering the focus of the interviews, quite naturally the first question presented to participants was that of interculturalism impacting teacher education – has there really been any impact? Interviewees seem to be rather evenly divided into three groups in their opinions on the subject.

Two participants considered the influence to be quite significant and positive at the same time. It was emphasized that changes in the classrooms happened quite rapidly and the education system responded quickly and appropriately with changes in teacher education programmes such as awareness raising in modules across the curriculum but also by sending intercultural education guidelines to schools (NCCA 2005 and 2006).

Another two interviewees agreed that there was an influence but initially it came from teachers themselves not the teaching colleges and the DES. This was referred to as a bottom up rather than top down approach. Secondly, the change took place on the conceptual level more than on the practical level. Here, both participants stressed two issues. First, there seems to be a lack of communication between the key stakeholders (teachers, teacher educators, the DES) and within those groups and, as a result, all the efforts are rather 'piecemeal' and only 'surface level when it should go deeper' (Diane). Consequently, a 'huge gap between theory and practice' (Tracy) was created. In order to bridge this gap, as suggested by some of the interviewees, teacher education programmes should be augmented with more inclusive content where issues connected to interculturalism permeate the whole curriculum. Furthermore, the student teacher should be exposed to multiculturalism which they might not have experienced as primary or secondary learners themselves (Diane and Tracy).

Finally, the remaining two teacher educators had a rather pessimistic outlook stating 'extremely limited impact' and 'no impact' (James, Alex). When asked to further elaborate on those answers familiar themes were present – 'Multiculturalism is disjointed. Teacher educators do it but it's each to their own. For it to have an impact it needs a common discourse' or 'Multiculturalism hasn't translated into teaching' and finally 'Teacher educators haven't had the exposure to multiculturalism themselves'. There is also some criticism of the Irish education system with Alex maintaining that multiculturalism is treated as a politically correct add-on character-ized by the lack of overarching policy while it should have been made a national priority with Ireland learning from countries with long traditions of immigration such as the UK or USA. Furthermore, James pointed out that an integrated curriculum based on intercultural foundations (here specifically understood as different ways/ traditions of thinking) should be implemented from primary to third level education.

English as an Additional Language and teacher education

The issue of linguistic diversity is nearly inseparable from discussions on interculturalism. Irish schools are currently a meeting ground for over 200 languages[9] and, as a consequence, multilingualism and multiculturalism is an everyday experience for many teachers. Therefore, in the next question the relationship between EAL learners, comprising an estimated 16 per cent of all pupils in Ireland (Byrne et al. 2009 xiv), and teacher education was explored.

9   Gallagher, <http://www.irishtimes.com/timeseye/whoweare/p3bottom.htm>

Only Charlotte had a rather positive opinion and emphasized not only the fact that multilingualism is discussed across the curriculum but especially in the modules devoted to language teaching and literacy in both Irish and English. Furthermore, Charlotte believed that principles of teaching Irish are similar to those of EAL so all teachers are indeed equipped with the knowledge and practical tools to help their EAL students, at least at the primary level.

Both Diane and Alex suggested that only a limited relationship existed and described the status quo as 'hit and miss'. They claim that there isn't much input available to student teachers and, as such, EAL and linguistic diversity is not integrated into the curriculum. These claims are consistent with Leung's criticism of the position of EAL within teacher education in England (Leung 2001, 2005, 2007).

James proposed that 'teacher-centred didactic should change into a learner-centred approach' and Diane stated that every future teacher should have EAL training. An interesting point was raised by Mia, who thinks that the EAL situation in terms of identifying pupils in need of language support is rather clear at the moment but teachers may face a much greater challenge with second generation migrants. This statement is very much in line with the recent OECD reports according to which many second generation immigrants experience considerable literacy difficulties in both languages – the mother tongue (or the language of their parent/s country) and the host country's language).

Student teachers' attitudes towards a multicultural work environment

Another interesting issue centred on how future teachers themselves feel about working in an intercultural and multilingual environment. Here all five participants saw both positive and negative sides. Firstly, on the more optimistic side, student teachers are perceived as positive and enthusiastic, very open, interested in other cultures and willing to learn about them. Although many students admit that multicultural classrooms might present various challenges, generally they meet those challenges with positive attitudes.

However, as reported by their tutors, even though student teachers might be ready theoretically, they definitely lack the practical skills and tools – 'Guidelines are helpful but not enough' (Tracy). At the same time a certain discourse of fear seems to be emerging, where student teachers are described as 'nervous and afraid to make a mistake' (Alex), 'afraid to get it hopelessly wrong' (Diane) and 'concerned with lack of knowledge' (Tracy).

How multicultural are we really?

It is interesting to note that this 'multicultural self-reflection' surfaced rather spontaneously without it being specifically prompted by the interviewer. All but one participant agreed that a majority of the student population up to now has been of Irish background thus creating a very homogeneous group. This situation is occasionally altered by exchange students coming mainly from western European countries, especially the UK, the USA or as part of the Erasmus programme. Although these students may add an interesting cultural aspect as well as present an alternative point of view, as the interviewees emphasize, cultural differences are not that pronounced and in some cases students share a common first language. Furthermore, most exchange students stay in Ireland only for one or two semesters and do not take part in student teaching practice; hence, their impact on the learning process of other student teachers is rather limited. This lack of diversity amongst student teachers translates into homogeneity of teachers in classrooms and as Diane said 'I would love for it to change. It would be a great model for children in schools'.

The situation is quite similar at the faculty level, especially in primary teaching colleges with the Irish language proficiency requirement in place. Here the participants claimed that cultural diversity among faculty could, first of all, help student teachers understand what multiculturalism in classroom really is as opposed to the 'imagine if' scenarios (Diane, Tracy). It was also pointed out by three of the interviewees that the quality of education could benefit from 'expertise from outside' (Alex) – from outside of Ireland and within the country. Teacher educators agreed that an alternative route of entry where the Irish language is not a requirement should be introduced, however, they had no specific ideas regarding implementation. As Alex said 'It's critical to get kids from traveller population and other backgrounds [into teacher education colleges] because they will be the faces of our schools and classrooms'.

Policy issues

Another important topic discussed was that of policy regarding multiculturalism and EAL. This was the only case where all the participants expressed very similar views. Three sub-themes emerged throughout the discussion.

Surprisingly, most participants started off with a clear concern about the 'short-sighted' (Diane) character of policies implemented, specifically in the context of EAL provision and the two-year funding cap applied to it. Interviewees are aware of the problems EAL students in schools are facing every day and admit that although some learners might have good conversational language skills, they still lack the necessary fluency to access the curriculum (Cummins 1992). As Mia said 'Language support is critical as language skills are critical for cognition, empowerment and enabling integration'. Furthermore, participants suggest this 'lack of vision' (Alex) will generate huge social costs in the future.

The second point emphasized by the participants was the aspirational character of the policy in place and its detachment from classroom reality. As emphasized by some interviewees, this aspirational nature of the strategies might be responsible for further shortages of funding as they lack a practical aspect.

Finally, all participants agreed that it is hugely important to have explicit policies in place and also commended on the DES inviting various parties to contribute to those documents (teacher educators, migrant representatives, teachers, parents etc) but the absence of implementation schemes results in policy documents being simply filed away in schools. It was suggested that policy should start at BEd (Bachelor of Education) level in order to give student teachers the necessary strategies they can implement in classrooms and exposure to interculturalism that many of them may have never had.

Samosas and saris

In the course of the interview with the first participant the issue of multi-culturalism being superficial in schools arose and the researcher decided to examine this question with other participants. According to Diane, teachers and schools attempt to represent cultural diversity through, for example, changing classroom displays, presenting songs or stories from different countries or inviting parents. However, she questioned the sufficiency of these actions. Alex suggested that although 'Africa days, food and dance are not enough it is a good start. It's awareness even if it's superficial'. This claim was also partially supported by Mia who agreed that visibility in schools is necessary but change happens at a deeper level in social contexts ('Tip of an Iceberg' Weaver 1986) and all those involved in education in intercultural settings should aim for those deeper levels.

Participants were then asked what it would mean to take a deeper and more meaningful approach to multiculturalism. All interviewees high-lighted the importance of cultivating links with a pupil's home and his/her local community because 'good quality interventions are needed, not hunches' (Mia). Every teacher should develop principles of inclusive learn-ing which would highlight the complexity of a lived experience (Tracy). A very interesting point was made by Diane who suggested that student teachers should begin by examining their own assumptions and prejudices. Understanding one's own identity as a person and the way this identity impacts one as a teacher, Diane elaborated, should be the starting point. Moreover, student teachers, but also experienced teachers, need time to reflect on themselves as practitioners and how their professional practice is influenced by what is happening in the wider context.

Reflective practice is very closely connected to continuous profes-sional development which is, in turn, one of the pillars of modern teacher education. Participants were thus asked to comment on the in-service development options available to teachers. Interviewees observed a lack of (or very little) knowledge on their part as to what development pro-grammes are offered by DES. It was also unanimously agreed that teachers tend to choose modules from within their own specialization followed by Information Technology and Special Needs Education. However, three of the participants emphasized the need for in-service training for mainstream teachers in the area of interculturalism and EAL. Furthermore, it was pointed out that although intercultural guidelines (NCCA 2005 and 2006) are a great resource, their publication should have been accompanied by a training day for teachers and/or school management. This resonates with findings reported by Devine where she states that the lack of explicit policies results in school practice being informed by teachers' own initiatives and interests rather than critical reflective approach supported by national guidelines and state investment (Devine 2005: 6).

A discourse of multiculturalism

Reflection on the language surrounding interculturalism emerged unprompted during three interviews and was elicited in the remaining three. Participants noticed a very clear dichotomy between an issue to be tackled/ a problem and a resource. It was indicated that there is a general negative perception of interculturalism and, moreover, it is problematized in the classrooms rather than perceived as a way to enrich one's learning experience. Some of the participants acknowledged that there are those who are trying to celebrate cultural diversity. However this phrase also seems to be turning into an empty slogan.

The second issue noted by the researcher, and already signalled in section focusing on linguistic face, is the discourse of fear which seems to be surfacing in relation to student teachers with words like 'fearful' and 'afraid' often being used. There are three suppositions which could be considered in this context. First of all, as reported by the interviewees, student teachers are not sure how to act in multicultural classrooms in a way that is not offensive to anyone. This uncertainty could be analysed from two interconnected perspectives – at a personal level (I as a person) and at a professional level (I as a teacher) – with the latter one being of interest to this research. Doubt in the professional sphere may further lead to student teachers feeling inadequately prepared to work in multicultural contexts, which may result in feelings of failure as teachers. Here the notion of face as public self-image comes to mind (Goffman 1967). Face, as further developed by Brown and Levinson (1978) is emotionally invested and as such can be lost, maintained or enhanced; therefore, it must be constantly attended to in interactions. Losing face in the classroom, however subjective a feeling this may be, might lead to undermining a teacher's authority and position in class which, in turn, could also negatively impact on the learning process. In some instances it might also possibly lead to forming negative attitudes towards multiculturalism, while as suggested by one of the participants our motto should be 'different is good' (Tracy).

Conclusions

The results of the study presented in this paper concur in many ways with research quoted earlier in the section devoted to international and Irish contexts; however, some additional suggestions are visible. As noted in IES '(...) a significant proportion of the current and future population are and will be immigrants. It is to be expected that immigrants will remain a definite feature of Irish society and education into the future.' (2010: Introduction). Therefore, the needs of those working in this hugely changed social context require prioritizing in terms of funding and time at two opposite ends of the educational continuum – students and teachers. On one hand, as other research suggests (e.g. DICE 2006, ESRI 2009), two years of language support is not sufficient for EAL learners to be able to access the curriculum on a par with their Irish peers. Furthermore, although assistance focused on a specific topic/ skill as that provided by the EAL teacher is vital, there is also a great need for in-class support, which would aid the learning process. Finally, as data suggests, interculturalism should permeate the curriculum in order to allow children to discover and understand other ways of thinking and perceiving our world. Such an integrated curriculum would be intended for both Irish and EAL learners as they will all live in one multicultural society. On the other hand, there might be also a growing need to integrate multiculturalism and multilingualism into initial teacher training and embed it in all subjects. In addition, as stated in IES 'All educators must be aware of the potential to systematically infuse language into their lessons and subject areas. They have a key role to play in developing and enhancing the language competence of all learners.' (2010: 51). It is especially important in those difficult times of economic downturn and spending cuts that mainstream teachers are equipped with appropriate tools enabling them to create a truly inclusive learning environment. These strategies should come from quality initial teacher education and well-structured in-service professional development programmes (see for example Leung 2001, 2005, 2007).

As statistical data clearly indicates, cultural and linguistic diversity is well represented among pupils in primary and secondary schools. However, student bodies and faculty on teacher education programmes still constitute a highly homogenous group; therefore, as suggested by the OECD (2009) and indicated by the participants of this study, steps should be taken in order to encourage migrants to to enter the teaching profession. Two major obstacles to this process, as suggested in the course of this research, seem to be the Irish language proficiency requirement present in some teacher training colleges and the predominantly Catholic school patronage system, with the latter being currently examined in relation to its suitability for a more diverse society (IES 2010: 36). It was agreed by the participants that alternative routes of entry into the teaching profession should be identified.

All participants highlighted the significance of policies which clearly indicate the importance of cultural diversity in modern Irish society; however, at the same time the clash between the aspirational character of policy and classroom reality was emphasized. Furthermore, as suggested by the interviewees, communication between policy makers and those implementing it could be improved as many teachers do not seem to be aware of the existence of those documents nor are sure how these resources could be used in their daily work. Consequently, there is a need for a point of dialogue and knowledge transfer between the key stakeholders: teachers, teacher educators, educational managers and policy makers (OECD 2009: 66). In addition, there is a need for structured workshops and training sessions aimed at improving classroom practice through the use of the policy tools and examples of best practice from both local and international contexts.

References

Arnesen, A-L., Hadzhitheodoulou-Loizidou, P., Bîrzéa, C., Essomba, M.A. and Allan, J. (2009). *Polices and practices for teaching sociocultural diversity: concepts, principles and challenges in teacher education.* Starsbourg: Council of Europe.

Ashworth, M. (2000). *Effective Teachers, Effective Schools: Second-Language Teaching in Australia, Canada, England And the United States.* Toronto: Pippin Publishing Corporation.

Banfi, C. (1997). 'Some thoughts on the professional development of language teachers', *ELT News and Views*, 4.1 (S), <http://www.essarp.org.ar/banfi/4.1S.pdf> accessed 10 June 2006.

Barrett, A. (2009). 'What do migrants do in a recession?' Paper presented at the ESRI Policy Conference *The Labour Market in Recession*, ESRI, 30 April 2009.

Bogdan, R.C., and Biklen, S.K. (2007). *Qualitative Research for Education*, 5th ed. Boston: Pearson International Edition.

Brown, P., and Levinson, S. (1987). 'Politeness: Some Universals in Language Usage'. In Jaworski, A., and Coupland, N. (eds), (2006). *The Discourse Reader*, 2nd ed., London: Routledge.

Burns, A. (2003). 'ESL Curriculum Development in Australia: Recent Trends and Debates', *Regional Language Centre Journal*, 34 (3), 261–283.

Byrne, D., Darmody, M., McGinnity, F., and Smyth, E. (2009). *Adapting to Diversity: Irish Schools and Newcomer Students.* Dublin: ESRI.

Carder, M. (2008) 'The Development of ESL provision in Australia, Canada, the USA and England, with Conclusions for Second Language Models in International Schools', *Journal of Research in International Education*, 7(2), 205–231.

Cohen, L., Manion, L., and Morrison, K. (2000). *Research Methods in Education*, 5th ed. London: Routledge.

Corson, D. (1998). *Changing Education for Diversity.* Buckingham: Open University Press.

Council of Europe (1950). *European Convention on Human Rights* <http://www.hri.org/docs/ECHR50.html> accessed 15 September 2009.

Council of Europe (1995). *Framework Convention for the Protection of National Minorities* <http://conventions.coe.int/Treaty/EN/Treaties/Html/157.htm> accessed 15 September 2009.

Council of Europe (2008). '*White Paper on Intercultural Dialogue – Living Together as Equals in Dignity*', Strasbourg: Council of Europe <http://www.coe.int/t/dg4/intercultural/source/white%20paper_final_revised_en.pdf> accessed 15 September 2009.

Council of Europe and Department of Education and Science (2008). *Language education policy profile: Ireland*, Language Policy Division Strasbourg and DES. <http://www.education.ie/servlet/blobservlet/language_education_policy_profile.pdf> accessed 18 September 2009.

Council of Europe (2009).'Languages in Education, Languages for Education: Language in Other Subjects'. <http://www.coe.int/t/dg4/linguistic/Source/LE_texts_Source/LangInOtherSubjects_en.doc> accessed 18 October 2010.

Creese, A. (2000). 'The Role of the Language Specialist in Disciplinary Teaching: In Search of a Subject?', *Journal of Multilingualism and Multicultural Development*, 21 (6), 451–470.

Creese, A., and Leung, C. (2003). 'Teachers' Discursive Constructions of Ethno-Linguistic Difference: Professional Issues in Working with Inclusive Policy', *Prospect*, 18 (2), 3–19.

Cummins, J. (1992). 'Language Proficiency, Bilingualism and Academic Achievement'. In P.A. Richard-Amato and M.A. Snow (eds), *The Multicultural Classroom: Readings for Content-Area Teachers*, pp. 16–26, New York: Longman.

Cummins, J. *Multiculturalism and multilingualism in Irish schools (2008)*. Seamus Heaney Lectures Series 2008/09; Lecture Two 17 November 2008; <http://www.spd.dcu.ie/main/news/shl-audio.shtml.> accessed 30 November 2008.

Cummins, J. and Swain, M. (1986). *Bilingualism in Education*. New York: Longman.

Davison, Ch. (2001). 'ESL in Australian Schools: from the Margins to the Mainstream'. In B. Mohan, C. Leung, and Ch. Davison (eds), *English as a Second Language in the Mainstream. Teaching, Learning and Identity*, pp. 11–29. Edinburgh: Pearson Education.

Department of Education and Skills and Office of the Minister for Integration (2010). *Intercultural Education Strategy 2010–2015*.<http://www.education.ie/home/home.jsp?pcategory=10856&ecategory=51881&language=EN> accessed 20 December 2010.

Department of Education and Science (2008). *Statement of Strategy 2008–2010*. Dublin: Department of Education and Science. <http://www.education.ie/servlet/blobservlet/des_strategy_statement_2008_2010.pdf?language=EN> accessed 20 December 2010.

Department of Education and Science and Equality Authority (2003). *Schools and the Equal Status*. Dublin. <http://www.educatetogether.ie/wordpress/wp-content/uploads/2010/02/ge_schools_and_equality.pdf> accessed 20 August 2009.

Department of Education and Science (2000). *White Paper on Adult Education, Learning for Life*. Dublin: Government Stationery Office. <http://www.aughty.org/pdf/learn_for_life.pdf > accessed 20 December 2010.

Department of Education and Science Circular 0053/2007.

Department of Education and Science Circular 0015/2009.

Devine, D. (2005). 'Welcome to the Celtic Tiger? Teacher Responses to Immigration and Increasing Ethnic Diversity in Irish Schools', *International Studies in Sociology of Education*, 15(1), 49–70.

Development and InterCultural Education (DICE) (2006). *Global education – teachers' view.* <http://www.diceproject.org/upload/uploadedFile/Global%20Ed%20combined%20new.pdf > accessed 18 February 2009.

Education Act 1998, No 51 of 1998. Dublin: Office of the Attorney General. <http://www.irishstatutebook.ie/1998/en/act/pub/0051/index.html> accessed 20 September 2009.

European Union (2000). 'Charter of Fundamental Rights of the European Union',<http://www.europarl.europa.eu/charter/default_en.htm> accessed 20 December 2010.

European Union Council (2004) 'Common Basic Principles for Immigrant Integration Policy in the European Union', <http: //www.enaro.eu/dsip/download/eu-Common-Basic-Principles.pdf> accessed 18 September 2009.

European Union Commission (2008). 'Green Paper – Migration and Mobility: Challenges and Opportunities for EU Education Systems', Brussels: EU Commission <http://ec.europa.eu/education/school21/com423_en.pdf > accessed 18 September 2009.

Franson, Ch. (2007). 'Challenges and opportunities for the Teaching Profession: English as an Additional Language in the UK'. In J. Cummins and Ch. Davison (eds), *International Handbook of English Language Teaching*, pp. 1101–1112. Springer Science and Business Media.

Gallagher, A. 'Speaking in Tongues', *Irish Times*, < http://www.irishtimes.com/timeseye/whoweare/p3bottom.htm>.

Goffman, E. (1967). 'On face-work: an analysis of ritual elements in social interaction'. In Jaworski, A. and Coupland, N. (eds), (2006). *The Discourse Reader*, 2nd ed., PAGES. London: Routledge.

Gundara, J.S. (2000). *Interculturalism, education and inclusion.* London: Paul Chapman.

Head, K., and Taylor, P. (1997). *Readings in Teacher Development.* Oxford: Heineman.

Kvale, S., and Brinkmann, S. (2009). *InterViews: Learning the Craft of Qulaitative Research Interviewing*, 2nd ed. Los Angeles: SAGE.

LeCompte, M., and Preissle, J. (1993). *Ethnography and Qualitative Design in Educational Research*, 2nd ed. London: Academic Press Ltd.

Leung, C. (2001). 'English as an additional language: distinct language focus or diffused curriculum concerns?', *Language and Education* 15(1), 33–55.

Leung, C. (2005). 'English as an additional language policy: issues of inconclusive access and language learning in the mainstream', *Prospect*, 20(1), 95–113.
Leung, C. (2007). 'Integrating School-Aged ESL Learners into the Mainstream Curriculum'. In J. Cummins and Ch. Davison (eds), *International Handbook of English Language Teaching*, pp. 249–269. Springer Science and Business Media.
Leung, C., and Franson, C. (2001a). 'England: ESL in the Early Days'. In B. Mohan, C. Leung, and C. Davison (eds), *English as a Second Language in the Mainstream. Teaching, Learning and Identity*, pp. 153–164. Edinburgh: Pearson Education.
Leung, C., and Franson, C. (2001b). 'Mainstreaming: ESL as a Diffused Curriculum Concern'. In B. Mohan, C. Leung, and C. Davison (eds), *English as a Second Language in the Mainstream. Teaching, Learning and Identity*, pp. 165–176. Edinburgh: Pearson Education.
National Council for Curriculum and Assessment (2005). *Intercultural Education in the Primary School: Enabling Children to Respect and Celebrate Diversity, to Promote Equality and to Challenge Unfair Discrimination.* Dublin: NCCA.
National Council for Curriculum and Assessment (2006). *Intercultural Education in the Post-Primary School. Enabling Students to Respect and Celebrate Diversity, to Promote Equality and to Challenge Unfair Discrimination.* Dublin: NCCA.
Office of the Minister for Integration. (2008). 'Migration Nation. Statement on Integration Strategy and Diversity Management', Dublin.
Organisation for Economic Cooperation and Development (2009). *OECD Thematic Review on Migrant Education – Country Report for Ireland.* Paris: OECD <www.oecd.org/dataoecd/8/22/42485332.pdf> accessed 20 September 2009.
Patton, M.Q. (1980). *Qualitative Evaluative Methods.* Beverly Hills: Sage Publications.
Schensul, S.L., Schensul, J.J., and LeCompte, M.D. (1999). *Essential Ethnographic Methods: Observations, Interviews and Questionnaire.*, London: Altamira Press.
United Nations (1948). *The Universal Declaration of Human Rights*, <http://www.un.org/en/documents/udhr> accessed 18 September 2009.
United Nations (1990). *The UN Convention on the Rights of the Child*, <http://www2.ohchr.org/english/law/crc.htm> accessed 18 September 2009.
Wallace, M.J. (1991). *Training Foreign Language Teachers – a Reflective Approach.* Cambridge: Cambridge University Press.
Watts, R.J. (2003). *Politeness.* Cambridge: Cambridge University Press.
Weaver, G.R. (1986). 'Understanding and coping with cross-cultural adjustment stress', in R.M. Paige (ed), *Cross-Cultural Orientation, New Conceptualisations and Applications*, pp. 193–225. Lanham, MD: University Press of America. <http://www.cso.ie>

Interview questions – teacher educators

1. **General information:** teaching areas, experience in years, gender.

2. **Multiculturalism and teacher education:**

    Do you think multiculturalism has impacted on the content of Teacher Education?

    - if yes: What sort of impact? How? Was it significant? What areas of teacher education? How would you describe the changes? (Good/bad?) How did the system respond? Has it had enough impact?
    - if no: Why do you think so? Should there have been a response from the system? If so, what?

    Is the concept of intercultural education included in Teacher Education programmes?

    - if yes: To what extent? Do you think it is sufficient?
    - if not: Why? Do you think it should be?

    Are any other approaches to education in multicultural and multilingual contexts incorporated in Teacher Education?

3. **EAL and teacher education:**

    a) Is this issue included in the curriculum?

- <u>if yes</u>: Do you think it's represented in a sufficient manner? Or should there be more attention/ space paid to it? How would you suggest this representation is improved?
- <u>if not</u>: Why do you think the issue is not represented? Do you think it should be represented? If so, to what extent?

b) To what extent do EAL learners impact on your own teaching?

- How do you talk about it with your students? (Readings? Activities?)
- Do you think you're discussing in sufficiently? Do you think you should spend more time on it? If so, why?
- If you're not incorporating EAL in your own teaching, why?
- If you're not incorporating EAL in your own teaching, would you like to?

c) Do you have any international students in your Teacher Education groups? If yes, do these students have an impact on your teaching?

4. **Policy issues**

a) Would you like to recommend any changes to the current policy regarding EAL learners and their education? If not how do assess current policy?

b) How do you assess the involvement of professional teaching organizations in the policy making and their general attitude towards multiculturalism in Irish education?

5. **Other comments.**

MARGARET HEALY AND KRISTIN ONDERDONK HORAN

6 Looking at language in hotel management education

Introduction

The development of the Cambridge, Limerick and Shannon (CLAS) Corpus is significant in that it is the first substantial corpus[1] of English language used in the hospitality industry. Language forms an essential part of success in hospitality, and this corpus will offer insights into the discourse of both native and non-native speakers of English, as well as providing researchers with data to map the progression of language use of speakers from an introductory level through to expert within the industry. The corpus data will be analysed using a specific software package called WordSmith Tools (Scott 2008) which provides a number of corpus linguistic tools for lexical analysis allowing the patterns of the discourse to be investigated from both a quantitative and qualitative perspective. This information is increasingly important for educators in the hospitality industry and hotel managers as successful interactions with clients are often based upon efficacious use of language, including the ability to master politeness norms, formality, and hospitality-specific lexis. Evaluation of the CLAS corpus will provide insights into the discourse currently used in education within the industry and into language-learner development for non-native English speakers. It will also provide and data for materials development which will assist in the creation of new course materials,

---

[1] A corpus is a collection of spoken (i.e. recordings) or written language which is stored on a computer and available for quantitative or qualitative analysis (Biber, Conrad and Reppen 1998).

particularly at the Upper Intermediate and Advanced levels. In the broader spectrum, the CLAS Corpus will be used to help further identify the Reference Level Language Descriptors for English linked to the Common European Framework of Reference for Languages (CEFR) and will feed into the English Profile Programme, 'where a focus on the C levels, both in functional and linguistic terms, has been prioritised' (http://www.eng-lishprofile.org).

Background to the study

Shannon College of Hotel Management

Shannon College of Hotel Management (SCHM) was approached in 2008 by corpus compilers and researchers from Cambridge University Press (CUP) and Mary Immaculate College (MIC), Limerick, and was invited to participate in this study. The suitability of SCHM for this research was determined as a result of numerous factors which included: the diversity of the student body (half of the student population are non-native English speakers), the availability of a range or recording contexts (such as: lectures, practical classes, presentations, interviews, meetings) and, specifically, its setting as a specialized academic location which had not previously been studied.

SCHM offers two main programmes of study: a Bachelor of Business Studies Degree in International Hotel Management (BBS) and a Bachelor of Commerce Degree with a National University of Ireland (NUI) Diploma in International Hotel Management (B. Comm). Both are Level 8 degrees awarded by the NUI, with the BBS being taught entirely in Shannon and the B. Comm having fourth year students complete their final year in NUI, Galway. It is a requirement that students complete two full-time placements in a hotel, an operative level placement during the second year of studies and a final trainee management placement following year four. As mentioned, there are a large number of international students, predominantly Asian, and the minimum English language entry requirement for non-native speakers is a B2-C1 CEFR level or International English Language Testing System (IELTS) 6.0.

Teaching materials for hospitality education

One of the aims of the CLAS corpus is to produce more teaching materials in the hospitality area, particularly for hotel English. There are a number of course books covering the topic of hospitality; however, there is a dearth of hotel-specific materials at the Upper Intermediate and Advanced levels. Most books available are the lower levels, many at Beginner (O'Hara 2002; Stott & Revell 2004; Walker & Harding 2006) and Intermediate (Harding & Henderson 1994; Stott & Pohl 2010; Walker & Harding 2007; Jones 2005). There are some at Upper Intermediate level (Jacob & Strutt 1997; Harding 1998; Walker & Harding 2009), however, these are mainly aimed at general tourism and are not hotel-specific. There is no formal published material widely available at advanced level.

While the jargon used in the hospitality industry (for example: greetings: *hello, how may I help you?*; use of politeness tokens such as *would you like?*) is present in materials from Intermediate level, for students training for a career at management level in a hotel there is a lack of materials presenting and practising complex vocabulary and linguistic structures in certain areas, for example, culinary terms (e.g. *terrine, focaccia*) often originate in other languages and can pose pronunciation difficulties; style-shifting may occur depending upon the relationship with the guest (Blue & Harun 2003); and linguistic treatment of politeness and softening in difficult areas such as hiring and firing can pose problems and needs to be addressed during training. The CLAS corpus will provide researchers with an opportunity to evaluate the discourse in SCHM diachronically over the four-year course and will identify the language features which will be most useful to these students and lead to future more relevant materials.

English profile

It is anticipated that the tie-in between the CLAS corpus and English Profile will prove mutually beneficial. As a multi-faceted collaborative research project which aims to enhance the learning, teaching and assessment of English worldwide, English Profile is seeking to define 'the language that learners can be expected to demonstrate at each level, offering a clear benchmark for progress that will inform curricula development as well as the development of courses and test material' (http://www.english-profile.org) for the benefit of both learners and educators alike. Work on defining these descriptors does not currently extend beyond the B2 level of the CEFR and, as mentioned, priority is being given to the C1/C2 level descriptors. This requires language research which will provide the actual data illustrating the different criteria between the various B and C levels and which can be characterized by significant linguistic features. While a CLAS corpus objective is to provide learner data related to the hospitality industry, in terms of the English Profile Project its contribution will be much more specific in that it will contribute to and assist in defining the differences in reference level descriptors around the B2, C1, C2 levels.

Related studies

Many corpora are still focused on written language, although more and more spoken corpora are now being compiled. The largest corpus currently publicly available covering spoken English is the British National Corpus (BNC) with ten million spoken words. While the focus now has shifted from written to spoken corpora, the tendency currently is also to create and develop new spoken corpora in specific vocational and professional areas, called specialized corpora (Koester 2010).

Specialized corpora

A key feature of the successful hotel, as previously mentioned, is often determined by direct face-to-face contact with the client, the personal touch in dealing with people while providing the service. The linguistic model of the service encounter has been investigated in relation to several other sectors: – in the business world, for example, in travel agents (Coupland and Ylanne-McEwen 2000); petrol stations/small shops (Binchy 2000); bookshops (Aston 1988). In the academic world too, where the CLAS corpus is also situated, specific small purpose-built corpora are being developed examining the professional discourse of that metier, for example Vaughan (2007) investigated teacher talk within the context of a community of practice (Wenger 1998), a parallel framework which can also be applied to the hospitality sector.

Training people (whether native or non-native speakers) in specialized areas requires the learner to 'control that subset of the English language which the particular community has extracted to form its particular style' (O'Toole 1994: 4). The relationship between communication skills and success in the hospitality industry cannot be underestimated. Sheridan (2004: 22) insists that 'strong communication both verbal and non-verbal between staff and guests is an essential component of customer service ... helping employees learn English produces a more cohesive and self-confident staff, better guest experiences and higher perceptions of value and professionalism.' Blue and Harun (2003: 77) noted that the hospitality register in English is vast and that a number of functions of hospitality language such as greeting a guest, requesting information and salutations necessitate some level of knowledge of the pertinent phrases before someone can operate successfully in guest-contact positions. Blue and Harun (ibid) go further to describe the minimum 'cluster' of language skills that staff dealing with guests should have acquired, namely: how to address a person; how to solicit and give the necessary information; how to respond to questions/requests; how to use prompts; how to use gestures; how to deal with difficult customers; and how to appease complaints.

Some hotels do offer training programmes for employees; however, many do not have the funding to provide such programmes and tailoring courses for each department to provide the necessary spoken skills for that department can prove expensive and time consuming. Thus, most hotels would expect that their staff members are trained in language skills before being employed, underlining the need for linguistic training in hospitality-focused educational institutions.

Community of practice

From the early 1960s, Gumperz (1962, 1968, 1971, 1972) did considerable and seminal work on speech communities and Swales (1985, 1988) developed these concepts further in terms of discourse communities. More recently Lave and Wenger (1991) and Wenger (1998) have expanded on the framework of communities of practice, taking the concept of *legitimate peripheral participation* as the basis for learning and induction into the relevant professional and vocational arena. This framework is particularly appropriate for the research being carried out at SCHM, a location where apprentices in the hospitality industry are trained through practical and legitimate participation in the work of the industry, as well as gaining the theoretical knowledge in an academic setting. Wenger (1998) identifies three key elements which constitute a community of practice and by which membership can be recognized, namely: there must be a *joint enterprise* which the members negotiate collectively, a common purpose; there must be *mutual engagement* of the members in the enterprise and its further-ance; and there must be a *shared repertoire* of expression by the members.

Analysis of the CLAS corpus is expected to reveal these key elements of community of practice at SCHM, and also to confirm through its discourse and legitimate participation (during the two off-campus placements) the furtherance of this community in operation.

Using the data

Shannon College was selected as a specialized and discrete locus for this linguistic research because it offers the opportunity to capture a broad spectrum of academic English across a range of both business topics and specific hotel-oriented modules. This will allow comparative analysis of the data with other corpora, for example, spoken corpora in the academic and business environments (MICASE, CANBEC, LIBEL) and general spoken corpora (CIC, LCIE, CANCODE).[2] Furthermore, the contribution of non-native English speaker data will facilitate comparisons with other non-native language use in other corpora, particularly the Cambridge Learner Corpus and will feed into the English Profile Programme, as previously mentioned.

O'Keeffe, McCarthy and Carter (2007: 5–6) point out that a spoken corpus is more time-consuming to create than a written corpus because the speech has to be transcribed and one hour of speech can take approximately two working days to transcribe. In addition to this, there is also the requirement to tag the recorded speech for many other elements which will allow for qualitative assessment of the data at a later stage. These tags would include many of the non-linguistic features of spoken language, such as laughter, overlap, hesitation, interruption, and other such vocalization traits.

Once a specialized corpus, such as the CLAS corpus, has been built with carefully selected materials, the next step is to analyse the data. As noted by Biber, Conrad and Reppen (1998), one of the benefits of using a corpus is that both quantitative and qualitative techniques can be used. Methods such as Discourse Analysis (DA) and Conversation Analysis (CA) have become widely used in investigating corpus data (Thornbury 2010). Sinclair (1991: 3) also points out that the growth in corpora, and more specifically the investigation of collocation, semantics and pragmatics, has

---

2   The corpora mentioned are: MICASE – Michigan Corpus of Academic Spoken English; CANBEC – Cambridge and Nottingham Business English Corpus; LIBEL – Limerick-Belfast Corpus of Academic Spoken English; CIC – Cambridge International Corpus; LCIE – Limerick Corpus of Irish English; CANCODE – Cambridge and Nottingham Corpus of Discourse in English (O'Keeffe et al., 2007: 285–293).

changed the way we study and teach language. Examination of these elements will be investigated and analysed based on the corpus findings, and the discourse of this community of practice at SCHM will be primarily evident through its shared repertoire (Wenger 1998).

In the past, examples of language use were created by teachers and materials writers to demonstrate grammar points and vocabulary use, which sometimes offered some rather stilted models of spoken language. In recent times, however, some newer textbooks are now corpus-based and they provide authenticity of contemporary language use by using examples of actual spoken interaction which maintain currency with up-to-date language change. The *Touchstone Series* (McCarthy, McCarten and Sandiford 2005) is such an example and, moreover, the grammar rules cater for descriptive use rather than just the prescriptive rules of formal grammar. One of the outcomes of this research is to develop further materials in the hospitality sector, in particular higher level English language pedagogic resources which reflect the discourse as it is used today.

In practical terms, data analysis will be constructed using computer software especially designed for corpus analysis, in this case Wordsmith Tools using the latest Version 5 issued in 2008 (Scott 2008). Details of the major features of this software will be explained later when discussing some of the preliminary findings.

Research methodology

The project leaders from CUP and MIC met the faculty and students at SCHM to present the project. Practical arrangements for data collection were put in place which began in November 2008 and continued over a twelve-month period, covering two academic years. 107 separate academic speech contexts, amounting to 120 hours of data, were recorded using a digital audio recorder and stored in MP3 sound file format. These recording events entailed either a single lecture period (one sound file), double lectures (two sound files) or some recording events (Culinary or Restaurant Practical, class presentations, English oral exams) had numerous files, all of which amount to 311 individual sound files in the overall corpus. The coding system for the recordings consisted of a three-part sequence: CLAS – to indicate this corpus; 001 to identify the numerical sequence of the recording; and a further two-digit number to identify the specific sound file within a recording event. For example, CLAS.075.14 nominates the fourteenth sound file in the seventy-fifth recording.

All students and relevant teaching staff members who participated in the project were required to complete certain documentation. The Speaker Information Sheet elicited some general personal and educational details, such as previous education (the majority of students were progressing from second level education), and the use of English and/or other languages in their daily lives (53 per cent of students were non-native speakers and all but one of the recorded teaching staff were native speakers). Each participant was allocated an individual I.D. number and that data has been stored in a database with approximately 450 entries listing students in First, Third and Fourth years over the two academic years, the academic staff and also some occasional participants. The corpus will be linked to this database, thus enabling the identity and personal profile of each speaker to be accessed and attributed to each speaker turn. Furthermore, each participant signed a Consent Form in respect of the data being collected and anonymity is guaranteed to the participants by the end users of the corpus.

For each individual recording event, the documentation included a Sign-in sheet for all present; an Individual Recording Details sheet; a Speaker Order sheet; a classroom layout, and lecture hand-outs, presentations and other class materials. The template for all these documents formed part of the Sub-Corpus Agreement contract which was signed on behalf of Cambridge University Press/Cambridge ESOL, Mary Immaculate College and Shannon College of Hotel Management in October 2009 and which covered all legal considerations and ethical guidelines in respect of the CLAS corpus.

The challenge in the CLAS corpus was to ensure a comprehensive matrix of speech events that represented a typical academic year in Shannon College. All types of recording events representative of daily college life needed to be reflected in the data collected. In summary, the distribution across the four main categories of recordings which included general business modules, hotel specific modules, language for non-native speakers, and student presentations (native and non-native speakers jointly or separately), were all represented across the three years of study. Figure 6.1 represents the breakdown by year and by content.

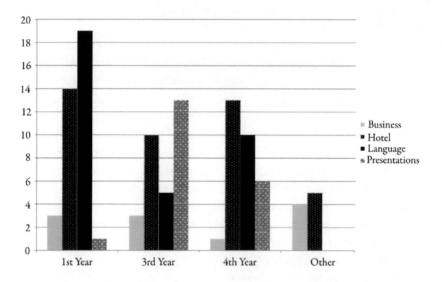

Figure 6.1 Summary breakdown of CLAS recordings by year and content

Thirty-seven recordings of first year students accounted for almost forty-four hours of speech; third years contributed over thirty-five hours in thirty-one recordings; fourth years provided in excess of thirty-two hours in thirty recordings and miscellaneous meetings and the Certificate in English Language Studies (CELS)[3] language classes amounted to another

3   CELS, Certificate in English Language Studies, is a year-long preparatory course offered to non-native speakers who hope to enrol in SCHM's degree course or other third-level colleges the following year. Students prepare for the Cambridge IELTS exam at the end of their course.

eight hours, totaling 120 hours overall in 107 recorded speech events. It must be noted that the higher number of recordings and time for first year students reflects the significantly increased teaching contact hours in the first academic year.

Recordings were made using a digital audio recorder. Audio recording was selected as the means of data collection for this corpus as it was generally believed to be the least intrusive method for all participants. In reality, the participants became rather oblivious to being recorded and conducted their participation in a most natural and uninhibited way. Nevertheless, it must be noted that there were the occasional incidents when the speaker(s) became conscious of the fact that they were being recorded. This usually happened after a particular utterance or exchange, for example when speaking about a commercially-sensitive topic, caused them to remember the recorder. Nonetheless, consideration had to be given to the observer's paradox (Labov 1972) which means that the very presence itself of the observer/investigator can influence the participation of subjects in the event or experiment. Labov outlined the inherent paradox stating that 'the aim of linguistic research in the community must be to find out how people talk when they are not being systematically observed; yet we can only obtain this data by systematic observation' (ibid: 3). Notwithstanding, the observer's paradox did not generally seem to become an inhibiting factor in the overall data collection for this corpus.

Having completed the data collection, the next phase was the transcription process, which is currently in train. This too presented initial challenges, particularly in terms of transcription conventions and tagging. Cambridge University Press's standard transcription conventions had to be expanded to cater for some of the linguistic features particular to this study, for example, non-standard contractions and vocalizations of an Irish-English variety, mispronunciations and other non-linguistic features of the recordings. To-date, over 520,000 words have been transcribed providing samples from each segment of the recordings by year and category. Using this significant sample from the anticipated one million words, hereafter called CLAS-1, certain linguistic features of this environment as a micro-cosm of the industry are beginning to emerge which will be discussed here-after. It is important to point out at this juncture that the CLAS corpus is a work in progress and the sample corpus used here is not a finalized, proofed document so there may be some variations in the data presented here when compared with the final, definitive version of the corpus.

Discussion of preliminary findings

One of the main purposes of the CLAS corpus is to identify the linguistic indices within the community of practice (Wenger 1998) of the hotel management training sector. WordSmith Tools 5.0 software (Scott 2008) was used to analyse the corpus. This is an integrated suite of computer programmes used to look at how words behave, the three main features of which are wordlists, keywords and concordances. Wordlists provide a large amount of statistical information regarding the variety and frequency of word tokens in the corpus. The word count in CLAS-1 amounts to 528,108 tokens providing 13,505 individual word types. Keywords are words which occur unusually frequently in this corpus when compared to their occur-rence in some kind of reference corpus (ibid) which is typically a much larger corpus. By comparing two corpora, the linguistic features of the hotel management training sector will become apparent and these can be analysed both quantitatively (wordlist frequencies) and qualitatively using a variety of approaches including Discourse Analysis and Conversation Analysis. This analysis will provide a synchronic overview of hotel training discourse and, furthermore, will document the process of initiation into this specific community of practice as demonstrated through the language use (Wenger 1998), in other words, the 'hotelspeak', across the three student years viewed diachronically.

Several linguistic indices are already evident from this sample corpus. These include anticipated ones such as: acronyms – *C & B* (Conference and Banqueting), *F & B* (Food and Beverage), *SOPs* (Standard Operating Procedures), *PMS* (Property Management Systems), *FIEs* (Foreign Investment Enterprises); culinary terminology (*velouté, béchamel, posset*); specific hotel technology (*Picasso, Opera, Fidelio* – these are software packages); jargon (*rack rate, on the pass, par stock*); and other culturally associated linguistic features (trade-names, place names, organizations).

Keywords

As indicated above, keywords, while not necessarily the most frequently occurring words in a corpus, are the most unusually frequent words when compared with a larger reference corpus. The reference corpus used for comparative purposes is the Limerick Corpus of Irish English (LCIE) (Farr, Murphy and O'Keeffe 2004), a one-million word corpus of casual Irish English conversations which uses the same variety of language as the CLAS corpus. For the purposes of this paper and based on the available CLAS-1 transcriptions, specific keywords are already identifiable. Table 6.1 records the first fourteen keywords of specific interest in this professional and academic environment, showing their keyword ranking, frequency and ranking in the overall wordlist. The wordlist refers to the raw frequency of all the occurrences of all the words in the corpus and these are displayed in rank order from most frequent to least frequent by the software.

Table 6.1 Comparison of keyword listing and wordlist in CLAS-1

Word	Keyword Ranking	Frequency	Wordlist Ranking
hotel	7	1128	74
management	12	417	172
staff	17	334	205
information	19	395	181
guest	25	232	271
manager	27	299	221

Word	Keyword Ranking	Frequency	Wordlist Ranking
system	32	441	163
protein	33	192	322
training	38	334	206
restaurant	44	236	270
hotels	45	227	275
guests	53	147	406
linen	55	125	467
room	60	505	147

As illustrated by this initial selection of keywords, an examination of the first 100 keywords further shows that thirty-four of them are linguistically oriented to the hotel training sector: it is revealing to note that they include an almost equal number of both hotel-specific (*guests, rooms, accommodation, service, wine*) and general business (*credit, software, energy, leadership, department*) terminology – it must not be forgotten that the students are studying for a business degree with a hotel management speciality. Words like *protein* and *linen* which have a specifically high keyness in this table came from first year lectures on Food Science and Accommodation modules which have been transcribed in CLAS-1.

Concordances

A concordance is the list of all the examples of a particular word or word clusters in the total text (Scott 2008). Concordances also display the words that surround a particular selected word; therefore, word patterns can be noted and explored. This can be a particularly useful, though sometimes challenging, corpus-based feature of language from a pedagogical point of view especially when working with non-native speakers who are still acquiring the language. From the concordance toolkit, the surrounding source text can be viewed in context for further information. Examining the various texts in which the particular word is embedded allows for a greater expansive understanding of the word with its many variations of meaning, nuance and indeed genre. The word *suite*, for example, illustrates this point to good effect. It ranks at no. 462 in the wordlist with fifty-one occurrences and at no. 226 in the keyword list. Investigating the source texts, however, reveals that, as in the first set below, the word *suite* is used to indicate the bedroom and its ancillary facilities in a hotel, the most common meaning of the word. These examples are taken from first year student presentations on designing a hotel bedroom as an assignment in the Accommodation module.

N Concordance
22 For example this is the bedroom in the honeymoon **suite**. As you can see with the um headboard they've
23 lake view and golf side bedroom five one bedroom **suite** two penthouse and one presidential suite. Only
24 bedroom suite two penthouse and one presidential **suite**. Only twenty-five bedrooms have been
25 a at a the theme of it was a New York penthouse **suite**. And um the people that are in the group are
26 a walk-in wardrobe and a beige rug. We have an en-**suite** with the standard shower sink toilet and now
27 the room so the furniture and fittings in our **suite** suits these very simple but smart. Um first we

---

Figure 6.2   Concordance for *suite meaning hotel bedroom* from CLAS-1

The second set of meanings for *suite*, used to indicate a group of related software programmes suitable for hotel use (the fifth meaning assigned to the word in the Longman dictionary, 1995), come from fourth year student presentations wherein they were required to assess various hotel software packages as an assignment in their Hotel Management Information Systems module.

N Concordance
8   the best uh most appealing feature of the Executive **Suite** is that they have a high speed of operation and
9   you go with? We we we're chosen the Executive **Suite** and cause it's all in one and you can upgrade it
10   restaurant or worldwide hotel chain. there's an Execu **Suite** Hotel PMS and uh it may improve work
11   they go uh Touch POS and the another they go uh **Suite** PMS. And the ones that you would
12   over here. We have two softwares Hotellinx **Suite** PMS and uh Executive Suite hotel PMS. And
13   softwares Hotellinx Suite PMS and uh Executive **Suite** hotel PMS. And the other features of both this
14   is a short description of Hotellinx and Executive **Suite** again. Uh the hotel sta= this suites this is

Figure 6.3 Concordance for *suite meaning software programmes* from CLAS-1

This is a particularly effective example of the purpose and benefits to be acquired from corpus linguistic studies. In this specific instance, the difference in meaning and usage of the same word by two different levels of students exemplifies one of the hypotheses within this research, namely that this community of practice is also evinced, supported and exemplified by the linguistic indices of this environment, demonstrating the diachronic nature of language acquisition in this particular academic and vocational setting. Furthermore, an examination of the source text contexts in the finalized corpus will reveal whether this word is used more frequently in relation to hotel rooms and furniture, or if its usage is more consistent with software terminology.

Another example of semantic variation is the use of the word *perishable*, a not-unsurprising word in a hotel management training college where students are taught about food under many headings, for example, nutrition, cooking, hygiene, health and safety considerations. However, the CLAS corpus invokes a further meaning which demonstrates the *shared repertoire* (Wenger 1998) specific to this particular community of practice, a meaning pertaining to the loss of potential revenue from an unoccupied table in the restaurant, as instanced in the following extract from a lecture to first years on Front Office Management.

> <$NS505> ... over the course of a breakfast or lunch or a dinner am how much time is somebody taking up sitting on a seat and that's what is perceived as a *perishable* item ... *perishability* that if you don't fill a table between six and seven tonight you'll never fill that table between six and seven tonight again.

Figure 6.4 Extract from recording CLAS.089.01 illustrating the *shared repertoire* (Wenger 1998) meaning of *perishable* and *perishability* in CLAS-1

If the table, or indeed a hotel room, is vacant at a particular time, there is never another opportunity to earn income from that facility, so these facilities are in fact *perishable* items in the hotel's inventory. As these concordances demonstrate, the various layers of meanings of a lexical item need to be borne in mind in the pedagogical context of acquiring the *shared repertoire* (Wenger 1998) of this community of practice for both the non-native speakers of English and, indeed, the native English speakers.

Pronouns as a key deictic device

Biber et al. (1998: 1042) confirm that pronouns are significantly more common in spoken language than in written language and they form a central role in establishing and maintaining successful interaction between participants in a conversation. The CLAS corpus is a spoken corpus so evidence of considerable pronoun use can be anticipated here. The educational context within SCHM provides an interactive location wherein lecturers and students collaborate together and demonstrate their *mutual engagement* (Wenger 1998) and, through their discourse, discover and decipher the shared meaning and the common purpose of their *joint enterprise* (ibid). Issues of positioning both in the immediate classroom interaction and in terms of students' future roles as hotel managers will be expressed through pronominal deictic use. Therefore, investigation of the frequency and function of personal deixis is of considerable importance in building and supporting this specific community of practice (ibid).

Carter and McCarthy (2006: 375) list the several classes of pronouns – personal, possessive, reflexive, reciprocal, relative, interrogative, demonstrative and indefinite. In CLAS-1, an initial investigation of personal pronouns only (subject, object, determiner, possessive and reflexive) reveals 51,420 occurrences, or 9.7 per cent of the overall words. 41,568 occurrences from this segment (81 per cent) are subject pronouns and Figure 6.5 shows the breakdown. With the exception of *she*, *he* and *ye* ranked at numbers 153, 171 and 206 respectively, all the other subject pronouns appear within the first thirty positions on the wordlist.

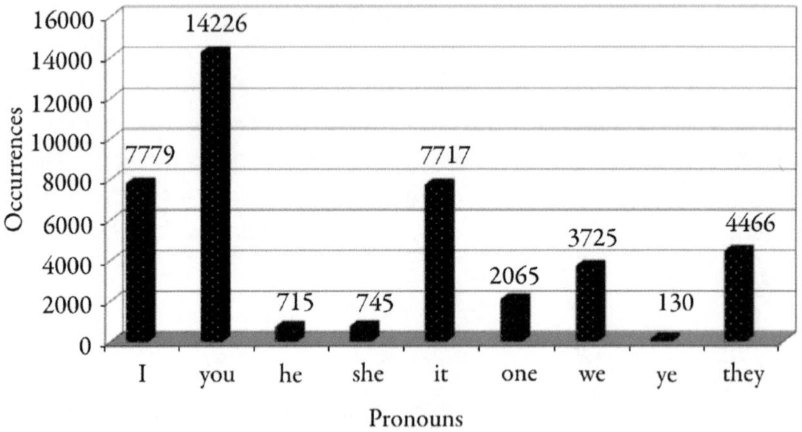

Figure 6.5 Distribution of subject pronouns in CLAS-1

You, the fourth highest frequency word in the wordlist with 14,226 tokens, has been examined from a random sample and its function sub-divided as follows: subject singular 33 per cent, object singular 7 per cent, subject plural 25 per cent, object plural 5 per cent, generic use 21 per cent, and discourse marker component 9 per cent. Combined with the high prevalence of the determiner *your* (48.3 per cent within its category), *you* and all its extensions figure predominantly within the discourse of this College. This finding is noteworthy as it shows that the lecturers through the use of this discourse are orientating their students towards their own future professional status. The following two examples illustrate this point and highlight this conscious focus as the extracts are taken from two separate academic years and two different recording event types. The first extract is taken from a first year Culinary Practical, the second one from a third year lecture in the Front Office module:

> <$NS516> ... *your* tarragon <-> so *you* fry off onion, add in *your* white wine, reduce it down by half and then add in *your* demi-glaze which is *your* brown stock and ...

Figure 6.6   Extract from recording CLAS.007.07 illustrating the use of *you* and *your* personal pronouns in CLAS-1

> <$NS505> ... *you* spend so long focusing on balancing *your* money, balancing *your* credit cards, balancing *your* cash, making sure everything is right, that the whole area of credit bills tend to be not viewed as important ... or they paid *you* credit cards or something, *you* have that money. The money *you* don't have is *your* credit bills ... So there's a lot of annoying little issues caused by Walkouts, I suppose with the most important being *your* financial loss in *your* hotel ...

Figure 6.7   Extract from recording CLAS.092.01 illustrating the use of *you* and *your* personal pronouns in CLAS-1

This use of *you* combined with *your* is not merely accidental or idiolectal. On the contrary, this discourse is a conscious choice used to embed into the students' psyche a sense of personal responsibility and engagement with the *joint enterprise* (Wenger 1998) of running a hotel or a kitchen and the consequences of their actions: in other words, in the real-life, projected future situation when the students are actually the Duty Manager or Chef, the responsibility will be theirs personally, it will be their money, their extended credit and ultimately their financial loss which will result if Standard Operating Procedures (*SOPs* – one of the many acronyms of hotel discourse) are not followed to the letter. Davies and Harré's (1990) concept of 'interactional positioning' is clearly evident in the discourse of these mentors within this community of practice (Wenger 1998), as evidenced in Figures 6.6 and 6.7 above, where the 'interactive positioning in which what one person says positions another' (Davies and Harré 1990: 48) is designed to get the students to foresee and project themselves into their future positions as responsible hotel managers.

This process of pre-positioning the students into their future roles through the discourse of the experts in this community of practice (Wenger 1998) can also be examined and, indeed, contrasted with the discourse from the business world, given that the CLAS corpus shares linguistic features of both the academic and business registers. The Cambridge and Nottingham Business English Corpus (CANBEC)[4] serves as a useful business corpus against which to review the CLAS corpus findings, particularly in terms of pronoun use and function. Although O'Keeffe et al. (2007) point out that in the spoken academic register, *we* is not found to be as frequent as it is in business discourse, Handford (2010: 155) remarks on the 'ubiquity of we in business and other forms of institutional communications'. *We* is used to reinforce strong corporate identity and participation, a collective responsibility approach and teamwork in business, contrasting strongly with the individual personal responsibility within the hotel world. In CANBEC *we* pronouns collocate strongly with verbs such as *need* and *have*, for example *we need to, we have to, we've got to* (O'Keeffe et al. 2007: 21), whereas in CLAS-1, these and other verbs collocate much more strongly with the pronoun *you*.

Looking at collocates of the verb pattern *you need* as an expression of obligation, CLAS-1 yielded 312 occurrences of *you need*, 228 of which were followed by an infinitive verb form. Figure 6.8 illustrates the main infinitive verbs which collocate with *you need* and these are contrasted with *we need*, many of which are basic delexicalized verbs.

4   This corpus project was established in the School of English Studies at the University of Nottingham, UK, and is funded by Cambridge University Press. It is copyrighted by Cambridge University Press 2003 (O'Keeffe et al. 2007: 206).

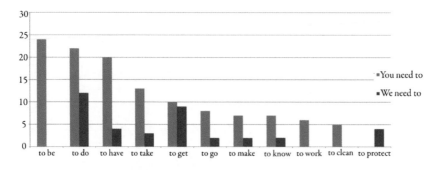

Figure 6.8 *You need to* and *we need to* collocating with infinitive verbs in CLAS-1

Given its recording location at Shannon, the opportunity that the CLAS corpus presents to examine this community to ascertain if there is any marked tendency towards the use of Irish-English in this hospitality training discourse is not to be overlooked. Examining in detail the pronoun patterns and, in particular, the high frequency of *you* in the corpus further encourages the investigation of the well-recognized feature of Irish-English, namely the use of *ye* (second person plural number) and also the less frequent but most distinctive Irish-English use of *yer* functioning as the second person plural determiner pronoun. Although not statistically significant in the overall context, the 130 occurrences were investigated and they reflect a feature more of individual idiolect rather than a pronoun usage pattern common throughout the corpus. The speech patterns of only three lecturers accounted for 111 occurrences of *ye*. One interesting example occurred in a Culinary Practical class where first year students were being taught how to cook by the Chef, the speaker in the following extract.

<$NS5 16> Now guys, it's not (girl's name)'s responsibility to make *yer* sauce. *Ye* should be doing it, so (girl's name), *you* go back over and look after *your* bench. That's how these boys are going to learn, by making mistakes ... *you*'re going to need more flour underneath that, it's stuck to it. <$sound of greaseproof paper /$> <$ loud voice /$> Okay when *ye*'ve the lined when *ye*'ve *yer* pastry lined like this <$ long pause /$> now rolled on the table behind *you* there *you'll* see I've the pastry pasta dough made ...

Figure 6.9 Extract from recording CLAS.007.04 illustrating the use of *ye* and *yer* from CLAS-1

One interesting feature in this extract is that the *yer* is syntactically very closely linked to the *ye*, and also that the speaker was able to use the *you* form with either a singular or a plural meaning as he chose. At first he spoke directly to the '*guys*', later referring to them as '*these boys*', indicating that the *yer sauce* was in fact their sauce. In the second example, the *you* in 'you're going to need' is actually used to address one particular student (names are excluded to safeguard anonymity), as can be interpreted from the larger textual context. However, the transcriber's comments <$ loud voice /$> is utilized throughout the CLAS transcriptions to indicate that the speaker, the Chef in this example, raises his voice deliberately when he is addressing the whole class who are spread across a large kitchen and he wants all the students to be able to hear him. Here, then, he is addressing the whole class with his *ye've yer pastry* but without any difficulty he subsequently chooses the more regular forms of *you/you'll* even though still addressing the whole class, albeit after a long pause.

The above extract also quite neatly illustrates Wenger's (1998) whole concept of novice and expert within the framework of community of practice. Here the spoken discourse captures the relationship between the Chef, the expert/lecturer, and the students, guys/these boys, in this *joint enterprise* (ibid) where the participants must together negotiate a common purpose, in this case the transference of culinary skills and knowledge, and become inducted through their own *legitimate peripheral participation* (ibid) into the professional community of hotel management. The kitchen is not a formal, seated lecture hall typical of an academic setting; instead it is a fast-paced, busy and demanding work setting located within an academic setting where the discourse at times reflects the rather informal relationship between the participants and the co-operative spirit that leads to successful learning outcomes for the novices.

Conclusion

There are several benefits from this project for the participant institutions involved. By opening its doors to this international project, SCHM now has a record of its own academic discourse in hotel management training. This collection of data can be accessed in the future and exploited as a resource for self-directed reflective professional development for faculty members. In the context of its own community of practice, the College can interrogate its own discourse and examine how its language contributes to the inherent *joint enterprise* (Wenger 1998) for both staff and students alike.

One of the objectives of the project was to record and investigate the English language itself, particularly as articulated by the non-native speakers in this College, and to chart their language learning acquisition and ownership over the four-year course of study. The objective is to design and develop future teaching materials more suited to their language needs, specifically at the higher levels within the hospitality environment. Empirical data from the CLAS corpus will inform such materials development.

Furthermore, the CLAS corpus will dovetail into the English Profile Programme by providing a further resource for language research into competency descriptors for non-native English speaking students at different levels. Competency descriptors to date have been largely defined by data obtained from written exams. The CLAS corpus data will enhance and refine these standard definitions because much of its learner English has been gathered in what may be regarded as less daunting environments such as in general language classes and oral presentations and not within exam scenarios.

References

Aston, G. (ed.) (1988). *Negotiating Service: Studies in the discourse of bookshop encounters*. Bologna: Coperativa Libraria Universitaria Editrice Bologna.

Biber, D., Conrad, S. and Reppen, R. (1998). *Corpus linguistics: Investigating language structure and use*. Cambridge: Cambridge University Press.

Binchy, J. (2000). *Relational Language and Politeness in Southern-Irish Service Encounters*. (Unpublished PhD thesis) University of Limerick.

Blue, G.M. and Harun, M. (2003). 'Hospitality language as a professional skill'. *English for Specific Purposes*, 22, 73–91.

Coupland, N. and Ylanne-McEwen. V. (2000). 'Talk about the weather: small talk, leisure talk and the travel industry'. In J. Coupland. (ed.), *Small Talk*, 163–182, Essex: Pearson Education.

Davies, B. and Harré, R. (1990). 'Positioning: The Discursive Production of Selves'. *Journal for the Theory of Social Behaviour*, 20 (1), 43–63.

English Profile. Available at <http://www.englishprofile.org> accessed 12 January 2011.

Farr, F., Murphy, B. and O'Keeffe, A. (2004). 'The Limerick Corpus of Irish English: design, description and application'. *Teanga*, 21, 5–29.

Gumperz, J. (1962). 'Types of linguistic communities'. *Anthropological Linguistics*, 4 (1), 28–40.

Gumperz, J. (1968). 'The Speech Community'. *International Encyclopedia of the Social Sciences*, pp 381–386. London: Macmillan.

Gumperz, J. (1971). *Language in Social Groups*. Stanford: Stanford University Press.

Gumperz, J. (1972). 'The Speech Community'. In P.P. Giglioli (ed.) *Language and Social Context*, pp. 219–231. London: Penguin.

Handford, M. (2010), The Language of Business Meetings. Cambridge: Cambridge University Press.

Harding, K. (1998). *Going International: English for Tourism*. Oxford: Oxford University Press.

Harding, K. and Henderson, P. (1994). *High Season: English for the Hotel and Tourist Industry*. Oxford: Oxford University Press.

Jacob, M. and Strutt, P. (1997). *English for International Tourism*. Essex: Addison Wesley Longman.

Jones, L. (2005). *Welcome! English for the travel and tourism industry 2nd ed.* Cambridge: Cambridge University Press.

Koester, A. (2010). 'Building small specialised corpora'. In A. O'Keeffe and M. McCarthy (eds), *The Routledge Handbook of Corpus Linguistics*, pp 66–79. London: Routledge.

Labov, W. (1972). *Sociolinguistic Patterns*. Oxford: Blackwell.

Lave, J. and Wenger, E. (1991). *Situated Learning: Legitimate Peripheral Participation*. Cambridge: Cambridge University Press.

Longman (1995). *Dictionary of Contemporary English, 3rd ed.* Essex: Longman Group Ltd.

McCarthy, M., McCarten, J. and Sandiford, H. (2005). *Touchstone Series*. Cambridge: Cambridge University Press.

O'Hara, F. (2002). *Be My Guest: English for the Hotel Industry*. Cambridge: Cambridge University Press.

O'Keeffe A., McCarthy, M. and Carter, R. (2007). *From Corpus to Classroom: Language Use and Language Teaching*. Cambridge: Cambridge University Press.

O'Toole, M. (1994). 'Training in a Second Language Environment.' *Journal of European Industrial Training* 18(1), 4–9.

Scott, M. (2008). *WordSmith Tools Version 5*. Liverpool: Lexical Analysis Software.

Sheridan, M. (2004). 'The Ten-Minute Manager's Guide to Improving Language Skills'. *Restaurant and Institutions*. March 15, pp. 22–23.

Sinclair, J. (1991). *Corpus, Concordance, Collocation*. Oxford: Oxford University Press.

Stott, T and Pohl, A. (2010). *Highly Recommended 2: English for the hotel and catering industry*. Oxford: Oxford University Press.

Stott, T. and Revell, R. (2004). *Highly Recommended: English for the hotel and catering industry*. Oxford: Oxford University Press.

Swales, J.M. (1985). 'A genre-based approach to language across the curriculum.' In Tickoo, M.L. (ed.), *Language Across the Curriculum*. Singapore: RELC, 10–22.

Swales, J.M. (1988). 'Discourse communities, genres and English as an international language.' *World Englishes*, 7(2), 211–220.

Thornbury, S. (2010). 'What can a corpus tell us about discourse?'. In A. O'Keeffe and M. McCarthy (eds), *The Routledge Handbook of Corpus Linguistics*, pp. 270–287. London: Routledge.

Vaughan, E. (2007). '"I think we should just accept ... our horrible lowly status": analysing teacher-teacher talk within the context of Community of Practice'. *Language Awareness*, 16/3: 173–189.

Walker, R. and Harding, K. (2006). *Tourism 1*. Oxford: Oxford University Press.

Walker, R. and Harding, K. (2007). *Tourism 2*. Oxford: Oxford University Press.

Walker, R. and Harding, K. (2009). *Tourism 3*. Oxford: Oxford University Press.

Wenger, E. (1998). *Communities of Practice: Learning, meaning, and identity*. Cambridge: Cambridge University Press.

NOEL P. Ó MURCHADHA

7   Caighdeáin, caighdeánú agus torthaí ar chaighdeánú na Gaeilge

Introduction

According to Coupland (2007: 42), standard involves more than a completed history of linguistic standardization, it involves an ideological contest and articulates a position or point of view in relation to that contest. Standard is thus considered not merely as a rigid object, but also as an ideology against which varieties of language are evaluated. This paper considers the history of linguistic standardization and the manner in which standardization was achieved in particular languages. The standardization of Irish, the current review included, is discussed in this context. Reporting on fieldwork data collected from teenagers in the Gaeltacht, it is argued that the creation of a written standard for Irish has been detrimental to the vitality of traditional Gaeltacht speech, as argued elsewhere (Ó hIfearnáin 2008; Ó hIfearnáin and Ó Murchadha 2011). Results from the fieldwork indicate that participants consider Gaeltacht youth speech and non-Gaeltacht speech more standard than traditional Gaeltacht speech.

It is argued that the official standard variety of Irish was developed based on the perceived necessity for unitary written norms. The efficacy of alternative models of standardization is considered and it is suggested that incorporating such models, in addition to the traditional models, in discussions on the standardization of Irish might prove a fruitful enterprise. It is further argued that the Official Standard ought to be considered as an instrument to invigorate Irish as a spoken language and to bridge the perceived gap between written and spoken Irish.

Teanga Chaighdeánach

Má ghlactar le léamh Coupland (2007: 42) ar an gcaighdeánú, tuigtear gur cheart an tuiscint idé-eolaíochtúil as a ngintear agus as a bhforbraítear an caighdeán mar choincheap, chomh maith le stair, feidhm, próiseas agus múnlaí an chaighdeánaithe, a bheith san áireamh in aon chur síos cuimsitheach ar an gcaighdeánú. Is féidir teacht ar thuiscint níos cuimsithí ná cuntais chaola ar fhoirmeacha caighdeánacha agus neamhchaighdeánacha teanga tríd an idé-eolaíocht a chur san áireamh sa phlé ar an gcaighdeánú. Sa tslí sin is féidir soiléiriú a dhéanamh ar an tslí a réadaítear teangacha caighdeánacha agus caighdeáin teanga (Deumert agus Vandenbussche 2003: 456) agus ar an tslí a n-úsáidtear iad le measúnú a dhéanamh ar úsáid na teanga.

Feidhm an Chaighdeáin

Is é atá i gceist leis an gcaighdeánú ag an leibhéal neamh-idé-eolaíochtúil ná noirm aonfhoirmeacha a chur in áit na héagsúlachta, faoi mar a deir Milroy (2001: 531): 'In respect of the internal form of language, the process of standardization works by promoting **invariance** or **uniformity** in language structure. We can therefore suggest a primary definition, which is non-ideological and which relates to the internal structure or physical shape of standardized objects: **standardization consists of the imposition of uniformity upon a class of objects.'** Is í an aonfhoirmeacht sprioc an chaighdeánaithe, sa mhúnla traidisiúnta ar a laghad, ionas an chumarsáid i measc lucht na teanga a éascú, a deirtear. 'The whole notion of standardization is bound up with the aim of functional efficiency of the language. Ultimately, the desideratum is that everyone should use and understand the language in the same way with the minimum of misunderstanding and the maximum of efficiency' (Milroy agus Milroy 1999: 19).

Féachtar ar chruthú leagan aonfhoirmeach teanga mar phróiseas ina leagtar amach rialacha na scríbhneoireachta agus ina dhiaidh sin is féidir leis an gcaighdeán aonfhoirmeach feidhmiú mar leagan oifigiúil den teanga, mar leagan den teanga a mbaintear leas as san oideachas agus mar mhúnla d'fhoghlaimeoirí na teanga. Cuireann ceannródaí na pleanála teanga, Einar Haugen, síos ar an gcaighdeánú mar 'the activity of preparing a normative orthography, grammar and dictionary for the guidance of writers and speakers in a non-homogenous speech community' (1959: 8). Sa tslí sin, creidtear gur uirlis fheidhmiúil é an caighdeán a shainíonn rialacha na teanga.

An Caighdeán agus Féiniúlacht

Is as brú suibiachtúil an aitheantais ghrúpa a eascraíonn an caighdeánú chomh maith le brú oibiachtúil na héifeachtúlachta (Lodge 1993: 23). Is féidir leis an gcaighdeán a bheith ina shuaitheantas aitheantais a aontaíonn lucht labhartha na teanga náisiúnta sa mhéid agus go bhfuil tréithe inmhianaithe an idéil náisiúnta go smior ann. Sa bhreis air sin, ní hamháin gur léiriú ar fhéiniúlacht an ghrúpa atá sa chaighdeán, ach úsáidtear chomh maith é mar mhodh gníomhach leis an bhféiniúlacht eitneach nó leis an bhféiniúlacht náisiúnta a neartú (Oakes 2001: 50). Pé slí a gcuirtear caighdeán aonfhoirmeach náisiúnta i dtoll a chéile, smaoinítear go minic air mar mheán trínar féidir dlúthpháirtíocht an ghrúpa nó an náisiúin a bhaint amach agus a chur in iúl. Ina choinne sin, tagann canúintí na teanga náisiúnta i gcoinne idéal sin na céannachta mar léiríonn siad an difríocht is dual do theangacha agus do dhaoine. Tá an méid sin tábhachtach óir sna stáit ina bhfuil leagan caighdeánach den teanga náisiúnta, is minic gurb é an leagan sin a aithnítear ar an bhfoirm ardghradaim teanga a mbaintear úsáid as san oideachas agus d'fheidhmeanna oifigiúla agus glactar leis mar shampla de cheartúsáid na teanga. Chítear gur ag imeacht ón gcaighdeán agus ón idé-eolaíocht náisiúnta teanga atá canúintí na teanga. Ní hamháin go bhfeidhmíonn an caighdeán mar uirlis a gceaptar gá a bheith léi don scríbhneoireacht, mar sin, ach mar leagan náisiúnta den teanga a chuireann seasamh aontaithe in iúl chomh maith.

Múnlaí Traidisiúnta an Chaighdeánaithe

Baintear leas go minic as múnla Haugen (1959) ar an gcaighdeánú teanga,
atá bunaithe ar an Ioruais, sa phlé sochtheangeolaíochta ar an gcaighdeánú
(féach, mar shampla Deumert agus Vandenbussche 2003; Lodge 1993;
Ó hIfearnáin 2006). Ba é an múnla sin ba bhunús ag creata pleanála teanga
i mórán stát a tháinig chun cinn le linn na 1960aidí agus na 1970aidí, bíodh
agus gur féidir é a úsáid le forbairt stairiúil an Bhéarla agus na Fraincise a
rianadh chomh maith, mar shampla. Sainítear ceithre chéim na pleanála
teanga sa mhúnla tuairisciúil seo. Is iad roghnú na bhfoirmeacha údarásacha,
códú na foirme, cur i bhfeidhm agus leathnú feidhme na céimeanna sin,
ach ní gá go gcuirfí i gcrích iad san ord sin.

Don teanga féin, chomh maith le foirm na teanga sin, a thagraíonn
roghnú na bhfoirmeacha údarásacha. D'fhéadfaí teanga fhormhór an
daonra, teanga idirnáisiúnta, teanga dhúchasach nó teanga chóilíneach
a roghnú. Agus an teanga roghnaithe, bunaítear an caighdeán go minic
ar chanúint réigiúnach nó ar chanúint shóisialta áirithe. Dála *Nynorsk* na
hIoruaise, is ar chaint na ndaoine a bunaíodh caighdeán na Nua-Ghaeilge.
Sainiú rialacha na teanga atá i gceist le códú na foirme, chomh maith le
soláthair foclóirí. Uaireanta aithnítear foghraíocht chaighdeánach mar chuid
den chódú. Glacann litriú caighdeánach agus gramadach chaighdeánach
údarás chucu féin de réir mar a chuirtear i bhfeidhm iad, go háirithe sa
chóras oideachais agus in obair an stáit. Ní bhíonn rath ar an gcaighdeán
go dtí go nglacann an pobal leis. Céimeanna suntasacha i gcur i bhfeidhm
an chaighdeáin isea a úsáid sa chóras oideachais, in obair an stáit agus sa
bhfoilsitheoireacht, agus tugtar stádas dlíthiúil dó babhtaí chomh maith.
Próiseas leanúnach atá sa leathnú feidhme agus is iad forbairt an fhoclóra,
na téarmaíochta agus na stíle na príomhchúraimí ionas an teanga a chur
in oiriúint d'feidhmeanna úra.

Caighdeán Labhartha

Ní chuirtear caighdeán i bhfeidhm ar an gcaint chomh fuirist céanna.
'Before we go on to ask how we are able to fool ourselves so thoroughly,
we must first deal more carefully with the question of the mythical

homogeneous standardized spoken language. Until the impossibility of such a thing is established incontrovertibly, people will continue to pine after it, and, worse, to pursue it.' (Lippi-Green 1997: 44).

Is leis an scríbhneoireacht is mó a bhaineann úsáid chaighdeánach na teanga (Milroy agus Milroy 1999: 8). Is féidir le foirm aonfhoirmeach chaighdeánach den teanga don scríbhneoireacht, áfach, daingniú a dhéanamh ar an tuairim gur amhlaidh atá an scéal i gcás na teanga labhartha, óir creideann an pobal go minic gur leagan neodrach den teanga atá sa chóras scríbhneoireachta (Sebba 2007). Baintear leas babhtaí as an teanga chaighdeánach scríofa, na rialacha agus an ghramadach ar a bhfuil sí bunaithe agus an idé-eolaíocht ar a bhfuil sí bunaithe, mar rúibricí agus mar chritéir nuair atá an teanga labhartha á meas. Glactar leis go minic gur ann do leagan labhartha den teanga atá níos cirte ná leaganacha eile. Glactar leis, ní hamháin gur féidir caint chaighdeánach, canúintí caighdeánacha agus foghraíocht chaighdeánach a bhaint amach, ach go bhfuil a leithéidí inmhianaithe chomh maith (Lippi-Green 1997: 44).

Chíonn an pobal i gcoitinne go bhfuil iompar áirithe sa teanga atá 'ceart' agus iompar eile atá 'mícheart' (Wilton agus Stegu 2011: 12). Bíonn dúil faoi leith ag an bpobal sa chaighdeán labhartha i dteangacha áirithe, dá réir sin (Grondelaers agus Van Hout 2010: 22; Smakman 2006: 44), ach pléitear anseo leis an gcaighdeán labhartha aonfhoirmeach mar mhiotas agus mar idéal in intinn daoine. I bprionsabal, is féidir labhairt de réir choinbhinsiúin chaighdeánacha na teanga scríofa. Is beag baint atá aige sin le foghraíocht, áfach. Is féidir caint chaighdeánach a bhaint amach i raon leathan canúintí agus stíleanna trí rialacha agus gramadach na teanga scríofa a chur i bhfeidhm sa teanga labhartha (Trudgill 1999: 118–119), ach, dar ndóigh, is ag géilleadh d'idé-eolaíocht an chaighdeáin a bheifí sa mhéid sin óir is bunaithe ar roghanna idé-eolaíochtúla a bhíonn teangacha caighdeánacha (Sebba 2007).

Coincheap cumhachtach atá sa teanga chaighdeánach mar gheall ar an nasc idir é agus institiúidí oifigiúla sochaíocha agus an gradam a théann leis an nasc sin (Auer 2005; Eckert 2000: 19; Haugen 1966: 933; Ó Donnchadha 1995: 296). Uaireanta tógtar an idé-eolaíocht gur ann do theanga chaighdeánach cheart amháin don scríbhneoireacht agus cuirtear i bhfeidhm ar an teanga labhartha é. Sa tslí sin, deirtear gur caighdeánach nó neamhchaighdeánach atá leaganacha labhartha den teanga. Is in idé-eolaíocht na teanga caighdeánaí atá fréamhacha an léargais sin ar an teanga.

Idé-eolaíocht an chaighdeáin

Feidhmíonn teanga chaighdeánach ag an leibhéal idé-eolaíochtúil chomh maith le leibhéal do-athraitheach aonfhoirmeach an struchtúir inmheánaigh (Milroy 2001: 531–532). Mar sin féin, dírítear an-chuid airde fós ar shainiú struchtúir inmheánacha na bhfoirmeacha caighdeánacha teanga. Léamh idé-eolaíochtúil ceannais atá i gcur síos mionsonraithe ar an teanga chaighdeánach agus is mó toradh a d'eascródh as dul i ngleic le critíc chasta idé-eolaíochtúil agus le díospóireachtaí idé-eolaíochtúla (Coupland 2000: 627). Is tábhachtach a aithint nach dual don teanga chaighdeánach bheith níos fearr ná níos deise ná saghsanna eile teanga (Foley 1997: 409), ach bronntar gradam uirthi mar gheall ar an nasc idir í agus grúpaí scothaicmeacha agus an nasc le hinstitiúidí cumhachta agus údaráis na sochaí (Eckert 2000: 19), gné nach n-aithnítear in idé-eolaíocht an phobail.

Is féidir smaoineamh ar an idirdhealú idir an caighdeán mar uirlis fheidhmiúil agus an caighdeán mar leagan idéalaithe den teanga i dtéarmaí teangacha caighdeánacha agus caighdeáin teanga. Do rialacha dochta saintreoracha na scríbhneoireachta a thagraíonn an teanga chaighdeánach, ach tagraíonn na caighdeáin teanga do mhúnlaí teanga a fheidhmíonn mar phointí tagartha agus measúnú á dhéanamh ar shlite difriúla leis an teanga a úsáid (Nevailanen 2003). Dá réir sin, is féidir díriú sa phlé ar an teanga chaighdeánach, ní hamháin ar an teanga mar chonstráid neamh-idé-eolaíochtúil, ach mar leagan idéalaithe teanga (Haugen 1966: 931; Swann et al. 2004) le tacar noirm theibí ar féidir le húsáid na teanga cloí leo a bheag nó a mhór (Milroy agus Milroy 1999: 19). Idéal é an caighdeán a mbronntar gradam air mar gheall ar an ról lárnach a bhíonn ag an teanga chaighdeánach san obair oifigiúil agus sa chóras oideachais (Auer 2005; Haugen 1966: 933; Ó Donnchadha 1995: 296).

Caighdeánú na Gaeilge

Stair na Teanga Aonfhoirmí sa Ghaeilge

Síneann úsáid na teanga aonfhoirmí don scríbhneoireacht Ghaeilge siar i bhfad i stair na teanga chomh fada leis an tSean-Ghaeilge ón séú haois go dtí an deichiú haois, ar aghaidh chomh fada leis an Meán-Ghaeilge ón deichiú haois go dtí an dara haois déag agus ar aghaidh arís chomh fada leis an Nua-Ghaeilge Mhoch, nó an Ghaeilge Chlasaiceach, a bhí i réim ón dara haois déag go dtí deireadh an tseachtú haois déag agus tosach na hochtú haoise déag. Caighdeán docht daingean a bhí sa Ghaeilge Chlasaiceach den chuid is mó, bíodh agus go bhfeictear beagán éagsúlachta ann chomh maith. Córas aonfhoirmeach scríbhneoireachta d'fheidhmeanna liteartha faoi leith, go háirithe scríbhneoireacht na bhfilí gairmiúla agus teagasc na mbardscoileanna, a bhí ann. D'fhan sé go réasúnta seasta in ainneoin agus go gcreidtear gur le linn an ama sin a tháinig éagsúlacht réigiúnach chun cinn sa teanga labhartha.

Ba í an uasaicme Ghaelach a chuir pátrúnacht ar fáil d'fhilí gairmiúla na tréimhse sin, nós a neartaigh úsáid na Gaeilge Clasaicí i réimse na filíochta gairmiúla. Ach, tar éis tús an tseachtú haois déag tháinig athrú mór ar an scéal. Cuireadh cosc ar an nGaeilge sa saol poiblí agus tháinig an Béarla go mór chun cinn sa tír mar ghnáth-urlabhra in áit na Gaeilge. Theith roinnt den uasaicme Ghaelach thar lear, díshealbhaíodh tailte an dreama a d'fhan go minic agus deineadh teanga an riaracháin den Bhéarla. D'fhág sin go raibh an Ghaeilge imeallach go maith faoi dheireadh na naoú haoise déag agus ní raibh mórán pátrúnachta ar fáil leis na filí gairmiúla a choimeád i mbun pinn. Le linn an ama sin, chuaigh úsáid na Gaeilge Clasaicí i léig agus tháinig an díchaighdeánú chun cinn. Bíodh agus gur leanadh le scríobh roinnt mhaith lámhscríbhinní faoi phátrúnacht cuid den chléir agus den uasaicme le linn na tréimhse sin, tá gnéithe iontu a léiríonn tionchar na gcanúintí ar an scríbhneoireacht agus imeacht i léig na Gaeilge Clasaicí (Ó hUiginn 2008: 8).

Caighdeánú na Nua-Ghaeilge

Ionas an t-athrú urlabhra ó Ghaeilge go Béarla a chur ar mhalairt slí,
leagadh béim faoi leith ar chaomhnú agus ar chothú na Gaeilge sa cheathrú
dheireanach den naoú haois déag agus ag tús na fichiú haoise. Sa tréimhse sin
bunaíodh Cumann Buan-Choimeádta na Gaeilge sa bhliain 1876, Aontacht
na Gaeilge in 1880 agus Conradh na Gaeilge in 1893, agus tugadh ról lárnach
don Ghaeilge sa chóras oideachais tar éis bhunú an Stáit i 1922. D'fhág sin
go raibh an-bhéim ar theagasc na Gaeilge agus ar chruthú litríochta sa Nua-
Ghaeilge ag an am. Faoin am sin, áfach, b'easnamhach í an Ghaeilge ó thaobh
téarmaíochta agus caighdeáin de, agus ní rabhthas aontaithe ar litriú, ar
ghramadach ná ar chló agus glacadh leis go forleathan gur cheart rialacha
agus gramadach na Gaeilge a shainmhíniú athuair chun uirlis aonadach a
chur ar fáil don teagasc agus don scríbhneoireacht (Ó Riain 1994: 64). Is
amhlaidh gur glacadh leis an ngá a bhí le teanga náisiúnta chaighdeánach
a chruthú d'aonghuth agus gan mórán díospóireachta (Ó Laoire 1997: 20).

Ceist an Chló

Is sa chló Gaelach a scríobhadh na lámhscríbhinní Gaeilge ar fad nach
mór agus leanadh leis an nós sin sa chlódóireacht tar éis gur cuireadh cló
clódóireachta ar fáil sa séú haois déag a bhí bunaithe ar stíl na lámhscríbhinní
sin. 'Is léir gur tháinig an cheist faoi chló na Gaeilge chun cinn nuair a
tugadh faoi *Irisleabhar na Gaedhilge* a fhoilsiú mar bhí tús curtha leis an
Athbheochan agus bhí méadú thar cuimse ag teacht ar líon na bhfoilseachán
as Gaeilge' (Ó Conchubhair 2009: 149). Ar chúiseanna praiticiúla, moladh
in áiteanna gur cheart glacadh leis an gcló Rómhánach in áit an chló
Ghaelaigh mar go bhfágfadh a leithéid de chinneadh nach mbeadh fearas
difriúil clódóireachta ag teastáil don Ghaeilge, nach mbeadh ar léitheoirí
dul i dtaithí ar chló amháin don Bhéarla agus cló eile don Ghaeilge agus gur
b'fhurasta d'fhoghlaimeoirí in Éirinn agus i gcéin plé leis an gcló Rómhánach
a raibh taithí acu air cheana féin (Ó Conchubhair 2009: 162–163). Seachas
cruth na litreacha, ba é cur in iúl an tséimhithe an phríomhdhifríocht idir
an dá chló óir is le ponc os cionn na litreach a dheintí sin sa chló Gaelach

agus le 'h' i ndiaidh na litreach a dheintí é sa chló Rómhánach. Bhí níos mó i gceist sa choimhlint ná an chuma a bhí ar na litreacha, áfach. Coimhlint idir dhá dhearcadh a bhí ann go bunúsach, dearcadh coimeádach agus dearcadh forbarach, idir an sean agus an nua, idir a raibh 'fíor' agus a raibh 'bréagach' (Ó Dochartaigh 1989: 120). Fréamhaithe sa náisiúnachas cultúrtha a bhí tuiscint an dreama a bhí ar son chaomhnú an chló Ghaelaigh sa mhéid agus gur chreid siad gur ghá idirdhealú a dhéanamh idir Gaeilge agus Béarla, idir Éire agus Sasana, agus go bhféadfaí an t-idirdhealú sin a léiriú leis an gcló (Ó Conchubhair 2009: 146–150).

Bíodh agus gur glacadh leis an gcló Rómhánach d'*Irisleabhar na Gaedhilge* ó 1898 ar aghaidh, lean an díospóireacht ar aghaidh go ceann roinnt mhaith blianta. Sa bhliain 1931 ghlac rialtas Chumann na nGaedheal go hoifigiúil leis an gcló Rómhánach, ach d'fhill rialtas Fhianna Fáil ar an gcló Gaelach bliain níos déanaí agus is sa chló sin a scríobhadh bunreacht 1937. I bhfábhar an chló Rómhánaigh a bhí Rannóg an Aistriúcháin, ach níor glacadh leis mar chló éigeantach don Ardteistiméireacht go dtí go raibh an bhliain 1972 ann (Ó Riain 1994: 65), cinneadh a chuir deireadh leis an díospóireacht a bheag nó a mhór. Sa lá inniu is é an cló Rómhánach is gnách le daoine úsáid, ach baintear leas as an gcló Gaelach go fóill mar mhaisiúchán agus ar roinnt chomharthaí.

An Córas Litrithe

Is as córas scríbhneoireachta an tseachtú haois déag a bhí leas á bhaint ag tús na hAthbheochana, córas a bhí bunaithe ar an nGaeilge Chlasaiceach agus scríbhneoireacht Sheathrúin Chéitinn den chuid is mó. Bhí buntáiste ag dul leis an gcóras sin sa mhéid agus go raibh sé socair seasta cheana féin agus níor ghá aon obair a dhéanamh ach é a mhúineadh agus a chur i bhfeidhm. San am céanna, áfach, deirtear go raibh an saghas sin Gaeilge seanaimseartha agus ársa le linn do Chéitinn a bheith i mbun pinn sa seachtú haois déag (Ó Baoill 1988: 111) agus deirtear nach raibh sí ar a dtoil ach ag beagán scoláirí (Greene 1972: 15). Mar leagan den teanga a bhí ag teacht go mór leis an scríbhneoireacht ar fad siar chomh fada le 1200, b'fhacthas go raibh sé difriúil go maith ó Ghaeilge bheo na Gaeltachta (Mac Mathúna

2008: 79). Bhí baol ann, mar sin, go ndéanfaí imeallú ar chainteoirí na Gaeltachta agus orthu siúd a bhí tar éis an teanga a fhoghlaim cheana féin dá nglacfaí leis an nGaeilge Chlasaiceach mar chaighdeán don scríbhneoireacht (Ó Baoill 1988: 111).

Bhí malairt tuairim ag teacht chun cinn an t-am céanna áit ar moladh gur cheart an córas nua scríbhneoireachta a bhunú, ní ar an nGaeilge Chlasaiceach, ach, ar chaint bheo na Gaeltachta. I ndeireadh na dála, is ag gluaiseacht chaint na ndaoine agus an tAthair Peadar Ó Laoghaire a bhí an lá nuair a socraíodh gur cheart an scríbhneoireacht a bhunú ar chaint bheo na Gaeltachta. Mar gheall ar an gcinneadh sin, is ar fhoghraíocht chanúintí na Gaeltachta a bhí scríbhneoirí ag bunú a gcuid saothar, iad fós ag baint leasa go minic as litreacha inmheánacha a bhí ina litreacha balbha sa chuid is mó de na ceantair Ghaeltachta faoin am sin (Ó Baoill 1988: 112). Bíodh agus go raibh réiteach ar an aighneas faoi chaint na ndaoine agus faoin nGaeilge Chlasaiceach, níorbh ionann sin agus a rá go raibh córas aonadach caighdeánach i bhfeidhm ar scríobh na teanga.

An caighdeánú faoi stiúir an Stáit

Scríbhneoirí agus lucht léinn a phléigh agus a shocraigh ceist an chaighdeáin ag tús na hathbheochana, ach ghlac an stát smacht ar an dualgas sin i ndiaidh a bhunaithe. Díríodh ar an mírialtacht ba dhual don scríbhneoireacht Ghaeilge ag an am a thabhairt chun réitigh tar éis gur cuireadh an-bhéim ar theagasc na Gaeilge sa chóras oideachais agus ar aistriú cáipéisí oifigiúla tar éis bhunú an Stáit i 1922. Is ar ghrúpa scoláirí Gaeilge agus stáitseirbhíseach a bhronn Éamonn de Valera an fhreagracht seo i dtosach báire, ach nuair a theip orthu siúd réiteach lena chéile ar bhuncheisteanna an chúraim is ar Rannóg an Aistriúcháin a thit an dualgas agus is iad a chuir an caighdeán i dtoll a chéile. Thar aon rud eile, is sa tóir ar sheasmhacht inmheánach na teanga a bhí Rannóg an Aistriúcháin mar gurb é a theastaigh uathu ina gcuid oibre féin.

Ar mhaithe le litriú aonfhoirmeach a chur ar fáil a foilsíodh *Litriú na Gaeilge: An Caighdeán Oifigiúil* sa bhliain 1945 agus leagan níos cuimsithí, *Litriú na Gaeilge: Lámhleabhar an Chaighdeáin Oifigiúil*, dhá bhliain níos déanaí. Is iontu sin a leagtar amach córas litrithe simplithe nua a thugann tús áite do litriú a bhí níos cóngaraí d'fhoghraíocht an ama (Ó Baoill agus Ó Riagáin 1990: 183; Ó Laoire 1997: 21). Fuarthas réidh le litreacha balbha agus cuireadh gutaí le síneadh fada ina n-áit sa tslí agus gur deineadh 'oifigiúil' de 'oifigeamhail', agus 'oíche' de 'oidhche'. Chomh maith leis sin, deineadh athchóiriú ar na consain i gcásanna áirithe ionas, mar shampla, 'dearfa' a chur in áit 'dearbhtha', 'scéal' in áit 'sgéal' agus 'Nollaig' in áit 'Nodlaig'. Bíodh agus gur cáineadh na hathruithe seo in áiteanna agus gur eascair córas gramadaí níos casta astu i gcásanna áirithe (Wigger 1979), glacadh leo don fhoilsitheoireacht agus deineadh litriú caighdeánach díobh.

Gramadach

Ba é foilsiú *Gramadach na Gaeilge: Caighdeán Rannóg an Aistriúcháin* i 1953 an chéad iarracht a tugadh ar ghramadach na Gaeilge a shainiú. Ba é an foilseachán sin ba bhunús do phróiseas comhairliúcháin náisiúnta ar an gcaighdeán áit ar lorgaíodh tuairimí agus moltaí ó dhaoine as gach ceantar Gaeltachta, ó mhúinteoirí agus ó dhaoine eile a raibh eolas faoi leith acu ar an teanga (Rannóg an Aistriúcháin 1958). Cuireadh na moltaí sin san áireamh chomh maith le moltaí ó shaineolaithe ar an teanga agus *Gramadach na Gaeilge agus Litriú na Gaeilge: An Caighdeán Oifigiúil* á ullmhú. Toradh ar bheagnach leathchéad bliain oibre agus díospóireachta a bhí sna foilseacháin sin agus ullmhaíodh iad agus an-bhrú ama ar na húdair.

Bíodh agus gur aithin na húdair go mbeadh an caighdeán ina threoir úsáideach don phobal agus do mhúinteoirí (Rannóg an Aistriúcháin 1958: viii), níor thuig siad go múnlódh a gcinntí ar an gcaighdeán foirm na Gaeilge i ngach saghas téacs Gaeilge, i leabhair bhunscoile agus iarbhunscoile sa Ghaeltacht agus lasmuigh den Ghaeltacht, i nuachtáin agus úrscéalta, i scrúduithe, i leabhair urnaithe agus sa scrioptúr naofa, i gcomharthaí bóthair agus i ndrámaí stáitse, ar an gcraolachán agus ar an teilifís, i leabhair do pháistí réamhscoile, agus i bhfógraí báis (Williams 2006: 2). Sin mar a thit amach, áfach, mar ghlac lucht scríofa na Gaeilge leis an gcaighdeán mar chaighdeán docht saintreorach (Mac Mathúna 2008: 82). Toradh i bpáirt ba ea é sin ar chinneadh na Roinne Oideachais glacadh leis go hoifigiúil, cinneadh a chinntigh ról lárnach don chaighdeán tríd an scolaíocht (Ó hIfearnáin 2008: 124; Ó hIfearnáin agus Ó Murchadha 2011). Mar sin a deineadh caighdeán deifnídeach don scríbhneoireacht Ghaeilge as caighdeán a dearadh go príomha mar uirlis d'úsáid inmheánach Rannóg an Aistriúcháin.

Tabhairt chun réitigh An Chaighdeáin Oifigiúil agus na canúintí

Tar éis gur réitíodh an plé faoi sprioc an chaighdeánaithe agus an lá ag caint na ndaoine, ba é an chéad dúshlán eile conas éagsúlacht shuntasach réigiúnach na teanga labhartha a chur san áireamh sa chaighdeán aonadach scríofa úr. Leagtar béim sa chaighdeán ar ról lárnach urlabhra na Gaeltachta agus maítear nach gcuireann foirmeacha roghnaithe an chaighdeáin teir ná toirmeasc ar úsáid ceartfhoirmeacha eile (Rannóg an Aistriúcháin 1958: viii). Luaitear ceithre phríomhriail ar deineadh an caighdeán dá réir:

1. Chomh fada agus ab fhéidir sin gan glacadh le foirm ná le riail nach bhfuil údarás maith di i mbeochaint na Gaeltachta;
2. Rogha a dhéanamh de na leaganacha is forleithne atá in úsáid sa Ghaeltacht;
3. An tábhacht is dual a thabhairt do stair agus litríocht na Gaeilge;
4. An rialtacht agus an tsimplíocht a lorg.
   (Rannóg an Aistriúcháin 1958: viii)

Is léir ó léamh beacht ar na rialacha sin, ní hamháin gur doiléir iad, ach go bhfuil siad ag teacht salach ar a chéile chomh maith. Ní gá, mar shampla, gurb í an fhoirm is coitianta sa Ghaeltacht an fhoirm is simplí agus is rialta, ná gurb í an fhoirm is láidre bunús í i stair agus i litríocht na teanga.

Bíodh agus go bhfuil an caighdeán an-láidir ar ról tábhachtach na Gaeilge sa Ghaeltacht, is é an toradh a bhí ar a fhorbairt ná gur tugadh aitheantas dó mar leagan údarásach gradamach den teanga don scríbhneoireacht a dhéanann imeallú ar Ghaeilge labhartha na Gaeltachta ar a bhfuil sé in ainm is a bheith bunaithe. Sampla de sin é taithí an cheannródaithe teanga, Niall Ó Dónaill, a bhí go mór i bhfábhar caighdeán a bhunú ar leagan neodrach den teanga a fheidhmeodh mar sprioctheanga don scríbhneoireacht agus don chaint araon (féach Ó Dónaill 1951, mar shampla). Chonaic an Dálach sular i bhfad an chumhacht a ghlac foirmeacha caighdeánacha chucu féin thar fhoirmeacha traidisiúnta a raibh údarás maith dóibh i gcaint na Gaeltachta (Ó hIfearnáin 2008). B'ionann sin agus imeallú na gcanúintí Gaeltachta agus is féidir a mhaíomh nach de thaisme atá na canúintí Gaeltachta ag imeacht i léig, ach gur toradh i bpáirt é sin ar chur chun cinn an chaighdeáin mar fhoirm ardghradaim teanga (Ó hIfearnáin 2008).

Chítear an choimhlint sin idir an caighdeán agus canúintí na Gaeltachta arís i ndiúltú don chaighdeán ag roinnt daoine, go háirithe ag muintir na Gaeltachta, ar an mbonn é a bheith saorga agus mínádúrtha agus na canúintí a bheith nádúrtha barántúil. Léiriú iad lipéid mhaslacha cosúil le Gaeilge na státseirbhíse, Gaelscoilis, Gaeilge na leabhar agus Gaeilge Bhaile Átha Cliath ar choimhthíos lucht labhartha na gcanúintí i leith an chaighdeáin. Cruthúnas isea é ar na dúshláin a bhaineann le bheith ag iarraidh caighdeán aonfhoirmeach don scríbhneoireacht a chruthú le feidhmiú taobh le canúintí na teanga.

Fiú go bhfuil cuma dhaonlathach ar bhunú an chaighdeáin ar chanúintí na teanga agus go gceapfaí é a bheith oiriúnach mar straitéis le scríobh agus labhairt na teanga a thabhairt chun réitigh, ní hamhlaidh atá. Mar gheall ar fhás agus ar theacht chun cinn an chaighdeáin agus a fhoirmeacha roghnaithe sa chóras oideachais, sa chlódóireacht agus in obair oifigiúil an Stáit, aithnítear anois é mar leagan den teanga ann féin atá difriúil go maith ó chaint na Gaeltachta. Agus caighdeán aonfhoirmeach don scríbhneoireacht á chruthú le suí taobh le canúintí beo na Gaeltachta, cruthaíodh cód aonfhoirmeach nach bhfuil ag teacht go hiomlán le haon cheann de na canúintí traidisiúnta (Ó Laoire 1997). Eascraíonn ceisteanna faoi dhlisteanacht, faoi stádas agus faoi ghradam na gcanúintí agus an chaighdeáin féin as an bpróiseas sin.

An t-athbhreithniú oifigiúil ar an gcaighdeán

Bíodh agus gur foilsíodh ábhair eile a shoiléirigh pointí áirithe sa chaighdeáin agus a chuir comhairle ar fáil in áiteanna a raibh éiginnteacht (mar shampla in An Coiste Téarmaíochta 2003; Ó hAnluain 1960; 1999; Ó Dónaill 1977), táthar fós míshásta faoina dhoiléire agus a mhírialta agus atá an caighdeán don scríbhneoireacht. Deirtear gur deacair an caighdeán a mhúineadh mar go bhfuil sé an-difriúil ón nGaeilge sa ghnáthchaint laethúil (Ó Béarra 2009: 270; Williams 2006: 6); go bhfuil neamhréir sa chóras iolraithe d'ainmfhocail chosúla (Ó Béarra 2009: 270); gur róchasta gan ghá é córas na n-uimhreacha (Ó Mianáin 2003); nach bhfuil na téacsanna údarásacha ar an gcaighdeán ag teacht lena chéile; gur casta í foirm ghiniúnach na n-ainmfhocal le lagiolra agus gur an-difriúil í ón méid a chloistear sa ghnáthchaint laethúil (Ó Béarra 2009); agus nach raibh an caighdeán ag teacht leis an gcaint chomhaimseartha nuair a foilsíodh é céad lá (Ó Béarra 2009). Ó shin, labhair roinnt daoine ar son athbhreithnithe, agus bhí dream áirithe i bhfábhar caighdeán leathan agus caighdeán cúng a bhunú (féach, mar shampla Ó Baoill 2000; Williams 2006).

Thug an Stát aitheantas oifigiúil don ghá le hathbhreithniú ar an gCaighdeán Oifigiúil i Mí na Samhna 2008 nuair a d'fhógair an tAire Gnóthaí Pobail, Tuaithe agus Gaeltachta go gcuirfí próiseas athbhreithnithe ar bun a mbeadh toradh air i Mí an Mheithimh 2011, a dúradh. Bunaíodh coiste chun an próiseas a stiúradh, coiste ar a ainmníodh an tAire, ionadaithe ainmnithe ón saol acadúil, ón gCoiste Téarmaíochta, ó fhoireann an fhoclóra úir Béarla-Gaeilge, ó Rannóg an Aistriúcháin, agus ó na meáin chlóite. Mholadh an coiste leasuithe agus d'fháiltíodh sé ansin roimh thuairimí an phobail ar na moltaí sin le linn tréimhsí comhairliúcháin. Is ar úsáid an tséimhithe i gcásanna áirithe a dhírigh an chéad tréimhse comhairliúcháin. Ar an ainmfhocal cáilithe agus an tuiseal giniúnach a bhí an dara tréimhse dírithe. Díríodh ar chóras na n-uimhreacha sa tríú tréimhse agus is iad na claochluithe tosaigh a bhí faoi chaibidil sa cheathrú tréimhse. Sa chúigiú tréimhse, is é córas na mbriathra a bhí faoi chaibidil. Tugann an coiste údar le gach moladh ag tagairt do sheasmhacht inmheánach na teanga, don tsoiléireacht, don tsimplíocht, do na foirmeacha is coitianta i gcaint na Gaeltachta agus do na foirmeacha a dtugtar aitheantas dóibh i dtéacsanna údarásacha an chaighdeáin. Próiseas níos follasaí ná iarrachtaí na gcaogaidí atá ann sa mhéid agus go n-eagraítear tréimhsí comhairliúcháin, go luaitear bunús le gach moladh, agus go n-ainmnítear an coiste. Is fiú aird a thabhairt don tosaíocht a thugtar do chaint na Gaeltachta arís ann, seachas aon saghas eile cainte, agus go mbronntar stádas údarásach ar chaint na Gaeltachta mar gheall air sin.

An Ghaeilge labhartha

Rangaítear an Ghaeilge chomhaimseartha labhartha anseo ar chontanam a shíneann ó chaint thraidisiúnta Ghaeltachta, go caint na hóige Gaeltachta agus ar aghaidh go caint iar-Ghealtachta. Seachas rangú docht daingean ar shaghsanna agus ar stíleanna na Gaeilge labhartha is contanam atá i gceist leis an múnla seo ar féidir an Ghaeilge labhartha a rangú air.

Gaeilge Thraidisiúnta Ghaeltachta

Creidtear gur le linn ré na Nua-Ghaeilge Moiche a tháinig éagsúlacht teanga ar bhonn réigiúnach chun cinn ar dtús sa Ghaeilge labhartha. Sa lá inniu, is iad canúintí Uladh, Chonnachta agus na Mumhan príomhchanúintí Gaeltachta na Nua-Ghaeilge. Tá siad ag teacht cuid mhór le bunfhoirmeacha comónta na Gaeilge (Ó Murchú 1969; Ó Siadhail 1989), ach tá difríochtaí áitiúla faoi leith le sonrú orthu san am céanna. Is féidir ina dhiaidh sin na príomhchanúintí a rangú ina bhfochanúintí bunaithe ar éagsúlacht réigiúnach mar atá na Déise, Múscraí agus Corca Dhuibhne i gcás na Mumhan, mar shampla. Bíodh agus gur ann do dhifríochtaí foclóra agus comhréire, tugann sonraí ó ghrúpaí fócais a eagraíodh le cuid de chohórt an taighde reatha, a ndéantar cur síos orthu thíos, le tuiscint gurb iad na difríochtaí foghraíochta agus prosóide is mó a scarann na canúintí traidisiúnta Gaeltachta óna chéile, dar leis na rannpháirtithe.

Agus Ó Siadhail (1989: 4) ag labhairt i dtéarmaí ginearálta, deir sé gur contanam atá i gceist leis na canúintí réigiúnacha agus é ag síneadh ó Chúige Uladh sa tuaisceart chomh fada le Cúige Mumhan sa deisceart agus an Ghaillimh mar phointe láir aige. Is don chaint choimeádach áitiúil a thagraíonn Gaeilge thraidisiúnta Ghaeltachta, más ea. Is beag tionchair de chuid an Bhéarla a chítear inti. Is i measc cainteoirí a rugadh roimh 1960 is mó a chloistear í (Ó Curnáin 2007; Ó hIfearnáin agus Ó Murchadha 2011) agus sonraítear difríochtaí réigiúnacha ann sa bhfoghraíocht, sa bhéim, sa phrosóid, sa bhfoclóir agus sa chomhréir (Ó hIfearnáin agus Ó Murchadha 2011).

Caint na hÓige Gaeltachta

Is iad canúintí traidisiúnta na gceantar áitiúla Gaeltachta na múnlaí follasacha ag caint na hóige Gaeltachta agus tá difríochtaí réigiúnacha le sonrú ó cheantar Gaeltachta go ceantar Gaeltachta, dá réir sin. Tá an saghas seo Gaeilge, áfach, ag imeacht ón gcaint thraidisiúnta áitiúil (Hickey 2011; Ó Curnáin 2007; 2012a; 2012b) agus ag bogadh i dtreo saghas cainte a bhfuil tionchar uirthi ag an mBéarla, ag Gaeilge na meán craolta, ag an nGaeilge ar scoil agus ag Gaeilge iar-Ghaeltachta an phobail athbheochanóirí (Ó hIfearnáin agus Ó Murchadha 2011). Tugtar é seo faoi ndeara sa bhfoghraíocht, sa bhfoclóir, sa ghramadach agus sa chomhréir.

Bíodh agus go gcoimeádtar roinnt de na gnéithe is suntasaí den chanúint áitiúil, tagann athruithe eile chun cinn chomh maith. I gcaint na hóige Gaeltachta sna Déise, mar shampla, coimeádtar an défhoghar [ai] i bhfocail cosúil le *im* [aim'] agus an défhoghar céanna taobh le consan coguasach srónach [ŋ'] i bhfocail cosúil le *tinn* [t'aiŋ'], *linn* [l'aiŋ'] agus *binn* [b'aiŋ'], ach san am céanna bogann na consain ailbheolacha chuimilteacha [r] agus [r'] i dtreo an ailbheolaigh [ɹ]. Tugtar athruithe faoi ndeara sa chóras fóinéimeach áit a mbaintear leas go minic as fóinéimí Béarla sa chás agus go bhfuil consain agus cairn chonsan na Gaeilge difriúil ón mBéarla. Mar sin, déantar [ɹ] de [r] agus [r'], fágtar séimhiú ar lár uaireanta ionas go ndéantar consain phléascacha [k] agus [k'] go minic as chonsain choguasacha chuimilteacha chiúine [x] agus [x'].

Ag baint leasa as rangú Dorian (1981: 19), áitíonn Ó hIfearnáin (2008: 120) gur féidir cur síos ar líon suntasach de chainteoirí óga na Gaeltachta mar chainteoirí óga líofa. I measc cainteoirí a rugadh tar éis 1980 is mó atá tréithe de chaint na hóige Gaeltachta le sonrú agus bíonn sí le cloisint go minic ar chláir don aos óg sna meáin chraolta Ghaeilge.

Caint iar-Ghaeltachta

Cleachtann cainteoirí lasmuigh den Ghaeltacht raon leathan stíleanna agus saghsanna Gaeilge. Díríonn cuid mhaith acu ar cheann de na canúintí réigiúnacha mar mhúnla. Glactar leis go forleathan, áfach, go bhfuil saghas eile Gaeilge tar éis teacht chun cinn i measc cainteoirí athbheochana lasmuigh den Ghaeltacht (Hickey 2011; Mac Mathúna 2008; Nic Pháidín 2003; Ó hIfearnáin agus Ó Murchadha 2011). Gaeilge iar-Ghaeltachta a thugtar ar an saghas sin Gaeilge anseo. Faoi mar atá amhlaidh ag a leithéid de chaint neamhthraidisiúnta sa Bhriotáinis (Hornsby 2005) agus sa Bhreatnais (Robert 2009), is beag an chomparáid idir an dearcadh a fhéachann ar chaint iar-Ghaeltachta mar leagan saorga den teanga agus an dearcadh a fhéachann ar bharántúlacht agus nádúracht na gcanúintí traidisiúnta Gaeltachta. Ceaptar gur ionann an saghas sin cainte agus caint chaighdeánach, fiú i measc cainteoirí iar-Ghaeltachta iad féin uaireanta. Bíodh agus nach bhfuil an méid sin iomlán cruinn, is dócha go dtagann sé ón nasc idir an saghas sin cainte agus an córas oideachais trí mheán na Gaeilge lasmuigh den Ghaeltacht agus suíomh lárnach an chaighdeáin mar mhúnla don teanga scríofa sa chóras oideachais ó bhreith an Chaighdeáin Oifigiúil sa bhliain 1958 (Ó hIfearnáin agus Ó Murchadha 2011).

Ní nasctar caint iar-Ghaeltachta le cohórt aoise faoi leith agus tá sí forleathan i measc cainteoirí óga agus aosta lasmuigh den Ghaeltacht. Is iad tionchar an Bhéarla ar an bhfoghraíocht, ar an gcomhréir agus ar an bprosóid na comharthaí sóirt lena n-aithnítear caint iar-Ghaeltachta agus is suntasach nach bhfuil múnla soiléir Gaeltachta le sonrú uirthi.

Sonraí Obair Pháirce

Cuirtear i láthair anseo cuid de na sonraí ó obair pháirce le 262 dalta,
iad ar fad in aois 15–19 bliana d'aois, ón tsraith shinsearach iarbhunscoile
i gceantair Ghaeltachta na Mumhan. Is le tástáil mheasúnú cainteora a
bailíodh na sonraí. Dhein na rannpháirtithe measúnú ar shamplaí cainte
a roghnaíodh ó RTÉ Raidió na Gaeltachta agus ó Raidió na Life. Bíodh
agus nach nglactar leis go huilíoch, glactar leis go forleathan faoin am
seo go mbíonn baint ag idé-eolaíocht cainteoirí i leith saghsanna difriúla
teanga leis an tslí a labhrann na cainteoirí céanna iad féin (Blommaert
2009; Garrett 2010; Kristiansen 2003; Niedzielski agus Preston 2003).
Déantar iniúchadh ar idé-eolaíocht na rannpháirtithe i leith na saghsanna
Gaeilge atá níos caighdeánaí, dar leo, ionas léargas a fháil ar an nasc idir an
idé-eolaíocht sin agus urlabhra an aos óig Ghaeltachta.

　　Mar fhorbairt ar obair Lambert et al. (1960) agus ag leanúint taighde
sa Danmhairg (Kristiansen 2003) agus san Ísiltír (Grondelaers agus van
Hout 2010), iarradh ar na rannpháirtithe measúnú a dhéanamh ar aon
sampla déag de chainteoirí baineannacha. Cúig shoicind déag an ceann
a mhair na samplaí. Roghnaíodh na samplaí ionas na saghsanna agus na
stíleanna Gaeilge atá luaite thuas a bheith san áireamh: caint thraidisiúnta
Ghaeltachta; caint na hóige Gaeltachta; agus caint iar-Ghaeltachta. San
aon sampla déag sin, bhí san áireamh aon sampla amháin den chaint iar-
Ghaeltachta agus deich sampla den chaint Ghaeltachta. Is ar chanúint
na nDéise, Mhúscraí, Chorca Dhuibhne, Chonnacht agus Uladh atá na
samplaí Gaeltachta dírithe. Cuireadh sampla de chainteoir traidisiúnta
agus de chainteoir óg i láthair do gach ceann de na ceantair Ghaeltachta sin.

　　Seinneadh na samplaí faoi thrí do na rannpháirtithe. Roimh thús
na tástála dúradh leis na rannpháirtithe go raibh siad le páirt a ghlacadh
i dtástáil agus go dtabharfaí breis eolais dóibh ina taobh ar ball. Agus na
samplaí á seinnt don chéad uair seinneadh gan stad iad ó thús go deireadh
agus níor cuireadh de chúram ar na rannpháirtithe ach éisteacht go cúramach
agus dul i dtaithí ar leagan amach na samplaí. Seinneadh na samplaí don
dara huair le sos cúig shoicind déag idir na cainteoirí agus iarradh ar na

rannpháirtithe freagairt ar ocht scála aidiachta ar a raibh seacht bpointe agus a thagair do phearsantacht an chainteora. Roimh sheinnt na samplaí don tríú huair dúradh leis na rannpháirtithe gurb í sprioc an taighde a dtuairimí agus a léamh siúd a fháil ar shaghsanna agus ar stíleanna difriúla Gaeilge, ach dúradh go raibh sé tábhachtach nach raibh an méid sin ar eolas acu roimh thús na tástála. Iarradh orthu smaoineamh ar an sprioc sin agus an chuid dheireanach den tástáil á chur i gcrích acu. Seinneadh na samplaí don tríú huair agus ag baint leasa as scálaí ar a raibh seacht bpointe ag síneadh ó 'Aontaím' go 'Ní aontaím' thug na rannpháirtithe freagra ar cheithre ráiteas maidir leis na saghsanna cainte sna samplaí. Chomh maith leis sin, luaigh na rannpháirtithe an áit arb as don chainteoir agus an chuma a bheadh uirthi, dar leo. Cuireadh leagan Gaeilge agus leagan Béarla de na huirlisí measúnaithe ar fad ar fáil agus ba é an leagan Gaeilge nó meascán de Ghaeilge agus de Bhéarla a roghnaigh formhór na rannpháirtithe (87.4 faoin gcéad).

Dírítear thíos ar chuid de na sonraí ón gcuid den taighde ina raibh cuspóir na hoibre ar eolas ag na rannpháirtithe, is é sin na freagraí a tugadh ar an ráiteas 'Labhrann an duine seo go caighdeánach'. Taispeánann na torthaí go bhfuil léamh na rannpháirtithe ar an rud atá caighdeánach ag teacht leis an saghas Gaeilge a chleachtar ina bpiarghrúpa féin. Is é sin go labhrann siad féin go caighdeánach, nó níos caighdeánaí ná cainteoirí traidisiúnta, pé scéal é. Tagann na torthaí i gcoinne áiteamh Labov (2001) ina ndéanann sé beag de thionchar na hidé-eolaíochta teanga ar an aistriú urlabhra. Tugann siad le tuiscint go bhfuil ról lárnach ag an idé-eolaíocht teanga sa phróiseas sin agus léiríonn siad, i gcás na Gaeilge, go bhfuil cumhacht faoi leith ag an saghas Gaeilge a shíltear a bheith caighdeánach sa phróiseas ina bhfuil urlabhra na Gaeltachta ag athrú. Bheadh breis iniúchadh agus breis taighde de dhíth, dar ndóigh, le féachaint an amhlaidh atá an scéal sna ceantair eile Ghaeltachta, ag cainteoirí iar-Ghaeltachta agus ag cainteoirí lasmuigh den aoisghrúpa ar deineadh staidéar orthu sa taighde seo.

Torthaí

Léiríonn Tábla 1 freagraí na rannpháirtithe ar an ráiteas 'Labhrann an duine seo go caighdeánach' agus iad ag tagairt do na samplaí a seinneadh dóibh. Ar mhaithe leis an gcur i láthair is iad torthaí Chorca Dhuibhne agus Uíbh Ráthaigh amháin atá san áireamh, ach is ionann an pátrún anseo agus an pátrún sa chohórt ina iomláine agus dá réir sin léirítear tuairimí na gceantar eile iontu chomh maith. Is é is tábhachtaí le tabhairt faoi ndeara anseo ná an t-ord ina ndéantar rangú ar na saghsanna agus ar na stíleanna difriúla Gaeilge ó thaobh caighdeánachta de. Ceaptar gur caighdeánaí í caint na hóige Gaeltachta i gCúige Mumhan agus caint na hiar-Ghaeltachta ná caint thraidisiúnta na Mumhan. Ceaptar gur caighdeánaí í caint óige Chonnachta, fiú, ná caint thraidisiúnta na Mumhan seachas caint thraidisiúnta Mhúscraí. Léargas ar choimhthíos na rannpháirtithe Muimhneacha seo i leith caint Uladh é a suíomh ag an taobh diúltach den scála. Diúltú do chaint Uladh mar fhoirm neamhchaighdeánach teanga a bhíonn mar thoradh ar an gcoimhthíos sin agus is féidir an méid céanna a mhaíomh i dtaobh cainteoir traidisiúnta Chonnachta agus a suíomh in aice lár an scála.

Tábla 7.1 Freagraí na rannpháirtithe ar an ráiteas
'Labhrann an duine seo go caighdeánach'

Labhrann an duine seo go caighdeánach		
Aontaím 1 2 3 4 5 6 7 Ní Aontaím		
Saghas Cainte	N	Meán
Óg, Áitiúil	91	2.84
Óg, Múrscaí	92	2.93
Óg, Na Déise	89	2.96
Iar-Ghaeltacht	92	3.12
Traidisiúinta, Múscraí	92	3.24
Óg, Connachta	91	3.36

Traidisiúnta, Na Déise	92	3.46
Traidisiúnta, Áitiúil	91	3.73
Traidisiúnta, Connachta	92	3.84
Óg, Ulaidh	92	4.29
Traidisiúnta, Ulaidh	92	4.38
N Bailí	88	

D'fhéadfaí tarraingt ar reitric agus ar dhioscúrsa comhaimseartha ina mbítear ag caitheamh anuas ar an rud atá caighdeánach go minic i dtaca leis na torthaí le maíomh gur léiriú atá sna torthaí ar dhiúltú na rannpháirtithe don rud a shíleann siad a bheith caighdeánach. Dá chaighdeánaí an chaint isea is measa í sa léamh seo agus, mar sin, diúltú do chaint na hóige Gaeltachta agus don chaint iar-Ghaeltachta ar an mbonn go bhfuil siad saorga a bheadh ina n-aithint mar leaganacha caighdeánacha teanga. Léiriú ar ghradam na gcanúintí traidisiúnta a bheadh ina n-aithint sin mar leaganacha neamhchaighdeánacha teanga. Ní dócha gur amhlaidh atá an scéal.

Is é is dócha atá amhlaidh ná go bhfuil aitheantas á léiriú ag na rannpháirtithe le caint na hóige Gaeltachta as Cúige Mumhan agus le caint iar-Ghaeltachta (agus caint óige Chonnacht go pointe áirithe) agus go n-aithníonn siad gurb iad is gaire dá gcuid cainte féin. Is ionann na rannpháirtithe ag ainmniú na saghsanna seo Gaeilge ar na leaganacha is caighdeánaí agus a rá go labhrann siad féin go caighdeánach agus gurb é an rud a shíleann siad a bheith caighdeánach a stiúrann a gcuid cainte féin. Is féidir a mhaíomh, más ea, gurb iad caint na hóige Gaeltachta agus caint na hiar-Ghaeltachta, seachas caint thraidisiúnta na Gaeltachta, a fheidhmíonn mar mhúnlaí teanga do chainteoirí óga Gaeilge i gceantair Ghaeltachta na Mumhan, fiú gur múnlaí iad nach n-ainmníonn siad go hoscailte. Mar thaca leis na torthaí thuas, léiríonn imeacht i léig na gcanúintí traidisiúnta Gaeltachta agus teacht chun cinn saghsanna úra cainte ina n-áit go bhfuil múnlaí úra teanga ag teacht chun cinn sa Ghaeltacht seachas na múnlaí traidisiúnta. Tá na múnlaí sin intuigthe sna hathruithe atá ag teacht ar urlabhra chomhaimseartha na Gaeltachta. Toradh i bpáirt é an t-aistriú urlabhra seo ar idé-eolaíocht agus ar dhearcadh na hóige Gaeltachta a aithníonn caint na hóige Gaeltachta mar mhúnla don teanga labhartha a bhronnann gradam ar na saghsanna cainte seo a shíleann siad a bheith níos caighdeánaí (mar a mhíníonn Ó Murchadha 2012).

Plé

Bhí ról tábhachtach ag caighdeánú na teanga ar fhorbairt noirm don litriú agus don ghramadach sa Ghaeilge trí roghnú na bhfoirmeacha údarásacha, códú na foirme, cur i bhfeidhm agus leathnú feidhme. Múnla éifeachtach é don scríbhneoireacht Ghaeilge agus tugtar aitheantas dó as sin, in ainneoin roinnt aimhrialtachta. Fiú go raibh rath ar an gcaighdeán i sainiú córas scríbhneoireachta don Ghaeilge, ní aithnítear é mar leagan scríofa den teanga a thugann tús áite do na canúintí ar fad Gaeltachta bíodh agus gurb é seo a bhí ar cheann de phríomhspriocanna an chaighdeáin. Seachas sin, leagann an caighdeán béim ar chásanna ina bhfuil na canúintí ag imeacht ón rud atá caighdeánach agus léiríonn sé cé chomh difriúil agus atá na canúintí i gcásanna áirithe, faoi mar a aithníodh áiteanna eile (Dorian 1981: 19). Baintear an bonn den chaint thraidisiúnta Ghaeltachta, a fheidhmíonn cheana féin mar theanga 'L' sa tsochaí dhébhéascnach, mar gheall ar an mothú íslechta seo.

Sa tslí sin, tagann na torthaí thuas le taighde eile ar ról lárnach na hidé-eolaíochta teanga sa phróiseas ina dtagann athrú ar an urlabhra (féach, mar shampla, Blommaert 2009; Garrett 2010; Kristiansen 2003; Niedzielski agus Preston 2009). Léiríonn na torthaí gur gaire í caint na hóige Gaeltachta don chaint atá níos caighdeánaí, dar leis na rannpháirtithe, ná don saghas cainte a dtugann siad aitheantas dó mar mhúnla follasach don chaint údarásach ghradamach .i. an chaint thraidisiúnta áitiúil.

Ó thús na fichiú haoise is ar bhunshainmhíniú an chaighdeáin a dhírítear sa phlé ar chaighdeánú na Gaeilge – cruthú córas aonfhoirmeach scríbhneoireachta. Ní thugtar aird chuí ar thábhacht ná ar thionchar cruthú leagan aonfhoirmeach den teanga. Tá débhrí ag gabháil le gradam agus le caighdeánacht na teanga Gaeilge mar thoradh ar leagan caighdeánach aonfhoirmeach den teanga a chruthú don scríbhneoireacht gan aird chuí a dhéanamh de chumhacht ná de shainmhíniú idé-eolaíochtúil an chaighdeáin. In iomaíocht lena chéile ar mhaithe le gradam atá coincheap na teanga caighdeánaí agus canúintí na Gaeltachta. Tá na canúintí traidisiúnta Gaeltachta ag imeacht i léig agus saghsanna eile cainte a shíltear a bheith níos caighdeánaí ag teacht chun cinn ina n-áiteanna. Tá an méid sin ag titim amach san am céanna a gcuirtear an caighdeán chun cinn mar leagan gradamach den teanga, go háirithe tríd an gcóras oideachais.

Mar straitéis dírithe ar chaomhnú na gcanúintí traidisiúnta, theip glan ar chur chun cinn agus ar aithint na gcanúintí traidisiúnta mar mhúnlaí teanga. Chomh maith leis sin, d'fhéadfadh an cur chuige sin imeallú a dhéanamh ar chainteoirí iar-Ghaeltachta mar nach dtugtar an t-aitheantas céanna do ról an tsaghais sin cainte sa ghné sin d'athneartú na teanga. Is suntasach é sin óir is lasmuigh den Ghaeltacht is mó a chítear méadú ar líon na gcainteoirí laethúla Gaeilge i bhfigiúirí an daonáirimh.

D'fhéadfadh torthaí fiúntacha teacht as féachaint ar mhúnlaí malartacha an chaighdeánaithe, go háirithe tabhairt chun réitigh na saincheisteanna údaráis agus barántúlachta a théann le saghsanna agus stíleanna difriúla Gaeilge. Chomh maith le dhá chaighdeán a aithint don scríbhneoireacht, cuireann múnla na hIoruaise reachtaíocht ar fáil le go gcuirfeadh múinteoirí a gcuid cainte in oiriúint don chanúint áitiúil agus cuirtear canúint áitiúil an cheantair chun cinn i measc na ndaltaí. Teanga il-lárnaíoch í an Ocsatáinis a thugann tosach áite don éagsúlacht réigiúnach sa chóras scríbhneoireachta. Bíodh agus gur bunaithe ar mhúnla na Fraincise atá caighdeán na Briotáinise agus gur theip air mar phróiseas, glactar ann le noirm áitiúla ('badume', atá bunaithe ar nath sa Bhriotáinis a chiallaíonn 'timpeall na háite seo) seachas noirm lárnacha a cuireadh i bhfeidhm ar an teanga (Hornsby 2010). Tá lucht na Corsacaise le tamall anois ag cuimsiú choincheap an 'polynomie'. Féachtar ar an gCorsacais mar theanga ina bhfuil éagsúlacht inmheánach na teanga ina gné lárnach den phleanáil teanga agus déantar iarracht aontas teangeolaíochta a bhaint amach trí struchtúr cuimsitheach na teanga a dhiúltaíonn don chéimlathas.

Is fiú smaoineamh ar na múnlaí malartacha agus caighdeánú na Gaeilge
á phlé mar is féidir a mhaíomh gur ar aimhleas na gcanúintí Gaeltachta
a bhí cruthú an chaighdeáin aonfhoirmigh agus go mb'fhéidir gur chuir
sé lena n-imeacht i léig, fiú. Ní ceart gurb í an tseasmhacht inmheánach
agus cruthú leagan aonfhoirmeach den teanga ar mhaithe leis an gcóras
scríbhneoireachta amháin a bheadh mar sprioc ag caighdeánú na Gaeilge,
ach cur chun cinn agus cothú na héagsúlachta ag léibhéal réigiúnach. Tá
géarghá le hathmheasúnú ar Chaighdeán Oifigiúil na Gaeilge agus an ról
a d'fhéadfadh a bheith aige i gcaomhnú na héagsúlachta teangeolaíochta
leis an sprioc seo a luaitear sa chaighdeán a bhaint amach. D'fhéadfadh
gurb é réiteach na ceiste glacadh le múnla malartach nó straitéisí a chur
i bhfeidhm ina dtugtar aitheantas do dhifríochtaí teangeolaíochta
réigiúnacha sa chaighdeán athbhreithnithe. Níl na cúinsí cuí ann faoi láthair
le go mairfeadh caighdeán aonfhoirmeach don scríbhneoireacht taobh le
canúintí na Gaeltachta.

Is le cúnamh maoinithe ón gComhairle um Thaighde sna Dána agus sna
hEolaíochtaí sóisialta a cuireadh an taighde seo i gcrích.

Tagairtí

An Coiste Téarmaíochta (2003). *Moltaí faoi Úsáid an tSéimhithe i gCásanna ar Leith*.
   Baile Átha Cliath: An Coiste Téarmaíochta.
Auer, P. (2005). 'Europe's sociolinguistic unity: Or, a typology of European dialect/
   standard constellations'. In N. Delbeque, J. Van Der Auwera, agus D. Geeraerts
   (eagí), *Perspectives on Variation*, pp. 7–42, Beirlín: de Gruyter.
Blommaert, J. (2009). 'A Sociolinguistics of globalization'. In N. Coupland agus
   Jaworski (eagí), *The New Sociolinguistics Reader*, pp. 560–573, Basingstoke: Pal-
   grave Macmillan.
Coupland, N. (2000). 'Sociolinguistic prevarication over standard English', Review
   Article: Review of T. Bex agus R. Watts (eagí 1999) *Standard English: The Wid-
   ening Debate*, Londain: Routledge, *Journal of Sociolinguistics* 4(4): 630–642.

Coupland, N. (2007). *Style: Language Variation and Identity*. Cambridge: Cambridge University Press.

Deumert, A. agus Vandenbussche, W. (2003). 'Research directions in the study of standard languages'. In A. Deumert agus W. Vandenbussche (eagí), *Germanic Standardizations: Past to Present*, pp. 455–470, Philadelphia: John Benjamins.

Dorian, N. (1981). *Language Death*. Philadelphia: University of Pennsylvania Press.

Eckert, P. (2000). *Linguistic Variation as Social Practice*. Oxford: Blackwell.

Foley, W. (1997). *Anthopological Linguistics: An Introduction*. Oxford: Blackwell.

Greene, D. (1972). *Writing in Irish Today*. Baile Átha Cliath: Mercier Press.

Grondelaers, S. agus van Hout, R. (2010). 'Is Standard Dutch with a regional accent standard or not?, *Language Variation and Change*, 22, 221–239.

Haugen, E. (1959). 'Planning for a standard language in modern Norway', *Anthropological Linguistics*, 1(3), 8–21.

Haugen, E. (1966). 'Dialect, language, nation', *American Anthropologist*, 68(4), 922–935.

Hickey, R. (2011). *The Dialects of Irish*. Beirlín: de Gruyter.

Hornsby, M. (2005). '*Neo-breton* and questions of authenticity', *Estudios de Sociolingüística*, 6(2), 191–218.

Hornsby, M. (2010). 'From the periphery to the centre: Recent debates on the role of Breton (and other regional languages) in the French Republic', *Marginal Dialects: Scotland, Ireland and beyond*, 171–197.

Kristiansen, T. (2003). 'The youth and the gatekeepers: Reproduction and change in language norm and variation'. In J.K. Androutsopoulos agus A. Georgakopoulou (eagí), *Discourse Constructions of Youth Identities*, pp. 279–302, Amsterdam: Benjamins.

Labov, W. (2001). *Principles of Linguistic Change: Social Factors*. Oxford: Blackwell.

Lambert, W., Hodgson, R.C., Gardner, R.C. agus Fillenbaum, S. (1960). 'Evaluational reactions to spoken language', *Journal of Abnormal and Social Psychology*, 60, 44–51.

Lippi-Green, R. (1997). *English With an Accent*. Londain: Routledge.

Lodge, R.A. (1993). *French: From Dialect to Standard*. Nua Eabhrac: Routledge.

Mac Mathúna, L. (2008). 'Linguistic change and standardization'. In C. Nic Pháidín agus S. Ó Cearnaigh (eagí), *A New View of the Irish Language*, pp. 76–92, Baile Átha Cliath: Cois Life.

Milroy, J. (2001). 'Language ideologies and the consequences of standardization', *Journal of Sociolinguistics*, 5(4), 530–555.

Milroy, J. agus Milroy, L. (1999). *Authority in Language: Investigating Standard English*. Londain: Routledge.

Nevalainen, T. (2003). 'English'. In A. Deumert agus W. Vandenbussche (eagí), *Germanic Standardizations: Past to Present*, pp. 127–157, Philadelphia: John Benjamins.

Nic Pháidín, C. (2003). 'Cén fáth nach: Ó chanúint go críól'. In R. Ní Mhianáin
    (eag.), *Idir Lúibíní*, pp. 103–120, Baile Átha Cliath: Cois Life.
Niedzielski, N. agus Preston, D. (2009). 'Folk linguistics'. In N. Coupland agus
    A. Jaworski (eagí), *The New Sociolinguistics Reader*, pp. 356–373, Basingstoke:
    Palgrave Macmillan.
Oakes, L. (2001). *Language and National Identity: Comparing France and Sweden*.
    Philadelphia: John Benjamins.
Ó Baoill, D.P. (1988). 'Language planning in Ireland: The standardization of Irish',
    International Journal of the Sociology of Language, 70, 109–126.
Ó Baoill, D. agus Ó Riagáin, P. (1990). 'Reform of the orthography, grammar and
    vocabulary of Irish'. In I. Fodor agus C. Hegege (eag.), *Language Reform: History
    and Future*, pp. 73–95, Hamburg, Helmut Buske.
Ó Béarra, F. (2009). 'An Ghaeilge nua agus triall na Gaeilge'. In M. Mac Craith agus
    P. Ó Héalaí (eag.), *Diasa Díograise: Aistí in Ómós do Mháirtín Ó Briain*, pp. 259–
    276, Indreabhán: Cló Iar-Chonnachta.
Ó Conchubhair, B. (2009). *Fin de Siècle na Gaeilge*. Indreabhán: Cló Iar-Chonnachta.
Ó Curnáin, B. (2007). *The Irish of Iorras Aithneach, Co. Galway*. Baile Átha Cliath:
    Institiúid Ard-Léinn Átha Cliath.
Ó Curnáin, B. (2012a). 'An Ghaeilge iarthraidisiúnta agus pragmataic a chódmheasctha
    thiar agus theas'. In C. Lenoach, C. Ó Giollagáin agus B. Ó Curnáin (eagí), *An
    Chonair Chaoch: An mionteangachas sa dátheangachas*, pp. 284–365, Indreab-
    hán: Leabhar Breac.
Curnáin, B. (2012b). 'An chanúineolaíocht'. In T. Ó hIfearnáin agus M. Ní Neachtain
    (eagí), *An tSochtheangeolaíocht: Tuairisc agus feidhm*, pp. 83–109, Baile Átha
    Cliath: Cois Life.
Ó Dochartaigh, L. (1989). 'Cúis na Gaeilge – Cúis ar strae'. In E. Ó hAnluain
    (eag.), *Léachtaí Uí Chadhain 1 (1980–1988)*, pp. 116–133, Baile Átha Cliath: An
    Clóchomhar.
Ó Dónaill, N. (1951). *Forbairt na Gaeilge*. Baile Átha Cliath: Sáirséal agus Dill.
Ó Dónaill, N. (1977). *Foclóir Gaeilge-Béarla*. Baile Átha Cliath: An Gúm.
Ó Donnchadha, D. (1995). *Castar an Taoide*. Baile Átha Cliath: Coiscéim.
Ó hAnluain, L. (1960). *Graiméar Gaeilge na mBráithre Críostaí*. Baile Átha Cliath:
    An Gúm.
Ó hIfearnáin, T. (2006). *Beartas Teanga: An Aimsir Óg, Páipéar Ócáideach 7*. Baile
    Átha Cliath: Coiscéim.
Ó hIfearnáin, T. (2008). 'Endangering language vitality through institutional devel-
    opment: Ideology, authority and Official Standard Irish in the Gaeltacht'. In
    K. King, N. Schilling-Estes, L. Fogle, J.J. Lou agus B. Soukup (eagí), *Sustaining*

Linguistic Diversity: Endangered and Minority Languages and Language Varieties, pp. 113–128, Washington: Georgetown University Press.

Ó hIfearnáin, T. agus Ó Murchadha, N.P. (2011). 'The perception of standard Irish as a prestige target variety'. In T. Kristiansen agus N. Coupland (eagí), *Standard Languages and Language Standards in a Changing Europe*, pp. 97–104, Osló: Novus Forlag.

Ó hUiginn, R. (2008). 'The Irish language'. In C. Nic Pháidín agus S. Ó Cearnaigh (eagí), *A New View of the Irish Language*, pp. 1–10, Baile Átha Cliath: Cois Life.

Ó Laoire, M. (1997). 'The standardization of Irish spelling: An Overview', *Journal of the Simplified Spelling Society*, 22, 19–23.

Ó Mianáin, P. (2003). 'Na bunuimhreacha sa Chaighdeán Oifigiúil', *Taighde agus Teagasc*, 3, 116–144.

Ó Murchadha, N.P. (2012). 'Authenticity, authority and prestige: Teenagers' perceptions of variation in spoken Irish'. In T. Kristiansen agus N. Coupland (eagí), *Experimental Studies of Changing Language Standards in Contemporary Europe*, Osló: Novus.

Ó Murchú, M. (1969) 'Common core and underlying forms. A suggested criterion for the construction of a phonological norm for Modern Irish', *Ériu*. 21, 42–75.

Ó Riain, S. (1994). *Pleanáil Teanga in Éirinn 1919–1985*. Baile Átha Cliath: Carbad.

Ó Siadhail, M. (1989). *Modern Irish*. Cambridge: Cambridge University Press.

Rannóg an Aistriúcháin (1958). *Gramadach na Gaeilge agus Litriú na Gaeilge: An Caighdeán Oifigiúil*. Baile Átha Cliath: Oifig an tSoláthair.

Robert, E. (2009). 'Accommodating "new" speakers? An attitudinal investigation of L2 speakers of Welsh in southeast Wales', *International Journal of the Sociology of Language*, 195, 93–116.

Sebba, M. (2007). *Orthography and Society: The cultural politics of spelling around the world*. Cambridge: Cambridge University Press.

Smakman, D. (2006). *Standard Dutch in the Netherlands: A Sociolinguistic and Phonetic Description*. Utrecht: LOT Publishers.

Swann, J., Deumert, A., Lillis, T. agus Mesthrie, R. (eagí) (2004). *A Dictionary of Sociolinguistics*. Dún Eideann: Edinburgh University Press.

Trudgill, P. (1999). 'Standard English: What it isn't'. In T. Bex agus R.J. Watts (eagí), *Standard English: The Widening Debate*, pp. 117–128, Londain: Routledge.

Wigger, A. (1979). 'Irish dialect, phonology and problems of Irish orthography'. *Papers in Irish Phonology*, 173–199.

Williams, N. (2006). *Caighdeán Nua don Ghaeilge: An Aimsir Óg, Páipéar Ócáideach 1*. Baile Átha Cliath: Coiscéim.

Wilton, A. agus Stegu, M. (2011). 'Bringing the "folk" into applied linguistics: An introduction', *AILA Review* 24, 1–14.

8 Online reflections: The implementation of blogs in language teacher education

Introduction

The implementation of technology within education is rapidly expanding, and keeping at the fore of technological advancements should be essential for language teachers and language teacher educators alike. Research indicates that apposite technologies have the capacity to enhance teachers' practices by promoting reflection (Pryor and Bitter 2008), and the asynchronous modes of communication in particular are reported to foster this type of metacognitive activity (Kunz et al. 2003; Preece and Moloney-Krichmar 2003; Riordan 2011). To this end, one specific online application being dealt with in this chapter is blogging, and the role that blogs play as reflective diaries within language teacher education (LTE).

The main aims of this research are therefore, in the context of an initial teacher education programme, to investigate the integration of blogs, to examine the use of blogs as reflective diaries, and to gain empirical evidence on student teachers' perceptions of such a tool for their personal and professional development. The key questions stemming from these aims are thus:

1. Can blogs be used as reflective diaries, and if so, to what extent do they promote reflective practice?
2. How can we capture evidence of reflective practice within this mode?
3. What levels of reflection (descriptive, comparative and critical reflection as put forward by Jay and Johnson 2002) are present within the student teachers' blogs?

4. Is there evidence of any other activity or discourse type present within
   the blogs?
5. Do the student teachers feel/believe they can reflect effectively within
   this mode?
6. What are the student teachers' perceptions/reactions towards the use
   of blogs?

These aims are deemed important, firstly, as the present world we live in
is saturated with technology, and accordingly, it been suggested that 'the
energy and intelligence students invest in these new technologies is much
too valuable for the language teaching profession to ignore' (Lafford and
Lafford 2005: 702). The introduction of online technologies to student
teachers is therefore vital, as it is only fair to impart upon them the complete skill sets they may need to utilize as future teachers. Furthermore,
there is consensus that the potential of various technologies in LTE has not
been fully exploited (Barton and Haydn 2006; ChanLin et al. 2006), and
this research aims at filling this gap not only by providing data regarding
student teachers' use and perceptions of blogs for language pedagogy, but
also by presenting an insight into the possibilities that blogs offer in aiding
reflective practice (Schön 1991: 179). Accordingly, teacher educators can
draw on information concerning the use of online tools in LTE to promote
student teachers' professional development, while simultaneously preparing them to employ technology in their future careers. Lastly, the notion
of reflective practice is something which is difficult to define as well as
depict, therefore this study endeavours to build on our understanding of
reflection, to identify possible indicators of reflection, and to investigate
levels of reflective activity.

A corpus-based discourse analysis of the student teacher reflections
while blogging is thus employed in order to delve into the possible merits
such a tool may hold for the promotion of reflective practice (Schön 1991).
Further analyses emanating from questionnaires based on the student teachers' perceptions of this online application are also included. The following
section deals with these areas in more detail.

Background

Technology in LTE

What is clearly relevant to this research is that 'today's technologies can serve as a catalyst in their efforts to create a community of scholarship (reflection) around the practice of teaching that extends well beyond the geographic confines of any given school of education or teacher preparation institution' (Gomez et al. 2008: 128). Technology thus allows teachers to interact in ways that previously were not possible, and teacher education should undoubtedly draw on such a resource. Online technologies are increasingly making their way into LTE programmes to support teachers in initial education for a variety of reasons; current technologies can promote interaction and collaboration, and through this they can minimize student teachers' possible feelings of isolation (Kamhi-Stein 2000; Arnold and Ducate 2006). They can also foster the formation of communities of practice (Arnold et al. 2005; Wenger et al. 2005; Hanson-Smith 2006) whereby teachers can share information, offer support and advice, and inevitably, learn from each other and from experienced teachers.

Online mentoring can also be facilitated, and one particular study on the promotion of peer mentoring was implemented by McLoughlin et al. (2007) as a result of pre-service teachers gaining only face-to-face models of teaching, which they believe causes problems when one thinks about the emphasis currently put on technology integration. Within this particular study, the novice teachers used a collaborative blog to communicate with one another, and content analysis on the blog postings indicated some recurring themes from their exchanges. These included their teaching practice (TP) experiences and reflections, issues surrounding their students, topics regarding pedagogical theory and practice, giving support and advice, sharing information, and expressing future intentions (ibid). Although their study utilized a collaborative blog, in contrast to the personal blogs being employed within this study, the aforementioned themes arising from the discourse, and the affordances that blogs can offer are very similar, as will be seen later in the analysis section.

Reflective practice and professional development

With particular reference to this research, the use of online communication technologies are said to improve reflective practice, and professional development (Kunz et al. 2003; Coffman 2005; Murray and Hourigan 2006; Margalef García and Roblin 2008; Murray and Hourigan 2008; Pryor and Bitter 2008; Yang 2009; Riordan 2011), and while reflective practice is difficult to define (Jay and Johnson 2002; Mena-Marcos et al. 2008), it is an important feature within education contexts (Lloyd and Bahr 2010; Farr and Riordan 2012).

Although there are many descriptions of reflective practice (Dewey 1933; Schön 1991), the framework drawn upon here emanates from the work of Jay and Johnson (2002). Their typology of reflective practice, which derives from the work of teacher educators on the University of Washington's Teacher Education Programme, comprises three dimensions. The first, *Descriptive Reflections,* 'involves the intellectual process of "setting the problem;" that is, determining what it is that will become the matter for reflection' (Jay and Johnson 2002: 77). This is where the student teacher describes the issue (a problem in class, a feeling, an experience, a theory etc.), so it sets the scene for the metacognitive activity. The next dimension is *Comparative Reflections,* and this involves thinking about the issue from a number of different perspectives in order to understand it more fully. This is an important step as '[w]hen we consider alternative perspectives or varying ways to approach a problem, we discover meaning we might otherwise miss' (ibid: 78). The final dimension, *Critical Reflections,* is the end result of deliberating on the issue from a number of varied perspectives, whereby 'one makes a judgement or a choice among actions, or simply integrates what one has discovered into a new and better understanding of the problem' (ibid: 79). The above three dimensions work together, and thus evolve from dealing with an issue, to looking at the issue from 'multiple perspectives', to gaining an overall appreciation and understanding of the issue (ibid: 78).

To this end, the notion of reflective practice within this study is seen to encompass the student teacher in a constant cycle of thinking and deliberation, with an aim to mediate action or change in their practice or understanding. This may involve student teachers thinking about themselves, and their roles as teachers; their students; classroom issues; their own practice and the general concept of pedagogy, and in doing this, they negotiate meaning, evaluate, draw conclusions, and act upon their thoughts to make informed decisions. Accordingly, it has been pointed out that '[t]he crucial goal of a teacher education programme is to develop teachers who can independently contemplate' and critically assess their own performances to mediate judicious change' (Farr 2005; 2011: 73). It is acknowledged that further research is needed to more fully understand reflective practice, and although Akbari (2007) finds that there is no evidence to suggest improved teacher performance through reflective practice, Farr (2011: 13) cautions that '[...] to say that this means that it is not an effective tool, among others, is perhaps taking it a step too far'. Indeed as Morrison (1996: 328) reveals '[w]here reflection prospers it is seen by many students as a major significant feature of their development in all spheres. [...] it can promote self-authentication, existential self-realization, empowerment and transformation'.

In an attempt then to promote reflective practice, the teacher educator or peer mentor can coach the student teacher using tools such as discussions or journals (Ferraro 2000), the latter of which have had long tradition in LTE, as they are deemed useful for teachers for reviewing their values and their reasons for teaching (Richards et al. 2005). In this digital age, there has been a shift from the use of diaries and journals to that of blog writing (Margalef García and Roblin 2008; Higdon and Topaz 2009; Yang 2009), as blogs, despite their perceived limitations, are 'versatile in their application', and have a lot of potential as online journals (Kunz et al. 2003: 286).

A blog or weblog is a website which is 'usually maintained by an individual with regular entries of commentary, descriptions of events, or other material such as graphics or video' (WikiPedia 2011). Blogs are easy to create and maintain, and are therefore very attractive to the education arena (Coffman 2005). They have been used with language students and teachers alike and are said to promote reflection, self-expression and to aid student writing skills (Murray and Hourigan 2006). In research conducted by Murray and Hourigan (2008), with the use of blogs for language and technology students, their findings suggest that blogs allowed their students another means of communication, while also promoting reflection. Moreover, they observed that higher level language students reflected on a more critical plane, while the lower levels were more descriptive in their reflections (Murray and Hourigan 2008), something echoed in other similar studies (Lucas and Fleming 2011).

Furthermore, a study by Yang (2009) details the use of a collaborative blog for reflective practice with forty-three English as a Foreign Language (EFL) student teachers stemming from two teacher education programmes. Within his study, the course instructors set up the blog and the student teachers were required to reflect weekly on their teaching experiences. They were also encouraged to comment on one another's posts to promote collaboration. When analysing the blog contents, he sorted the postings into the following five categories: theories of teaching; instructional approaches and methods; teaching evaluation methods and criteria; self-awareness; and questions about teaching and requests for advice (Yang 2009: 15), which are somewhat similar to those outlined by McLoughlin et al. (2007). Yang's overall findings suggest that the student teachers were often more descriptive in their reflections than critical, however, he asserts that the instructors played a role during the process in that they posted questions in order to encourage more critical deliberations (Yang 2009).

In summary, it is therefore believed that online communication is a cost-effective method of promoting professional development, without time and space restrictions (Anderson and Kanuka 1997; Kanuka and Anderson 1998). A diversity of asynchronous devices are hypothesized to facilitate metacognition, reflection, support, and collaborative problem-solving (Hawkes and Romiszowski 2001; Han and Hill 2006; Montero et al. 2007; Margalef García and Roblin 2008; Higdon and Topaz 2009), and research indicates that if student teachers use technology in their teacher education programmes, they perceive its use as learners, which may aid them in evaluating the technology when they themselves begin their careers, thus expanding their knowledge and expertise and, in turn, possibly increasing integration (Arnold and Ducate 2006). The following section moves on to the details surrounding the study in question.

Methodology

This research makes up part of a larger project, using a variety of data collection techniques, such as questionnaires, interviews, and face-to-face as well as online discussions within three modes (blogs, chatrooms and discussion forums). However, for the purposes of this chapter, data emanating from the blogs and interviews is analysed and presented.

Data collection

The data was collected in the Autumn Semesters from September to December 2007,[1] 2008 and 2009 from three cohorts of students enrolled in a one-year University MA in ELT programme. Prospective participants were briefed on the project and those who volunteered to partake were offered a one-hour training session where they were introduced to the different tools that would be used. The participants were then invited to join activities for the duration of the semester. They used <http://www.blogger.com> to set up their personal reflective online journals, and were given topics that could be used to focus their reflections, however, they were free to add their own. Some suggested topics for consideration included their feelings about teaching and being observed, opinions on lesson planning, relationships with their students, what they feel their students gain from their classes, and any unexpected situations that arise in class and how

---

1   The first year was a pilot study which is included in the analysis here as only one
     student blogged in 2008, as a result of participation being voluntary. The pilot study
     was very successful with regards those who used blogs therefore is deemed important
     for inclusion within the analysis. The methodology employed for the pilot study and
     the main study was similar, in fact the only minor change was a rewording of some
     questions, for reasons of clarity, on the questionnaire. The methods of data collection
     techniques remained constant. Similarly, others accept the inclusion of pilot study
     data if it offers valuable data, and if the research design remains stable (Altman et
     al. 2006; van Teijlingen and Hundley 2001).

they are dealt with. Although no training in reflective practice was given to participants for this study, there is a strong culture of reflective practice running through their MA programme, so they are indeed familiar with the process.

The student teachers were asked to commence their blogs in Week 7 of the fifteen-week semester and were invited to blog until the end of the semester or as long as they wished. The researcher/peer mentor was the only other person reading the reflections, and she did not post comments directly to the blogs, in order to maintain as much privacy for the participants as possible. A final, albeit significant, point to note is that these blogs were un-assessed, in formal summative terms. Participation was voluntary and not proposed or encouraged by a lecturer, and this may have had an impact on the interpersonal meanings created and divulged within the discourse of the blogs, something which will be returned to in later sections.

The data

A total of twelve students completed blogs (four in 2007, one in 2008 and seven in 2009), and the content varied from very lengthy and frequent posting to minimal posting, however for the purposes of this chapter, all are included for the linguistic analysis. Once all student teachers had completed their blog entries, a corpus was compiled, following the criteria set out by Farr et al. (2004) for the Limerick Corpus of Irish English (L-CIE), and was analysed using Wordsmith Tools (Scott 2008). The BLOG corpus thus consists of approximately 31,000 words in total, and is analysed for indications of reflection using a corpus-based discourse analysis approach.

Methodological issues

The main methods used for this analysis are corpus-assisted discourse analysis/studies (CADS – Partington 2003), as well as content analysis. Corpus-based discourse analysis is seen as beneficial in that it adds a quantitative dimension to a qualitative framework (McCarthy 2001), and is utilized here to obtain an overview of the blogs and to illustrate what is present within them. Therefore frequency and keyword lists,[2] as well as the manual examination of concordances are generated for the analysis. Content analysis is then used to get further behind the discourse, and to categorize the recurring themes within the blogs in order to expand on the analysis. Finally, data from semi-structured interviews administered after the student teachers had participated in the blog writing are dealt with in order to depict their perceptions on the use of blogs for the purposes of reflective practice.

In addition, although it has been pointed out that '[q]ualitative researchers have no "golden key" to validity' (Silverman 2005: 211), several measures were taken to maximize validity. Namely, the data and methods utilized in this study are triangulated, for example, questionnaire data, interview data, and blog data, as well as quantitative, qualitative and corpus-based methods, thus this combination of different types of data and types of methods aims to reduce threats against validity (Berg 2009). Moreover, the interviews were recorded and transcribed, and follow the format of informal interviews, a technique, which Jorgensen highlights, allows for systematic questioning where the researcher has a 'definite sense of precisely what questions are relevant' (1989: 89). These are also known as standardized open-ended interviews, and the consistent wording of questions is said

2   A frequency list is a list of the words that appear in a corpus with their frequencies and the percentage they contribute to the corpus as a whole. A keyword list compares a chosen corpus to a general corpus in order to illuminate words which are 'unusually frequent' compared to their frequency in other texts (Scott 2008).

to reduce bias and minimize variation and probing (Quinn-Patton 2002).[3] The researcher was therefore very aware of her interview techniques (i.e. not leading the participants, not asking more than one thing of them at a time, allowing participants to get clarity on questions, and asking internal checking questions).

Furthermore, the researcher adhered to considerations set out by practitioners to maximize validity during data analyses. For example, Silverman (2005) considers looking at all possible interpretations of the data rather than making assumptions that appear logical or easy, looking for and analysing deviant cases, and using comprehensive data sets to ground the analysis, and Quinn Patton (2002: 544–566) suggests the following:

1. Testing rival explanations: looking for things that oppose findings
2. Negative cases: investigating something that does not fit the pattern
3. Triangulation (in this case, there is triangulation of methods (quantitative, qualitative, and corpus-based), as well as triangulation of data (questionnaires, interviews, blog interactions))
4. Keeping data in context and not making generalizations.

The results obtained from the data are presented in the following section.

Analysis

Quantitative and qualitative corpus-based analyses are presented in the first two sections here as a means of obtaining an initial overview of the BLOG corpus, and the following section then moves into a more content analysis approach in order to identify connections or yield new findings

---

3   It must be noted that for this study, there was slight variation in what questions were asked, as not all questions were relevant to all participants, due to the mixed participation within the study as a result of it being voluntary and non-assessed.

without losing the richness of the blogs data. These are the first steps taken in order to provide some framework to capture aspects of reflection within the data, however it is acknowledged that more detailed analyses will be needed in future in order to establish the full extent of critical reflection. This section then closes by examining interview results with the aim of getting behind the discourse by investigating the student teachers' perceived efficacy of blogs in promoting reflective practice.

Word frequency and keyword analysis

The generation of frequency lists was utilized as this type of analysis is considered a useful starting point for corpus investigations (Baker 2006), and it has the capacity to 'give very strong clues about the communicative function and nature of specific contexts' (Farr and Riordan 2012: 139). Table 8.1 therefore shows the top fifty most frequent items from the BLOG corpus compared to the Limerick Corpus of Irish English (L-CIE), a 1-million word corpus of spoken, casual conversation (Farr et al. 2004), and to the written component of the British National Corpus (BNC) sampler corpus of 1 million words (1999).

Table 8.1 Top fifty most frequent words across corpora[4]

F.	BLOG	L-CIE (Spoken)	BNC (Written)
1	THE	THE	THE
2	TO	I	OF
3	AND	YOU	AND
4	I	AND	TO
5	A	TO	A

---

4   Words highlighted are those which may signify reflection and are therefore worthy of discussion.

6	OF	IT	IN
7	IN	A	FOR
8	IS	THAT	IS
9	THAT	OF	THAT
10	IT	IN	WAS
11	NOT	YEAH	IT
12	AT	WAS	ON
13	MY	IS	BE
14	FOR	LIKE	WITH
15	AS	KNOW	AS
16	BY	HE	BY
17	WAS	THEY	I
18	HAVE	ON	AT
19	ON	HAVE	ARE
20	BE	BUT	HE
21	THIS	NO	FROM
22	YOU	THERE	THIS
23	WITH	WHAT	HAVE
24	ARE	FOR	NOT
25	BUT	BE	BUT
26	STUDENTS	SO	YOU
27	THEY	DO	HIS
28	AM	WE	AN
29	ME	IT'S	WHICH
30	DO	AH	HAD
31	ABOUT	SHE	OR
32	WHAT	NOW	THEY

33	SO	ALL	WERE
34	WOULD	OH	WILL
35	GOOD	ARE	ALL
36	OR	AM	WE
37	AN	JUST	ONE
38	ONE	ONE	HAS
39	HOW	THIS	THEIR
40	CAN	AT	BEEN
41	CLASS	WITH	THERE
42	FROM	OR	SAID
43	THINK	NOT	SHE
44	THERE	WELL	HER
45	HAD	THAT'S	WOULD
46	ALL	DON'T	IF
47	WE	IF	UP
48	LANGUAGE	GOING	MORE
49	THEM	THEM	CAN
50	WHEN	GO	WHO

There are words which fall into five main categories here. These appear to suggest reflection and include personal narration, metalanguage, affective engagement, cognitive engagement and evaluation. These are somewhat similar and based upon those found by Farr (2007a; 2011), who analyses reflection within a corpus of spoken and written teaching practice feedback. What is first apparent here, is the use of items which reflect personal narration, *I*, *my*, *was*, *am*, *me* and *we*. Words such as these may indicate that the student teachers are using this mode to give personal recounts, or simply personal information, and it may be proposed that a focus on the self is somewhat evident of introspection and reflection. What is also noteworthy is that *my* and *me* are unique to the BLOG corpus top fifty (relative to L-CIE and the BNC), and this may again indicate the intended personal nature of this mode. Further qualitative analysis through a random sample of concordance lines of *I* indicates that much of the data refers to the student teachers introducing themselves online, possibly creating a web presence and an online voice (Stevens 2003). Also relevant here, is that they are thinking about their pedagogical experiences. From the selected examples in Figure 8.1, we can see that the student teachers focus their thoughts on themselves as novice teachers (see lines 1, 2, 4, and 10 for example) while also on their students and their lessons (lines 7 and 8), and the art of teaching (lines 6 and 9), which is what we encourage novice teachers to reflect upon so that they can get a better understanding of their practice. If we then attempt to map these against the dimensions put forward by Jay and Johnson (2002), it appears that the student teachers are being mostly descriptive in their reflections, although in lines 6 and 9 they may be veering more towards comparative reflection as the examples point to issues of outside knowledge (methods of language teaching), and therefore the teachers are drawing on research (using multiple perspectives) to further their understanding of certain issues.

N	Concordance
1	If only I would have realized earlier that I could have challenged myself in the
2	the first time I was formally observed. I was nervous, about everything. Even
3	pointed out. never mind. i do know that i have lots and lots of faults and i have
4	plan your lessons? Why/why not? Yes! I am a natural planner by nature (and at
5	becoming confused and uninterested. I think teaching is difficulty enough
6	than skim over three or four things, and I think students prefer that too. I think
7	so I hope the students did too. Also I had built up a nice rapport with the two
8	of their school publications. certainly, i do not consider myself to be a "good"
9	far is the community learning method. i like the fact that learners can be in a
10	I really want to hang in there. I guess I will have good and bad days so with the

Figure 8.1 *I* concordance

Furthermore, the use of *we* may indicate their feeling of belonging to a community of practising teachers (Lave and Wenger 1991; Wenger 1998), and indeed a concordance search of this item proves that this is the case, with approximately 60 per cent of occurrences of *we* referring to the participants themselves as a group of novice teachers. Additional examination of the other features signifying personal narration might illuminate this idea further.

The second group of items highlighted in Table 8.1 is the metadiscourse surrounding teaching: *students, class*, and *language* being specific to the top fifty BLOG corpus, as anticipated. From the salience of this metadiscourse, we may assume that the student teachers are referring to, and therefore thinking about, the art of teaching, and reflecting to some degree on their practice. The last three groups of words specific to the BLOG corpus include those representing affective engagement, cognitive engagement and evaluation. For example, *think* may signify both affective opining or cognitive activity, *about, how* and *when* may indicate self-inquiry where the teachers are posing questions based on their teaching, *and good* may denote evaluation, all of which may suggest, albeit tentatively, metacognition and reflection. These items will be returned to in more detail in the next section.

Following the compilation of frequency lists, it was considered necessary to generate a keyword search in order to further examine the corpus. For this, the BLOG corpus was compared against L-CIE, and also against the BNC sampler corpus. What became apparent when compared against both reference corpora was that the items found to be key to the BLOG corpus often fell into the aforementioned categories. Therefore, keywords in the BLOG corpus include items possibly representing personal narration (*me, I* and *am*), metadiscourse (*teach, lessons* and *students*), cognitive engagement (*think*) and affective engagement and/or evaluation (*feel*). What is found here again resonates somewhat with Farr's (2007a: 2011: 76) findings, as she notes that

> Searching through and extracting from the top 200 most frequent items in POTTI and POR,[5] reflection is suggested primarily through the high occurrences of interrogative/relative pronouns, verbs of reflection/cognition/perception, and narrative verbs especially in past tense forms.

5   These are corpora compiled in the teacher education context in Ireland. POTTI (Post Observation Trainer Trainee Interactions) is a spoken corpus of feedback delivered after teaching practice sessions, and POR (Post Observation Reports) is a written corpus consisting of written reports compiled by tutors and subsequently returned to the student teachers after their teaching practice.

The brief examination of the frequency and keyword lists above therefore suggests reflection within the corpus, although additional analysis is necessary in order to explore this in more depth.

Indicators of reflection

In order to get a more comprehensive representation of possible reflection within the data, it was decided to analyse the blogs in terms of personal narration, cognitive engagement, affective engagement (Farr 2007b; 2011), and evaluation. These can be assessed through the investigation of the presence of stance which, expressed through grammatical, lexical, and paralinguistic devices (Biber et al. 1999), 'is generally understood to have to do with the methods, linguistic and other, by which interactants create and signal relationships with the propositions they utter and with the people they interact with' (Johnstone 2009: 30–31). The framework for this section of the analysis is thus similar to that utilized by Farr and Riordan (2012), which was also undertaken for the same purposes of investigating reflective practice. In this case, the categories of verbs and adjectives were chosen for the analysis, and Table 8.2 depicts the most frequent verbs having the potential to indicate reflection (all forms of the verbs have been included in the frequencies and have been normalized to words per million). It must firstly be noted that only verbs used in the first person were selected for generating statistics in order to focus on the use of these verbs from the student teachers' individual perspectives, because although second and third person speaker contributions 'express some kind of attitude or evaluation, they do not necessarily reflect the personal stance of the speaker/writer' (Biber 2006: 91). Secondly, all other functions other than those expressing stance have been disregarded from the investigation (for example, the use of the hedge *you know*). The results can be seen in Table 8.2.

Table 8.2 Verbs as indicators of reflection

Verbs	W/pm
Think*[1]	3131
Feel*	1677
Know*	999
Try*	806
Like*	742
Find*	581
Hope*	419
Believe*	387
Wish*	258
Understand*	258

1   * denotes that all forms of the verbs were searched for (i.e. think, thinks, thinking, thought etc.)

What is noteworthy here is that the cognitive verb *think* is the most frequent (as was also demonstrated in both frequency and keyword analyses in previous sections), and within the same category of possible cognitive items are *know, believe* and *understand*. These types of mental processing verbs are exactly what we hope to find in a corpus of reflective activity, and as can be seen in the examples in Figure 8.2 below, *think* is being used by the student teachers to focus on themselves (lines 4, 5 and 10), and their teaching and students (lines 1, 2, 8, and 9), thus possibly implying consideration and reflection. What becomes evident here, is that the levels of reflection appear to fall into the dimensions of both descriptive and possibly comparative (in line 3 the teacher uses some previous experience to inform her knowledge about herself as a teacher) (Jay and Johnson 2002). Added investigation, which lies outside the scope of the present analysis, is needed here to fully depict the levels of reflection.

N Concordance
1	Yes I do. Sometimes it may not be much but I do **think** students always learn something. This is
2	information about Ireland while I was doing the tp. I **think** that was good but at the end of the lesson, the
3	matter what the teacher does. everything is lost. i **think** i should not teach in groups where there are
4	because I know it is a result of my own efforts. I **think** my strengths are my ability to empathise with
5	I was never aware of up until then (and now). I **think** I'm a good teacher, and I've had loads of
6	better than i do mine.) i came over to ul because i **think** i am not a good teacher and i need/ed to
7	to be tactful while still getting their point across. I **think** that most student teachers don't have a big
8	WEDNESDAY, OCTOBER 24, 2007. 1. I **think** my teaching is improving. My nerves are
9	rather than skim over three or four things, and I **think** students prefer that too. I think that the
10	something from my classes? Yes, absolutely. I **think** I'm pretty good at knowing how much to teach

Figure 8.2 *Think** concordance

Furthermore, as seen in Table 8.2, the category of emotive/affective verbs *feel, like, find, hope* and *wish*, make up a large part of the overall frequencies, and can express opinions, affect, and add to the personal narrative of the corpus. The examples taken for *feel* in Figure 8.3 demonstrate how the student teachers express their personal feelings and attitudes (lines 4 and 6), how they feel about their teaching (lines 5 and 9), and their students (lines 1 and 10), and all of the examples here appear to indicate, yet again, descriptive reflections (Jay and Johnson 2002).

N Concordance
1 stress level. When I start teaching I will certainly feel sympathetic to students when they don't get the
2 has an effect on teachers and students? Yes I do feel this. I feel that when the class is arranged in a
3 TUESDAY, OCTOBER 27, 2009 How do I feel about student teachers being observed? I think
4 I'm looking forward to the weekend away but I feel very guilty for going away the weekend before
5 not feeling very positive. Though it is early days, I feel my progress hasn't been as good as it should
6 everything else college related. In a nut-shell, I feel that college so far is just that of teaching. I
7 by limericklady ee at 10.46 AM 0 comments How I feel about my own teaching... At the moment I am
8 before hand and I practiced the transcribing. I feel I didn't get the chance to diosplay what I know,
9 like my science and maths. Well thats how I feel about teaching! Gotta go FRIDAY, OCTOBER 2,
10 by limericklady ee at 11.28 AM 0 comments Do I feel students learn something from my class... I like

Figure 8.3 *Feel** concordance

Finally, the verb *try* adds to the evaluative aspect of the blogs. The student teachers are retelling events and expressing what they themselves have done or strived to do in a classroom, and most of the data (see Figure 8.4) suggests that they are very much focussed on themselves, which is not surprising as they are novice teachers. It may be interesting to point out that although the reflections appear to indicate descriptive narratives, line 9 may fall into the critical reflection dimension (Jay and Johnson 2002), whereby the student teacher translates experiences from previous actions into a new understanding of something.

N Concordance
1   method by putting sentences on the board and **trying** to elicit the rules on the modal verbs from
2   hanging over your head, finding when to do them and **trying** to organise them around your own time table.
3   a particular lesson to a particular student, and I don't **try** to give them too much at one time. I prefer to cover
4   my take on it. Just wait until next semester when I **try** student teaching and I'll be eating my words.
5   i do not consider myself to be a "good" teacher but i **try** to accept myself with all my faults and i love them
6   experiences and what they can bring to the class. I **try** to balance between being professional as a teacher
7   and thoroughly understand. I don't see much point in **trying** to "trip them up" with unexpected exam
8   useful one. Google itself is not the problem, and it is **trying** to become part of the answer with intiatives
9   and i was not observed. i had taken the decision to **try** something "new" and i did it. it took me quite a
10 is good, then i get some energy for the next day, to **try** again. i am not a perfectionist and i do not believe

Figure 8.4: *Try** concordance

The next section of the analysis moves on to investigate adjectives as indicators of reflection as they can often mark stance and evaluation (Farr and Riordan 2012). As with the verbs above, only items indicating stance are included, and are presented in Table 8.3.

Table 8.3 Adjectives as indicators of reflection

Adjectives	*W/pm*
Good	3099
Great	710
Important	613
Bad	581

Hard	548
Easy	355
Difficult	322
Positive	322
Better	290
Happy	225

Firstly, *good* appears as the most frequent item, which is not surprising as it emerged as a prominent feature from the frequency list analysis discussed earlier. What may be interesting to note here is the divide between positive and negative evaluative items. Some of the items within the examples below, which at first glance appear as being positive, indicate that not only do the student teachers use these words to indicate positive evaluations (*good, great, important, better* and *happy*), but they also evaluate negative or less positive situations (*easy* and *positive*). Nevertheless, these evaluations encompass the area of teaching and pedagogy.

1. I think I'm a *good* teacher
2. I have had some *great* and some awful lessons
3. Relating to students is *important*
4. With adults, however it isn't as *easy* to gauge how things are going
5. At the moment I'm not feeling very *positive*
6. It [a lesson] couldn't have gone *better*
7. I felt *happy* and excited at the same time [after a lesson]

While investigating the examples of negative evaluative items, it was found that the student teachers are focussing on what they perceive as challenging for them as teachers.

8. I guess I will have good and *bad* days
9. I have improved on the *bad* stuff [re. teaching]
10. [...] it is very *hard* to judge how you did or what grades you are getting

11. I just find it so *hard* to distinguish between all the different word classes
12. Also I am finding it *difficult* judging their [students] previous knowledge
13. At first I found it *difficult* to relate to ERASMUS students

In summary, the use of adjectives within the corpus suggests that regardless of whether the student teachers are being positive or negative about certain situations, they appear to be focussed on discussing their teaching and their students, albeit in a rather descriptive manner. This, along with the analysis of the verbs, therefore leads us to believe that they are reflecting on some level about their experiences in their newfound practice. There are, however, similar reservations here to those expressed by Farr and Riordan (2012) regarding the quality of these reflections and whether they are indeed critically reflecting or talking about reflecting, and more extensive analysis, which lies outside the scope of this present chapter, will illuminate this further. The following section now turns to some themes that arose from exploring the content of the blogs in order to get a fuller picture of the data.

Recurring themes

As was mentioned previously, the student teachers were given questions they could use to focus their blog postings, although they were free to blog as they wished, and different participants chose varied routes. From a more content analysis approach, the blogs were explored and recurring features found within them are now presented. Although, this may appear a rudimentary endeavour, the analysis of recurring themes is considered worthwhile in order to build upon previous assumptions, or indeed generate further insights. What needs to be forwarded here is the fact that although the blogs were to encourage reflective practice, they were un-assessed, and read only by the researcher, who was not in an authoritative role. This may have had an impact on what the student teachers blogged about, and how the interpersonal meanings within the blogs may differ from those when interacting with a lecturer, for example.

What is noticeable, firstly, is the student teachers often expressed their personal problems and anxieties with regards their teaching as well as their students, and the two examples below illustrate this clearly:

14. I have no idea how I could make my classes more successful
15. I hope I can be a good teacher

These examples also relate back to the issue of affective engagement mentioned in earlier sections. Furthermore, the student teachers appeared to use the blogs as somewhere they could vent and complain. They did so about their students, their classes, their lecturers and often their own teaching. These complaints may be due to a number of factors. As was previously mentioned they were very much aware that the peer mentor/researcher was not in an authoritative role therefore they may have felt more at ease expressing their true feelings, and secondly the blogs were private and confidential, so they knew they could be as honest as they wished. Another factor that may have influenced the frequent expression of complaints was that they were online rather than face-to-face so they were possibly more open, something also expressed in research on distance learning (Kostina 2011). This is also something Farr (2011: 89) suggests as she notes 'Any confrontational tendencies they may have often surface in their own written reflections which come in their TP diaries'. Again this may relate to issues of affective engagement in that the student teachers may find it easier to express their feelings and attitudes in written form (blogs) than in face-to-face interactions.

Something which also emerged was that the blog postings were very personal, and sometimes centred on subjects outside the realm of teaching, and this may be due the confidentiality factor discussed earlier. There was also a lot of humour being displayed within the blogs, and as the researcher was familiar with all students outside of this project, she noticed that often quite shy students in a face-to-face setting were those who came out of their shell within the online setting, something which has been indicated in other research on chatrooms discussions (Beauvois 1998). The humorous example from the student below concerns a lecturer who appeared to reprimand the student teacher in front of her peers, and she notes:

16. The whole class seemed to be structured around my weaknesses, which did nothing to lower my affective filter, Mr Krashen.

What is most interesting here is that, while she is in fact complaining about something, she does so through the use of humour (possibly softening the effect), but she also uses her prior knowledge of Krashen's (1985) Affective Filter Hypothesis (a theory they cover as part of their MA programme) to create the effect. This suggests that she is indeed using the content of what she was learning on the course (the aforementioned cognitive aspect), and inputting the information into her blog by reflecting on what she knows and how she interprets it (the aforementioned evaluative aspect), and this may be thus aligned with the dimension of comparative reflection.

The final major theme arising from the analysis of the blogs was the student teachers seem to be contemplating a number of elements: their students, themselves as teachers, their MA course and their classes. As was seen also in the previous sections, these postings were both positive and negative, and they mainly fall under both descriptive and comparative reflections rather than moving into the critical plane.

17. I think I'm pretty good at knowing how much to teach in a particular lesson to a particular student
18. After thinking about it, I decided that I used poor strategy planning for the exam
19. I obviously hope students do learn from my classes but between my lack of experience and the structure of the book I sometimes feel they are just going through the motions of the class and not actually taking anything from it

Additionally, some keywords appear, for example, affective items (*feel*, *hope*), and cognitive items (*think*, *know*) are often recurring tokens.

What can be surmised from this analysis is that the blogs offered the student teachers a place to voice their opinions on various subjects, and the possibility of evaluating and thinking about certain pedagogical areas, which may lead to deliberation and reflection. What has also been observed is that the topics divulged by the student teachers (the strong focus on their teaching, areas connected to pedagogy, evaluation, and their own self-awareness) are somewhat similar to those categorized by previous researchers (McLoughlin et al. 2007; Yang 2009). Furthermore, the themes of sharing personal information, divulging personal anxieties, complaining, expressing humour, and deliberating on their teaching and their students, which dominate the BLOG corpus may be a result of the fact that no power relationships existed between the student teacher, and the researcher, thus possibly allowing more honesty and freedom to express true opinions and judgements. Overall, the deliberations of the student teachers appear very much descriptive. This may not mean that the student teachers are not critically reflecting, but the 'framework' outlined above may be more suitable at capturing evidence of descriptive reflections and further analyses may indeed bring more critical reflections to light.

Student teacher perceptions

This final section now moves away from the reflective aspect of the language and into the student teachers' perceptions of blogs for reflection. Although in total twelve student teachers created blogs, only eight of those were available for an interview, and despite this being quite a small number, the results should offer an insight into general reactions towards the tool for those involved. The data presented here does not attempt to suggest that the perceptions are universal, nor does it attempt to provide evidence of reflective practice through blogging, but it is merely used to add further qualitative data to examine attitudes towards blogs.

During the interview, each participant was asked whether they liked using blogs, and all reported to enjoying the use of such a tool. As was mentioned earlier, this was part of a larger research project also involving the use of chat and discussion fora, hence the participants were asked which online application they preferred, and 62.5 per cent preferred the use of blogs above the other applications. Reasons set out for this included that they felt blogs were easy to set up and maintain, the process provided them with ideas for the use of this tool in their future lessons, the blogs gave them a space to express their thoughts and opinions (as is demonstrated from the sections above where personal narration, opining, and affective engagement are evident), and the asynchronicity of the mode offered more of an opportunity to think about what they were writing and therefore reflect more. However, one student commented that he did not reflect much on his teaching but reflected merely on a personal level (which is evident from previous examples, and is possibly a result of the blogs being un-assessed). Another student teacher aptly pointed out that those who fully participated in this specific project might be the students who reflect more anyway.

Bearing this in mind, the use of blogs within this project appear to be looked upon favourably by the participants for a diversity of reasons, and while they feel they had the opportunity to reflect within this mode, they seem to be descriptively reflecting rather than critically reflecting, something which warrants further investigation. The final section offers a discussion of the key findings as pertaining to the original research questions.

Conclusions and recommendations

As previously underlined, blogs have been described as a 'promising candidate' for encouraging online reflection (Kunz et al. 2003: 286), and what becomes apparent from the analysis above is that from a corpus-based linguistic investigation, there is some evidence of reflection through the presence of specific language occurring within the BLOG corpus, and this type of reflection is quite descriptive (Jay and Johnson 2002). If we return to our original research questions as set out in the first section, we may get a better representation of what blogs offered in terms of reflective practice:

1. *Can blogs be used as reflective diaries, and if so, to what extent do they promote reflective practice?*

It appears that blogs do have the potential to be used as reflective diaries, the asynchronicity of the mode fosters reflection, and there is evidence of reflective discourse within the blogs, albeit on a descriptive plane, rather than a critical plane. Further analysis is required to examine the extent to which they promote critical reflective practice.

2. *How can we capture evidence of reflective practice within this mode?*

Frequency and keyword analyses, and concordance analysis of possible indicators of reflection indicate that elements set out by Farr (2005; 2007a; 2011), pertaining to evaluation, affective engagement, cognitive engagement and personal narration, are visible in the corpus, therefore tentatively suggesting the presence of reflection. The language emerging from these proposed indicators of reflection demonstrates that the student teachers are using such devices to talk about themselves as teachers, their students, and the art of teaching. Moreover the themes recurring from the content analysis (personal problems and anxieties with regards teaching and students; complaining; being personal; centring on subjects outside the realm of teaching) allow further aspects of the discourse to emerge.

3. *What levels of reflection (descriptive, comparative and critical reflection as put forward by Jay and Johnson 2002) are present within the student teachers' blogs?*

The reflections appear to be generally descriptive, findings which are indeed similar to other research (Murray and Hourigan 2008; Yang 2009). However, it has been suggested that '[j]ust because reflection is not critical does not mean it is unimportant or unnecessary' (Brookfield 1995: 8), and therefore it is surmised that although they are not reflecting on the critical dimension, their descriptive reflections are still worthwhile, and possibly over time they can make the transition. Furthermore, it may also be worth a note that the student teachers in question here did not have the guidance of a TP tutor/lecturer to promote critical reflection, and therefore this could have had an impact on the levels of reflection found, something that will be focussed on in future analyses. What is necessary now is to move forward with a framework to investigate critical reflective practice, and to uncover features or items that may indicate this level of reflection.

4. *Is there evidence of any other activity or discourse type present within the blogs?*

The blogs appeared to offer the student teachers a space for other activities, which lie outside the realm of professional reflection, in that they often complained and expressed very personal information, often without a focus on their teaching or their students, and this is possibly something which warrants further investigation. The role of the researcher as a peer mentor may also have an impact here as the interpersonal meanings may shift depending on the type of activity (an un-assessed task), and type of interaction (student teacher and peer mentor).

5. *Do the student teachers feel/believe they can reflect within this mode?*

The student teachers reported that they did believe they got the opportunity to reflect within this mode, however it must be acknowledged that firstly they might be the ones who reflect more (as was pointed out by one participant), and also they may merely be reporting on the basis of what they know the researcher was looking for.

6. *What are the student teachers' perceptions/reactions towards the use of blogs?*

The participants appeared to be positive about the use of blogs for reflective practice, and indeed some highlighted that they would like to use such a tool in their future teaching. The notion of technology integration is also something to be expanded upon in future analyses.

What therefore comes to the fore is that there does appear to be evidence of descriptive reflection throughout the BLOG corpus. The items discussed appear to demonstrate this level of reflection, and the students overall generally favoured writing on their blogs, and saw the benefits of doing this. What is vital for ongoing research in this area is a focus on the depth of reflection being executed and any other factors that may influence such reflective practices. As was stated previously, the depth and quality of reflection has not been truly investigated in this chapter, but is very worthy of scrutinization for the purposes of evaluating the levels of thinking and metacognition on the part of the student teachers. Therefore, subsequent research needs to concentrate on frameworks for evaluating critical reflection and what its possible outcomes are. What this current chapter does offer to this area is an insight into the value of blogs, in that they are perceived in a positive light by the student teachers in question, and that they also have the potential to promote some degree of reflective activity, and it is surmised that if teachers begin their career on a path of reflective activity, this may give them a better understanding of themselves and their students, which can only serve to benefit them in their future careers.

References

Akbari, R. (2007). 'Reflections on reflection: A critical appraisal of reflective practices in L2 teacher education', *System*, 35, 192–207.

Altman, D., Burton, N., Cuthill, I., Festing, M., Hutton, J. and Playle, L. (2006). 'Why do a pilot study?' *NC3Rs Experimental Design Working Group*. <www.nc3rs.org.uk/downloaddoc.asp?id=400> accessed 20 February 2012.

Anderson, T. and Kanuka, H. (1997). 'On-line forums: New platforms for professional development and group collaboration', *Journal of Computer Mediated Communication*, 3 (3) <http://jcmc.indiana.edu/vol3/issue3/anderson.html> accessed 17 June 2009.

Arnold, N. and Ducate, L. (2006). 'Future foreign language teachers' social and cognitive collaboration in an online environment', *Language Learning and Technology*, 10 (1), 42–66.

Arnold, N., Ducate, L., Lomicka, L., and Lord, G. (2005). 'Using Computer-mediated communication to establish social and supportive environments in teacher education', *CALICO Journal*, 22 (3), 537–565.

Baker, P. (2006). *Using Corpora in Discourse Analysis*. London: Continuum.

Barton, R. and Haydn, T. (2006). 'Trainee teachers' views on what helps them to use information and communication technology effectively in their subject teaching', *Journal of Computer Assisted Learning*, 22, 257–272.

Beauvois, M.H. (1998). 'Conversations in slow motion. Computer-mediated communication in the foreign language classroom', *Canadian Modern Language Review*, 54, 198–214.

Berg, B.L. (2009). *Qualitative Research Methods*. Boston: Pearson Education.

Biber, D. (2006). *University Language. A Corpus-based Study of Spoken and Written Registers*. Amsterdam: John Benjamins.

Biber, D., Johannson, S., Leech, G., Conrad, S., and Finnegan, E. (1999). *Longman Grammar of Spoken and Written English*. London: Longman.

BNC (1999). *The BNC Sampler Corpus*. Oxford: Oxford University Computing Services.

Brookfield, S. (1995). *Becoming a Critically Reflective Teacher*. San Francisco: Jossey-Bass.

ChanLin, L.J., Hong, J.C., Horng, J.S., Chang, S.H., and Chu, H.C. (2006). 'Factors influencing technology integration in teaching: A Taiwanese perspective', *Innovations in Education and Teaching International*, 43 (1), 57–68.

Coffman, T. (2005). 'Weblogs and wikis in the classroom', *Virginia Society for Technology in Education Journal*, 19 (2), 2–8.

Dewey, J. (1933). *How We Think: A Restatement of the Relation of Reflective Thinking to the Educative Process*. Boston: DC Heath and Company.

Farr, F. (2005). 'Reflecting on reflections: The spoken word as a professional development tool in language teacher education'. In R. Hughes (ed.), *Spoken English, Applied Linguistics and TESOL: Challenges for Theory and Practice*, pp. 182–215. Hampshire: Palgrave Macmillan.

Farr, F. (2007a). 'Spoken language as an aid to reflective practice in language teacher education: Using a specialised corpus to establish a generic fingerprint'. In M.-C. Campoy and M.J. Luzón (eds), *Spoken Corpora in Applied Linguistics*, pp. 235–258. Bern: Peter Lang.

Farr, F. (2007b). 'Engaged listenership in spoken academic discourse: The case of student-tutor meetings'. In W. Teubert and R. Krishnamurthy (eds), *Corpus Linguistics: Critical Concepts in Linguistics*, pp. 67–85. London: Routledge.

Farr, F. (2011). *The Discourse of Teaching Practice Feedback: A Corpus-Based Investigation of Spoken and Written Modes*. London: Routledge.

Farr, F., Murphy, B., and O'Keeffe, A. (2004). 'The Limerick corpus of Irish English: Design, description and application', *Teanga* 21, 5–29.

Farr, F. and Riordan, E. (2012). 'Students engagement in reflective tasks: an investigation of interactive and non-interactive discourse corpora', *Classroom Discourse*, 3 (2), 129–146.

Ferraro, J.M. (2000). 'Reflective practice and professional development', *ERIC Clearing House on Teaching and Teacher Education*, <http://searcheric.org/digests/ed449120.html> accessed 3 June 2008.

Gomez, L.M., Sherin, M.G., Griesdorn, J. and Finn, L. (2008). 'Creating social relationships: The role of technology in preservice teacher preparation', *Journal of Teacher Education*, 59 (2), 117–131.

Han, S. and Hill, J.R. (2006). 'Building understanding in asynchronous discussions: Examining types of online discourse', *Journal of Asynchronous Learning Networks*, 10 (4), 29–50.

Hanson-Smith, E. (2006). 'Communities of practice for pre- and in-service teacher education'. In P. Hubbard and M. Levy (eds), *Teacher Education in CALL*, pp. 301–315. Amsterdam: John Benjamins.

Hawkes, M. and Romiszowski, A. (2001). 'Examining the reflective outcomes of asynchronous computer-mediated communication on inservice teacher development', *Technology and Teacher Education*, 9 (2), 285–308.

Higdon, J. and Topaz, C. (2009). 'Blogs and wikis as instructional tools: A social software adaptation of just-in-time teaching', *College Teaching*, 57 (2), 105–110.

Jay, J.K. and Johnson, K.L. (2002). 'Capturing complexity: A typology of reflective practice for teacher education', *Teaching and Teacher Education*, 18, 73–85.

Johnstone, B. (2009). 'Stance, style, and the linguistic individual'. In A. Jaffe (Ed), *Stance: Sociolinguistic Persepctives*, pp. 29–52. Oxford: Oxford University Press.

Jorgensen, D.L. (1989). *Participant Observation. A Methodology for Human Studies*. London: Sage Publications.

Kamhi-Stein, L.D. (2000). 'Looking to the future of TESOL teacher education: Web-based bulletin board discussions in a methods course', *TESOL Quarterly*, 34 (3), 423–455.

Kanuka, H. and Anderson, T. (1998). 'Online social interchange, discord, and knowledge construction', *Journal of Distance Education*, 13 (1) <http://cade.athabascau.ca/vol13.1/kanuka.html> accessed 25 November 2006.

Kostina, M. (2011). 'Three surprising ways that students view distance learning: Distance education hot topics', *Effective Online Teaching and Training* <http://effectiveonlineteaching.org/2011/09/07/3-surprising-ways-that-students-view-distance-learning/> accessed 12 December 2011.

Krashen, S. (1985). *The Input Hypothesis: Issues and Implications*. London: Longman.

Kunz, P., Dewstow, R., and Moodie, P. (2003). 'A generic tool to set up metacognitive journals and their serendipitous use', *The 20th Annual Conference of the Australasian Society for Computers in Learning in Tertiary Education (ASCILITE)*, Adelaide, Australia, ASCILITE.

Lafford, P.A. and Lafford, B.A. (2005). 'CMC technologies for teaching foreign languages: What's on the horizon?', *CALICO Journal*, 22 (3), 679–709.

Lave, J. and Wenger, E. (1991). *Situated Learning. Legitimate Peripheral Participation*. Cambridge: Cambridge University Press.

Lloyd, M. and Bahr, N. (2010). 'Thinking critically about critical thinking in higher education', *International Journal for the Scholarship of Teaching and Learning*, 4 (2), 1–16.

Lucas, P. and Fleming, J. (2011). 'Critical reflection: Journals versus blogs', *New Zealand Association for Co-operative Education Conference*, Eastern Institute of Technology (EIT). Napier, Hawkes Bay, New Zealand: EIT, 29–33. <http://www.nzace.ac.nz/conferences/papers/Proceedings_2011.pdf> accessed 21 September 2011.

Margalef García, L. and Roblin, N.P. (2008). 'Innovation, research and professional development in higher education: Learning from our own experience', *Teaching and Teacher Education*, 24, 104–116.

McCarthy, M. (2001). 'Discourse'. In R. Carter and D. Nunan (eds), *The Cambridge Guide to Teaching English to Speakers of Other Languages*, pp. 48–55. Cambridge: Cambridge University Press.

McLoughlin, C., Brady, J., Lee, M.J.W. and Russel, R. (2007). 'Peer-to-peer: An e-mentoring approach to developing community, mutual engagement and professional identity for pre-service teachers', Paper presented at the *Australian Association for Research in Education (AARE) Conference*, Fremantle, Western Australia, <www.aare.edu.au/07pap/mcl07393.pdf> accessed 25 November 2009.

Mena-Marcos, J.J., Sánchez, E., and Tillema, H. (2008). 'Teachers reflecting on their work: Articulating what is said about what is done', *Teachers and Teaching. Theory and Practice*, 14 (2), 95–114.

Montero, B., Watts, F., and García-Carbonell, A. (2007). 'Discussion forum interactions: Text and context', *System*, 35 (4), 566–582.

Morrison, K. (1996). 'Developing reflective practice in higher degree students through a learning journal', *Studies in Higher Education*, 21 (3), 317–332.

Murray, L. and Hourigan, T. (2006). 'Using micropublishing to facilitate writing in the foreign language'. In L. Ducate and N. Arnold (eds), *Calling on CALL: From*

Theory and Research to New Directions in Foreign Language Teaching, 149–179. San Marcos: CALICO.

Murray, L. and Hourigan, T. (2008). 'Blogs for specific purposes: Expressivist or socio-cognitivist approach?', *ReCALL Journal*, 20 (1), 82–97.

Partington, A. (2003). *The Linguistics of Political Argument*. London: Routledge.

Preece, J. and Moloney-Krichmar, D. (2003). 'Online communities: Focusing on sociability and usability'. In J. Jacko and A. Sears (eds), *Handbook of Human-Computer Interaction*, pp. 596–620. Mahwah: Lawrence Erlbaum.

Pryor, C.R. and Bitter, G.G. (2008). 'Using multimedia to teach inservice teachers: Impacts on learning, application, and retention', *Computers in Human Behavior*, 24, 2668–2681.

Quinn-Patton, M. (2002). *Qualitative Evaluation and Research Methods*. London: Sage Publications.

Richards, J.C., Sylvester, T., and Farrell, C. (2005). *Professional Development for Language Teachers: Strategies for Teacher Learning*. Cambridge: Cambridge University Press.

Riordan, E. (2011). 'Assessing the integration and quality of online tools in language teacher education: The case of blogs, chat and discussion forums'. In T. Hourigan, L. Murray and E. Riordan (eds), *Quality Issues in ICT Integration: Third Level Disciplines and Learning Contexts*, pp. 94–119. UK: Cambridge Scholars Publishing.

Schön, D.A. (1991). *The Reflective Practitioner. How Professionals Think in Action*. Aldershot: Ashgate.

Scott, M. (2008). *Wordsmith Tools Version 5.0*. Liverpool: Lexical Analysis Software.

Silverman, D. (2005). *Doing Qualitative Research*. London: Sage Publications.

Stevens, V. (2003). 'Teacher professional development in online communities of practice: How does this impact on language learning?', Paper presented at the *Computer Assisted Language Learning Symposium*, Cairo, Egypt, <http://www.vancestevens.com/papers/egypt/tpd_online.htm> accessed 14 July 2008.

van Teijlingen, E.R. and Hundley, V. (2001). 'The importance of pilot studies', *Social Research Update*, Department of Sociology, University of Surrey (Winter). <http://sru.soc.surrey.ac.uk/SRU35.html> accessed 20 February 2012.

Wenger, E. (1998). *Communities of Practice. Learning, Meaning, and Identity*. Cambridge: Cambridge University Press.

Wenger, E., White, N., Smith, J.D., and Rowe, K. (2005). 'Technology for communities', *CEFRIO*, <http://technologyforcommunities.com/CEFRIO_Book_Chapter_v_5.2.pdf> accessed 28 April 2008.

WikiPedia (2011). 'Blog', *Wikipedia*, <http://en.wikipedia.org/wiki/Blog> accessed 10 January 2011.

Yang, S.H. (2009). 'Using blogs to enhance critical reflection and community of practice', *Educational Technology & Society*, 12 (2), 11–21.

Notes on Contributors

JOANNA BAUMGART is a lecturer in English Language Teaching at the University of Innsbruck, Austria. Her current work focuses on interculturalism in Irish second level education and specifically teacher talk in multilingual mainstream classrooms. She is also interested in the use of classroom data for reflective practice in educational contexts as well as continuous professional development of teachers.

MANDY COLLINS is a PhD student at the Department of German and School of Education, University College Cork. Her current research explores cross-curricular teaching strategies for the contemporary post-primary classroom in Ireland, focusing on supporting the academic language development of all learners, including international pupils learning through English as an additional language. Her work draws on sociocultural perspectives of learning, genre theory and systemic functional linguistics. Her research interests include language pedagogy, academic English, collaborative learning, learning through drama, teacher education and critical discourse analysis. She has taught English to speakers of other languages, both adults and young learners, in many contexts in Kenya, France, Peru, London, Hong Kong, Sri Lanka and Ireland. Her current studies aim to address the linguistic challenges facing post-primary teachers and pupils in contemporary Ireland by exploring the extent to which techniques used to teach English to speakers of other languages transfer to the multilingual mainstream post-primary classroom.

COLIN FLYNN is a doctoral researcher in the School of Linguistic, Speech and Communication Sciences at Trinity College Dublin, where he teaches Irish language modules and undergraduate modules in applied linguistics and second language acquisition. He holds degrees in History and Irish Studies (New York University), Education (University College Dublin) and Applied Linguistics (Trinity College Dublin) and his research interests include the psychology of language learning and use, minority/heritage language education and language maintenance. His doctoral thesis focuses on the attitudes of adult learners of Irish towards the achievement of native speaker norms. From 2005 to 2010 he worked with the Irish language organization Gaelchultúr where he was involved in developing syllabuses, lesson plans and teaching materials for adult Irish language courses.

MARGARET HEALY has been the EFL/EAP course leader at the Department of English Language and Literature, Mary Immaculate College, Limerick, since 2007. She also tutors on the TEFL module of the Liberal Arts Degree programme. She is the course co-ordinator and trainer for the Preparatory Certificate in ELT for State Qualified Teachers delivered to graduating primary school teachers from the Faculty of Education at Mary Immaculate College. A Bachelor of Arts graduate in French and Italian from University College Dublin, she completed her MA in ELT at the University of Limerick in 2007. Currently working on her PhD in Applied Linguistics, she is compiling an oral corpus, recorded at the Shannon College of Hotel Management, which will provide research data for a linguistic case study of the development of a community of practice in the hospitality training sector. Her main research interests include corpus linguistics, the language of the hospitality industry, community of practice, Business English and ESP, language and gender, and ELT classroom interaction.

TINA HICKEY has published extensively on immersion education, the acquisition of Irish as first and second language, bilingualism, second language reading in Irish, family language transmission and minority language maintenance. She was awarded a Government of Ireland fellowship (2008), and was a Visiting Scholar at the ESRC Centre for Research on Bilingualism at the University of Bangor (2009). She is a former Convenor of the AILA Child Language Commission, and former Treasurer of the International Association for the Study of Child Language. She has served as President of the Irish Association for Applied Linguistics and of the Reading Association of Ireland, of which she was made an Honorary Lifetime Member in 2011. She is a member of the editorial boards of the *International Journal of*

Bilingual Education and Bilingualism and the *Journal of Immersion and Content-Based Language Education*. She is currently collaborating with Prof. Nancy Stenson on a Marie Curie funded project on Irish reading, and with Dr Ciara O' Toole on a Foras na Gaeilge funded study adapting the CDI. Tina Hickey lectures on language acquisition, bilingualism and psycholinguistics in the School of Psychology at University College Dublin.

LAUREN KAVANAGH is a PhD candidate in the School of Psychology, University College Dublin, where she was also awarded her BA in Psychology in 2007. She is conducting mixed methods research on parental involvement and home-school relations in Irish immersion education, under the supervision of Dr Tina Hickey. She has received a funded studentship from An Comhairle um Oideachas Gaeltachta agus Gaelscoilaíochta to undertake this research. She has presented her research at various conferences at a national, European and international level, including the International Symposium of Bilingualism and the European Conference on Educational Research. Her research interests include immersion education, home-school partnerships, second language acquisition and eye tracking.

MALGORZATA MACHOWSKA-KOSCIAK was born in Poland. She took her primary degree (Bachelor of Arts in English Language Philology) at the Foreign Language Teacher Training College, operating under the supervision of the Jagiellonian University Krakow, and her Master's Degree (in English Language Teaching) at Trinity College Dublin. She has also been a PhD student at Trinity College Dublin since 2009. She has been employed as a teacher of English as a Second Language in County Louth's Vocational Education Committee since 2007. Her central research interests include first and second language socialization, language ideology, identity negotiation, language maintenance, acculturation and power relations inherent in human interactions and society. She is also interested in second language learning from a variety of perspectives (pedagogy, curriculum design), children's attitudes to and experiences of language learning and multilingualism/migration.

NOEL Ó MURCHADHA completed his PhD in 2012 at the University of Limerick, where he also taught courses on the Irish Language and on Subject Pedagogics for Irish. His current research focus is on elucidating the link between subjective responses to linguistic variation and the direction of linguistic change in Irish. He has published articles on the standardization of Irish, on the use of experimental methods and folk linguistic methods in the study of language ideology, and on the role of socio-psychological factors in linguistic change. He has recently taken up a position at the Celtic Studies Department at the University of St Michael's College, University of Toronto, for the year 2012–2013.

KRISTIN ONDERDONK HORAN is Head of English as Foreign Language (EFL) at the Shannon College of Hotel Management. She has taught English in Ireland, the United States and the Czech Republic. Prior to teaching, she worked in broadcast media and academic publishing. She is currently involved in the development of the Cambridge, Limerick and Shannon (CLAS) corpus, a 1-million word corpus of hospitality and tourism-related language. Her research interests include discourse in the hospitality industry, media discourse, and cross-cultural discourse analysis.

ELAINE RIORDAN is a PhD student at the University of Limerick, Ireland. Her thesis entitled 'Virtual Learning Environments in Language Teacher Education for a Community of Practising Teachers' analyses online and face-to-face communication between student teachers. She is also a lecturer in TESOL/Second Language Acquisition, and programme leader for the MA in TESOL and the MA in TESOL with Translation at the University of Hull, UK. Her research interests include English language teaching and teacher education, corpus linguistics, new technologies and language teaching/learning and computer mediated communication.

Index